ENT and Oral Surgery of the Dog and Cat

A Veterinary Practitioner Handbook
Series Edited by Neal King BVSc MRCVS

ENT and Oral Surgery of the Dog and Cat

J. G. Lane BVetMed, FRCVS

Lecturer in Veterinary Surgery
University of Bristol

WRIGHT · PSG

Bristol   London   Boston
1982

Published by:
John Wright & Sons Ltd, 823–825 Bath Road, Bristol
BS4 5NU, England

John Wright PSG Inc.,
545 Great Road, Littleton, Massachusetts 01460, USA.

British Library Cataloguing in Publication Data

Lane, J. G.
    ENT and oral surgery of the dog and cat.—(A Veterinary
    practitioner handbook)
    1. Dogs—Surgery   2. Cats—Surgery
    I. Title   II. Series
    636.7'0897'371   SF991

ISBN 0 7236 0659 5
Library of Congress Catalog Card Number: 82 50756

Typeset and printed in Great Britain by
John Wright & Sons (Printing) Ltd, at The Stonebridge Press,
Bristol.

Preface

Surveys of small animal practice show that veterinarians devote a large proportion of their consultation and surgical time to the treatment of diseases of the head and neck. Therefore, it is surprising that few texts have been published on this special region when compared, for example, with the steady stream of books on ophthalmic and orthopaedic procedures, which occupy relatively little time outside specialist hospitals and referral centres. Thus, the purpose of this book is to meet a possible need, but no attempt is made to provide the definitive text on the subject. In keeping with the other volumes in this series, the emphasis is on a practical approach, in this case aimed at the differential diagnosis and management of the diseases of a special region. It is hoped that the text has adopted a sufficiently logical approach to be useful to practitioners and final year veterinary students in the solution of diagnostic problems and in the organization of treatment of the disorders that commonly afflict this area. Some subjects, such as cervical swellings or airway obstructions, lend themselves well to a presentation based upon an orderly diagnostic regimen, while others, such as the superficial lesions of the head, must be dealt with by a more direct description. I confess that my major interest is in operative surgery and, therefore, although I recognize that considerable advances in knowledge have been made in recent years on the infectious diseases of the canine and feline upper respiratory tracts, detailed discussions of the microbiology, epidemiology and prevention of these infections are not included here. Many veterinarians are deterred from the challenge of surgery of the head and neck through lack of confidence in their anatomical knowledge, which might explain why there are so few specialists in the field! Throughout the text, attention is drawn to the anatomical details that are relevant to an understanding of the disease processes and necessary for mastering the surgical procedures.

I wish to express my appreciation to Professor H. Pearson, who has encouraged me throughout this venture, and to Professor G. H. Arthur and the series editor, Neal King, who provided the stimulus at the outset. Elaine Mason has acted as both guide and goad along the way and she has sub-edited the script to steer it into print. Without their help, this book would never have come to fruition. Colleagues in the Department of Veterinary Surgery, University of Bristol, have also given freely of their time and experience to assist me in the preparation of the text. I am particularly grateful to Dr Christine Gibbs, whose radiological expertise has been invaluable and who has so willingly allowed me to use illustrations prepared in her unit. I also wish to thank John Conibear and Malcolm Parsons for their skilful photography, and Valerie Beswetherick and Carol Francis, who have painstakingly typed the manuscript.

J. G. L.

Contents

Chapter 1

Introduction

Sound surgical practice consists of a logical progression through the evaluation of each patient presented for treatment, the reasoned use of aids towards a diagnosis, the provision of a useful prognosis and finally the decisive performance of a clearly formulated line of therapy and aftercare. ENT and oral surgery does not differ from the other branches of general surgery and a similar disciplined approach to management of disorders in this region applies. A sound knowledge of normal organ structure and function and of the abnormalities that can afflict individual structures is essential if diagnostic skills are to be effectively employed to determine the nature and extent of disease or injury or to assess how these may influence the overall health of the patient. Commonsense is required to combine diagnoses with the pertinent circumstances of patients and their owners so that helpful information can be given before treatment is begun. Whenever possible, surgical procedures should be carefully planned beforehand from the stage of patient selection to the completion of the necessary aftercare. Thus, although technical skill and manual dexterity are essential attributes of the competent surgeon, they are worthless in the absence of the ability to make accurate diagnoses and clearly considered decisions.

A comparison between medical and veterinary ENT and oral clinical practice shows considerable differences of emphasis. Although deafness of dogs and cats represents a significant disability, its major importance to the owner stems from a failure to be able to communicate commands and consequent disobedience. In these days of frequent litigation owners should be advised of the potential damages which could be awarded against them if a deaf pet were to be the cause of a traffic accident. Nevertheless, by no stretch of the imagination could deafness

1

in an animal be equated with the handicap which hearing deficiencies bring to people. Thus, it is not surprising that much of the time of an ENT surgeon in medical practice is occupied by hearing assessments and surgery to preserve or restore hearing. By the same token, speech forms a fundamental role in communication, and vocal capacity is a major consideration for the human patient undergoing palatine, pharyngeal and laryngeal surgery. The preservation of an animal's voice is of little or no concern to veterinary surgeons; on the contrary, it is far more likely that his services will be sought to reduce the voice of his patients! The cosmetic result of diseases and their surgical treatments is more important on the head and neck than other regions, so that appearance is an important factor irrespective of whether the patient is human, canine or feline. Nasal, oral and aural disorders frequently express themselves by the production of a discharge which, understandably, animal owners may find objectionable. A bloody or purulent discharge which is voided by sneezing in the home is not only unpleasant and unhygienic but may cause expensive damage to furniture and fabrics. A frequent role of the veterinary ENT and oral surgeon is to render patients more wholesome companions. The relief of pain and maintenance of life are fundamental objectives of all clinicians but the presence of many vital structures in the head and neck and their susceptibility to injury carries added responsibilities.

SELECTION OF PATIENTS

The selection of patients to be subjected to surgery of the head and neck depends upon an organized diagnostic procedure to assess the nature and the extent of the disease or injuries present and to determine the urgency with which therapy should be instituted. Once a firm diagnosis has been established, the owners should be informed of the treatment which is likely to be necessary, together with a prognosis. An intimation should be given of the possible duration of symptoms after treatment and of the extent of the nursing which may be necessary when the patient is returned home.

Possible complications should be mentioned at this stage. Whenever disenchantment arises between veterinarians and their clients, it often stems from a failure to communicate adequate information at the stage when a diagnosis has been suggested but before treatment has commenced.

Diagnostic procedures

No regional disorder should be considered in isolation and a case history should take note of previous or concurrent systemic disease.

Information should be obtained on the duration of symptoms and their rate of onset. Inquiries should be made about the general well-being of the patient, including appetite, thirst, exercise tolerance and attitude to life as a whole. Any inclination to weight loss, lethargy, vomiting, diarrhoea, coughing or reluctance to take normal exercise should be noted. Naturally, the medical and surgical records of the patient should be examined for relevant factors and with referred cases particular care should be taken in the assessment of the response to earlier medication. The appearance and progress of discharges, whether they arise from the nostrils or ear canals, should be ascertained and in cases of nasal disease it is helpful to know whether the discharge is uni- or bilateral. When otitis is present a previous tendency to dermatitis may be relevant. Whenever an hereditary anomaly is suspected information regarding littermates and the breeding stock should be sought. Owners will usually volunteer information regarding recent traumatic episodes but may fail to mention accidents earlier in the patient's life. Their impressions regarding painful responses can be helpful and they should be quizzed about changes in behaviour, including temperament, hearing and bark. When oropharyngeal disorders are suspected a description of the patient's eating habits ranging from prehension to deglutition should be obtained. In the face of possible infectious diseases the vaccination history of the patient may give a lead and the likelihood of access to infected contact animals should be explored.

A preliminary examination and inspection of the patient takes account of the general bodily condition, temperature, pulse and character and rate of respiration. The colour of the mucous membranes is noted and the superficial lymph nodes are palpated for enlargement. Auscultation and percussion of the chest will be required if the patient is to be anaesthetized and, in any event, primary heart and lung disorders may require elimination even if the symptoms appear to arise in the upper respiratory or alimentary tract. The overall conformation of the head and neck is studied for swellings or asymmetry. Owners rarely fail to draw the clinician's attention to external lesions such as wounds, discharging sinuses or swellings. It is wise to question the owner about aggressive tendencies on the part of the patient before the examination of the head and neck is begun. Although a preliminary inspection of the nares, ear canals and oropharynx can be made in most conscious patients, the presence of painful lesions or aggression may necessitate a general anaesthetic before an accurate diagnosis can be made.

Simple endoscopy of the external ear canals, the nasal chambers, the oropharynx, larynx and trachea is a routine component of diagnosis of ENT and oral disorders. In order that these simple inspections may be achieved satisfactorily, certain criteria must be fulfilled. The patient must be rendered cooperative, suitable instrumentation must be available and the field under inspection must not be obscured. Resentment arising from pain or an aggressive temperament frequently prevents effective endoscopy of a conscious patient. All veterinary practitioners are familiar with the difficulties that can be encountered in auriscopy of a dog or cat whose ear canals are painfully inflamed. Not only is it more humane for this procedure to be conducted on an anaesthetized animal but the detail with which the examination may be performed renders it far more informative. Other procedures such as laryngoscopy and tracheobronchoscopy may be performed on standing horses but they are impracticable in conscious dogs and cats. Flexible fibrescopes are not normally required for the procedures under consideration here, so that simple light sources and rigid lens systems form the working components of most endoscopes used in general veterinary practice. The frustrations which arise from equipment with exhausted batteries, blown bulbs and poor electrical contacts will be familiar to many. Nowadays, there is available a range of light sources which depend upon a mains electrical supply and which can be used with various endoscopic attachments. Sometimes these incorporate a fibre light cable, and such a cold light system provides reliable illumination. Clearly, there is little virtue in the use of an instrument which cannot deliver light to the tissues under inspection and which cannot refer an image of those tissues to the examiner. For example, there has been a tendency to use human aural speculi for the examination of canine and feline ears. These speculi are designed to investigate the short human ear canal and are totally inappropriate to the long horizontal and vertical canals of veterinary patients. Useful endoscopy necessitates a clear field of view and it may require previous preparation of the patient to disperse inflammatory or other debris. The presence of mucus-based discharges renders most intranasal inspections useless but a preliminary forced nasal flush may contribute to a specific diagnosis by endoscopy. Similarly, wax-based otorrhoea may inhibit the diagnosis of diseases of the ear canal such as neoplasia and foreign bodies unless an effort is made to clear the field of view.

Radiography is a particularly pertinent aid to diagnosis of diseases of the head and neck. The air in the upper respiratory tract provides excellent negative contrast to the bones and soft tissues of this region and conversely the dental tissues are extremely radiodense. For some tissues, such as the nasal chambers, the changes sought by the radiologist are subtle and therefore high definition films are essential. These fine grained films are slower than those used in cassettes and require greater exposures; safety measures to prevent unnecessary exposure to radiation must be rigorously observed. Manual restraint of conscious patients for head and neck radiography cannot usually be achieved without hazard to the handlers. Radiography of this region is often best achieved on the anaesthetized animal.

Although a diagnosis can be suggested for many lesions of the ear, nose, throat and oropharynx based upon the physical appearance, radiological features, breed and sex predispositions and biological behaviour, the histopathological examination of biopsy samples by an experienced pathologist is frequently required for a definitive diagnosis and useful prognosis. Whenever possible the entire lesion should be excised and submitted for investigation but this is not always practicable so that a true biopsy sample is necessary. It is important that the sample which is taken is representative of the lesion as a whole. Tissue sections from the periphery alone should be avoided as these may comprise a zone of inflammatory reaction around a more specific focus. Conversely, there is no virtue in the submission of necrotic debris from the centre of a degenerate lesion. Samples should be submitted in a container which is large enough to contain adequate fixative and from which the fixed tissues can be withdrawn easily. It is helpful to the pathologist to provide details of the species, breed, age and sex of the patient together with a potted case history. Reference should be made to the location from which the biopsy was taken and a description of the lesion is invaluable. Evidence of metastasis to local lymph nodes or distant sites should be mentioned (*see Fig.* 10.9).

It is this author's view that veterinary clinicians have become excessively dependent upon the results of swab samples and microbiological tests. The rhetorical question 'Which microbes are present and which drugs should be used to eliminate them?' have displaced the more rational approach of 'Why are microbes present and what can be done to render conditions unfavourable for colonization by pathogens?'

It cannot be disputed that specific contagious viral infections of the upper respiratory tract in particular are of major significance to dogs and cats, but the clinical features of these disorders are well recognized and the indications for specific viral isolation are rare. Sometimes the results of microbial cultures are downright misleading; for example, it is more likely that opportunist bacteria will be cultured from the nasal discharges of dogs with intranasal *Aspergillus fumigatus* infections than that fungal colonies will be isolated. What can be the virtue of culture investigations of the pus voided through a chronic sinus when, by definition, a focus of suppuration such as a foreign body or sequestrum must be present? Great significance is attached by many veterinarians to the presence of *Pseudomonas aeruginosa* in aural discharges and efforts are made to check the sensitivity of this organism against all the antibiotics on the pharmacy shelf. Yet in practice it is unusual for cases of otitis externa to be brought to a more expeditious and successful conclusion as a result of culture and sensitivity tests unless, first, the aural micro-climate is assessed and corrected.

Clinical haematology can be helpful when a pyogenic response is suspected, for example, a high total white cell count with neutrophilia assists to differentiate intranasal aspergillosis from neoplasia in dogs. Measurements of clotting and bleeding times are indicated when a dyscrasia such as warfarin toxicity is suspected. It seems probable that the role of clinical immunology in the diagnostic repertoire will increase. This may range from the identification of antibody response to specific infections to the evaluation of the competence of the immune system of individual patients. Serum samples are used for antibody tests so that blood should be collected into glass containers where the clot will retract to permit easy collection of serum.

Timing of surgery

With the exception of aural, dental and oral procedures, elective surgery of the head and neck is best conducted at the beginning of each day's operation list. Interferences in this region may restrict the conducting airways and result in asphyxiation if postoperative oedema is severe or if haematomas form. Careful observation must be available during the recovery phase from general anaesthesia and, obviously, it is more sensible for this period of critical attention to occur during normal working hours. Many operations described in the chapters which follow should not be performed on an outpatient basis, nor in clinics where intensive care and overnight observation cannot be provided. It would be contrary to both clinical and ethical principles to discharge a patient home when there are significant risks of life-endangering complications. By the same token, no operation should be performed if the surgeon is unable to provide the necessary aftercare and nursing.

Operations such as the drainage of abscesses inevitably lead to the contamination of utensils and surfaces in the treatment room, not to mention the surgeon's hands, while other procedures such as ultrasonic dentistry contaminate the atmosphere by the production of a fine aerosol of infected particles. Under ideal conditions a separate room should be set aside for 'dirty' procedures. In any event the competent surgeon should plan his operation list so that those interferences which require a sterile technique are performed before those which are likely to introduce sepsis.

In a broader view of the timing of surgery, treatment should not be delayed for patients which are afflicted by respiratory obstructions, have sustained a serious extravasation of blood or are unable to eat and drink voluntarily. Nevertheless, preparatory measures such as whole blood or fluid infusions may be required prior to surgery. Longer term procrastination of diagnostic and surgical procedures may be prejudicial to the patient's survival, for example in cases of suspected neoplasia, and cannot be justified.

First aid

Animals which have sustained trauma to the head and neck or are afflicated by acute disease processes in this region warrant prompt attention because any delay in diagnosis and treatment may be detrimental to the outcome. First and foremost comes an evaluation of respiratory function. The rate and character of thoracic movements are gauged and the volume of air moved is assessed at the nostrils and mouth. The colour of the mucous membranes may reveal cyanosis, anaemia or failure of peripheral perfusion. Dyspnoeic patients must be handled with care; stress and rough technique can kill these patients and must be avoided.

Evidence of a defect of the conducting airways may take the form of an obvious laceration through the tracheal wall, visible aspiration of air through a wound in the neck or palpable emphysema around a puncture site. Unless the patient shows signs of dyspnoea, such as tachypnoea and cyanosis, emphysema through simple punctures should be treated conservatively. However, any major breach in the system demands immediate attention to restore an integral airway. In some cases, this will require tracheotomy tubing caudal to the site of injury: not only will this provide an alternative airway in the emergency but it will afford a means to maintain anaesthesia while the repair is effected rostrally. In the reconstruction of the trachea care should be taken to preserve the recurrent laryngeal nerves. Complete traumatic transections of the airway are most unusual so that wounds of the trachea usually take the form of a gaping split between cartilage rings. The dorsal ligament will often remain intact and can act as a basis for closure. Mattress sutures (3/0 or 4/0 silk) should be placed to avoid the edges of the wound itself but should be laid through the annular ligaments one ring distant from the defect.

After the patency and integrity of the conducting airways has been checked, it may be necessary to obtain radiographs of the chest if a ruptured diaphragm, pneumothorax or haemothorax are suspected. Violent placement of the patient into lateral or dorsal recumbency is a recipe for disaster when dyspnoea is already present. As far as possible, radiographs should be taken with the patient in a natural position and any alterations in posture should be made gently and slowly. Evidence of severe haemorrhage will have been obvious from the pallor of the mucous membranes if not from the outward appearance of extravasated blood. The control of haemorrhage at its source is a primary component of first aid but this may not be instantly apparent or accessible. Whole blood transfusions, plasma expanders or other fluid replacement may be indicated to reverse hypovolaemic shock before further investigations can be undertaken.

The principles of the management of lacerated wounds of the head and neck do not differ from those elsewhere on the body. Haemorrhage is controlled and every effort is made to cleanse gross contamination from the wound. Débridement of non-vital tissues precedes anatomical reconstruction which may include the reduction of dislocated joints and the fixation of fractures. Wounds on the ventral surfaces which remain contaminated should be left open to drain but dorsal wounds may require the creation of drainage channels or the implantation of Penrose drains to assist gravity. It is contrary to fundamental surgical principles to enclose particulate debris or necrotic tissues in the depth of repaired wounds.

Tracheotomy (*Fig.* 1.1)

Tracheotomy may be a specific first aid procedure to provide an emergency airway and to bypass an obstruction or defect of the proximal respiratory tract. Once the tracheotomy tube is in place the obstruction can be relieved or the defect repaired. In other circumstances tracheotomy may be performed as an elective procedure to provide a direct airway and route for anaesthesia whilst surgery is performed in the oropharynx, larynx or proximal trachea. Alternatively, if there is a likelihood of significant postoperative oedema and restriction of the conducting airways, for example after soft palate or laryngeal surgery, a tracheotomy tube may be used to provide a temporary bypass. A routine part of the preparation of patients for upper respiratory tract surgery should be to clip the hair from the skin overlying the mid-cervical trachea as this will expedite emergency tracheotomy should this become necessary in the postoperative period. A variety of tracheotomy tubes are available to veterinary surgeons and these include disposable plastic and 'hand-me-down' silver tubes formerly used frequently in human patients. Many of the silver tubes have relatively thin walls and comprise an inner sleeve which can be withdrawn easily for cleaning purposes: these are preferred by the author. Plastic tubes do not seem to be available in a wide range of sizes and in general the tubing material is thick. Whenever possible, a tube should be selected that will not only permit adequate normal resting respirations, but will allow a similar flow of air to pass around the tube through the natural airway. Thus, by closing the tube the surgeon is able to check periodically when its removal will be safe.

In emergency conditions tracheotomy may be performed under local anaesthesia. Alternatively, a short-acting intravenous agent, with or without an endotracheal tube, may be employed. A ventral midline skin incision is made (*Fig.* 1.1*a*) and the sternohyoid muscles are divided at their midline raphe (*Fig.* 1.1*b*). The loose connective tissue which overlies the trachea is bluntly divided. The trachea is entered by a transverse incision between cartilaginous rings (*Fig.* 1.1*c*). The tracheal

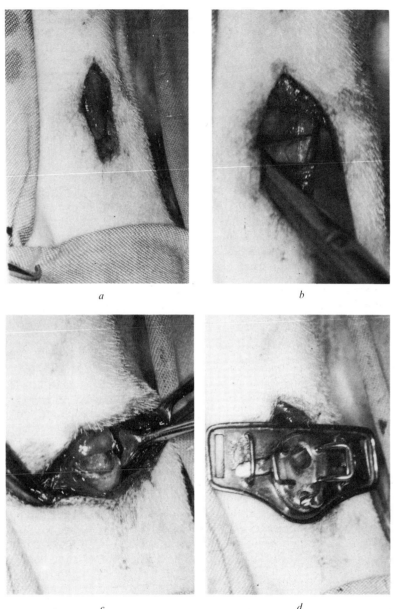

a   *b*

c   *d*

Fig. 1.1. Tracheotomy. (*a*) Ventral midline skin incision. (*b*) Division of sternohyoideus muscle. (*c*) Transverse incision between tracheal rings. (*d*) Silver
tracheotomy tube in place. Note the inner sleeve which can be removed for
cleaning.

incision may extend beyond 180° and the rings are held apart by the use of blunt hooks. Silver tubes are often provided with an introducer which is invaluable for atraumatic placement. Sutures may be required to close the muscle and skin layers if a long incision has been used. Nylon sutures are used to secure the tube to the skin (*Fig. 1.1d*) but care is necessary in their location otherwise they may encourage displacement of the tube. Umbilical tape may be passed through the eyes of the tube and around the neck to secure it in place. However, this tape may be caught by the claws of the patient if it attempts to scratch. The curvature of tracheotomy tubes is extremely variable so that gauze bolsters may be helpful to support the tube in a comfortable position.

Tracheotomy tubing is not a procedure to be taken lightly and it should never be performed where continuous intensive care observation is unavailable. A patient with a tracheotomy tube may asphyxiate through self-inflicted dislocation of the tube or otherwise through closure of the tube by dried blood and exudates. Tracheal exudation may be copious in the presence of a tube and regular removal of the inner sleeve for cleaning is necessary. Once the tracheotomy tube has fulfilled its purpose, it is removed and the residual defect left to heal by second intention. During the first 2 days after removal the exudate which persists should be bathed from the surrounding skin.

ANAESTHETIC CONSIDERATIONS

The provision and maintenance of a clear airway is a *sine qua non* for successful anaesthesia of all patients. The special considerations that apply to the general anaesthesia of animals undergoing pharyngeal, laryngeal and tracheal surgery are described in a later chapter. Blood, irrigation fluids and other debris may gather in the pharynx of patients subjected to a variety of surgical procedures of the head and neck. For example, routine dentistry may lead to the presence of loosened calculus and dental fragments in the mouth, together with free blood from extraction sites and, when ultrasonic instruments are used, water is sprayed into the buccal cavity. Even during procedures to cleanse the ear canal, fluid may pass through the middle ear and Eustachian tube to the pharynx. Thus, irrespective of the agents used, it is neglectful not to provide a cuffed endotracheal tube during general anaesthesia of most patients subjected to ENT and oral surgery. The oropharynx may be packed with a known number of surgical swabs or with a taped sponge pack to absorb fluids (*Fig. 1.2*). The cuff of the endotracheal tube should remain gently inflated until it has been withdrawn into the pharynx at the conclusion of the procedure.

The presence of surgical drapes conspires to obscure the head in many of the procedures described here. Patient observation may be extremely difficult and the anaesthetist must depend upon other

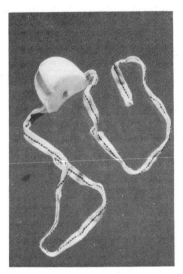

Fig. 1.2. Taped pharyngeal pack.

parameters such as the character of the femoral pulse, the respiratory rate and blind palpation of the jaw tone and lingual pulse to gauge the depth of anaesthesia. In these circumstances an oesophageal stethoscope is an invaluable aid. For the assessment of respirations the anaesthetist should observe the rebreathing bag rather than thoracic movements. A patient with an obstructed airway is likely to show significant thoracic efforts but may move small volumes of gas through the system. Periodic checks of the tubing and connections for kinking and disconnection should be made. Most surgeons develop a subconscious awareness of the colour of blood in surgical wounds but in ENT and oral surgery a conscious communication between the anaesthetist and the surgeon regarding this obvious evidence of satisfactory oxygenation should be developed.

PREPARATION OF THE PATIENT

Aseptic technique

The surgical techniques described in this book fall into two distinct groups. First, strict asepsis is not practicable within the mouth, nasal chambers and ear canals and yet in each of these sites, preliminary cleansing with antiseptic solutions will reduce significantly the concentration of potential pathogens. Secondly, invasions into the soft tissues, particularly of the throat, often lead to the creation of dead space so that thorough aseptic preparation of the operation site, surgeon and instruments is imperative if wound dehiscence is to be avoided. The surgeon and his assistants should beware of two potential hazards to the eyes at this stage. Care should be taken to avoid overspill of antiseptic solutions and spirit-based agents on to the corneal surface and conjunctival sac. These solutions can be extremely irritant to the cornea. Secondly, when the operation site is draped, the towel clips are best attached to the skin well away from the orbit.

Positioning of the patient

For each surgical procedure there is an optimal position for the patient, and this has four objectives:
1. To provide the most favourable approach to the surgical site.
2. To create tension in the tissues to be incised.
3. To allow the surgeon good visibility and a comfortable operating position.
4. To allow safe anaesthesia and observation.

Incisions through tense tissues make for safer blunt dissection and the identification of major vessels and nerves and this is particularly pertinent to the throat region. For ventral, ventrolateral and lateral incisions the neck may be extended over sandbags with the forelimbs drawn caudally and the nose or chin held by bands of adhesive tape (*Fig.* 1.3). Reference has already been made to some of the pitfalls of anaesthesia; the position of the patient must permit the presence of an endotracheal tube without kinking or accidental displacement from the airway. In this context, particular vigilance is required for techniques such as tonsillectomy and palatine surgery.

During irrigation procedures such as ultrasonic dentistry and cleansing of the external ear canal, the excess fluids may flood the operating surface so that the underside of the patient lies in a pool which includes blood and debris. This may be prevented by placing the head over a wire grid and thus the overspill can drain from the table without saturating the patient's coat, thus making it possible to return the pet to its owner in a more pleasing condition. Again, oral and nasal irrigation techniques lead to fluid accumulation in the pharynx. This may be absorbed by placing a known number of swabs or a taped sponge pack into the pharynx but care must be taken to remember to withdraw all this material at the end of the procedure.

AFTERCARE

Few would contest the statement that the results obtained by a surgeon show a direct relationship to the aftercare provided. The placement of the last suture does not represent the conclusion of a surgical procedure, nor even does removal of the sutures after wound healing by first

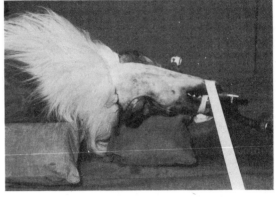

a

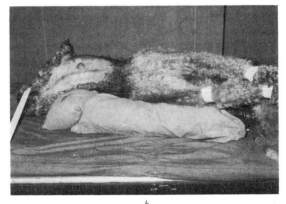

b

Fig. 1.3. (*a*) Patient positioned for ventral midline approaches, i.e. tracheal or thyroid surgery. (*b*) Patient positioned for ventrolateral approaches, i.e. to the submandibular salivary gland.

intention. Aftercare of surgical patients may range from intensive treatments in the immediate postoperative period to long term advice on diet and exercise, aimed to return the patient to normal activity.

Postoperative medication

The dependence on broad spectrum antibiotic therapy is no substitute for strict aseptic surgical technique. Antibiotics do have an important role to play in the control of postoperative infections and they should be used whenever contamination may be present within a wound and where a sterile technique is not practicable. Wound breakdown is likely in the face of suppuration and it must be remembered that commensal organisms may assume a pathogenic role in tissues traumatized by surgery. Thus, a course of broad spectrum antibiotics is indicated after surgery to the oral cavity, ear canals, nasal cavities and whenever other intraluminal procedures are performed on the upper respiratory tract. The length of the course provided depends upon the degree of tissue trauma and the likely duration of tissue repair. Transient bacteraemia is known to follow dental extractions and this is a specific indication for the provision of antibiotic cover.

Wounds of the head and neck are particularly vulnerable to self-trauma by scratching and rubbing, often on recovery from general anaesthesia. The tactical use of analgesic agents is recommended after any operation that is likely to be painful. Patients are likely to show discomfort after techniques that penetrate or scrape bony surfaces, and the structures of the external and middle ear are highly sensitive. The author's preferred analgesic régime consists of an intramuscular injection of pethidine as the patient lightens from general anaesthesia. This may be repeated 4 hours later if required.

Post-surgical oedema can cause a serious obstruction of the airway during recovery from oropharyngeal and laryngeal operations. The role of tracheotomy tubing in the recovery phase has been described above and this technique should be used whenever there is a risk of asphyxiation. To a lesser extent, oedema may be obviated by the intravenous or intramuscular injection of corticosteroids at the time of surgery.

Care of wounds

Incisions are more likely to heal by first intention if the tissues are spared the insults of infection and trauma. The choice of non-irritant suture material such as silk is indicated for the closure of skin wounds of the facial region. At this site, monofilament nylon may tickle the patient and stimulate scratching. Irrespective of the site, non-absorbable materials such as nylon and silk should be used as sparingly as is consistent with accurate apposition of the skin edges. Suture needle puncture wounds and suture tracts provide ideal sites for the inoculation and growth of bacteria. It has been shown that the frequency of wound dehiscence and suture abscessation increases in parallel with the number of skin sutures placed. Subcuticular suture patterns not only provide adequate strength but do not penetrate skin surfaces and there is the additional advantage of a good cosmetic result. Although the dried blood clot which forms over and between the edges of incised skin plays no active role in the process of repair, it does serve a vital function as a seal to protect the deeper tissues from invasion by bacteria. The over-zealous removal of crusted clots on wound surfaces is misguided as these should be left undisturbed as much as possible. Wounds of the ears and facial region are best protected from self-injury by the use of a head bucket or Elizabethan collar. Additionally, the dew claws should be covered with a light dressing. The indications for bandages in this region are very rare; in fact it is difficult to apply them securely and when they are displaced round the neck there is a risk of strangulation.

The role of non-absorbable materials in wound dehiscence and abscessation has been mentioned already. It is clear that these complications are more likely to arise at those sites where asepsis has not and/or could not be achieved, and in this respect aural surgical wounds are typical. Additionally, the longer the skin sutures remain in place, the more likely it is that suppuration within the wound will develop. Therefore, suture removal should not be delayed beyond the time when the strength of the tissue repair is sufficient to prevent a mechanical breakdown. Frequently the skin sutures may be removed on the ninth or tenth day after surgery and there are distinct disadvantages if this procedure is delayed until the twelfth or fourteenth day.

Dead space within surgical wounds represents an ideal focus for infection but this undesirable consequence of surgery may be unavoidable in loose tissues, especially of the neck. The judicious use of implanted tissue drains is to be commended but the technique must not be regarded as an alternative to an accurate anatomical closure. Tissue (Penrose) drains may also be indicated in the aftercare of large abscesses and whenever exudation between tissue layers is likely to cause a distension at the surgical site. The objective of a tissue drain is to provide a route for the gravity flow of tissue fluids such as blood, pus or serum. Simple plastic tubes prepared with a series of small holes to coincide with the extent of the site to be drained are suitable. The tubing should not be implanted through the surgical incision but by a separate channel created by a stab incision in the skin at the lowest point and blunt dissection by forceps through the subcuticular tissues. Attachment of the drainage tube to the skin below the exit point is necessary otherwise it will become displaced. The fixation of the tube can be achieved by a 'sandwich' formed by two layers of adhesive tape enclosing the tube and attached to the skin by sutures. Sutures which pass through the lumen of the tube itself should be avoided as these are inclined to leak and to encourage infection. More sophisticated systems which incorporate a vacuum pack are also available for tissue drainage. The maintenance of patency and the removal of the fluids discharged are the main requirements in the aftercare of wounds with drainage tubes. Occasionally, where infection is known to be present, a drainage tube acts as a suitable route for irrigation. Solutions such as hydrogen peroxide or povidone-iodine may be infused through the tube and it is of little consequence if they drain through or around the implanted material.

The virtues of the maintenance of drainage from infected sites such as abscesses require little further emphasis. Some abscesses show a tendency to heal by granulation before drainage is complete and the use of a bandage seton offers an alternative to tissue drainage tubes. Entry and exit points for the seton should correspond to the highest and lowest points of the abscess and the bandage material should be tied so that it is not possible for the feet of the patient to become entangled. Fresh bandage material should be introduced daily and this may or may not be impregnated with antiseptic medication. The old bandage is used to pull through the new at the daily changeover.

Intensive care

Whenever there is a danger of circulatory collapse or respiratory obstruction the patient should be kept under continuous observation. Temperature, pulse and respiratory characteristics should be monitored frequently. A written record is commended not only so that trends may be identified early, but to assist the nursing staff at changeover times. Data of food and fluids taken voluntarily, urination and defaecation, together with a full time schedule of medication, should be included on the case record. Pallor, a depressed temperature, increased pulse rate and poor capillary refill are signs of failing tissue perfusion and are indications for fluid therapy. Whenever haemorrhagic shock is evident the use of whole blood transfusions may be considered provided that the site of haemorrhage has been identified and controlled.

A patient with a tracheotomy tube must never be left unattended. The tube may represent the lifeline of the patient and it could be displaced in an instant. A more likely complication of tracheotomy is the obstruction of the temporary airway by dried tracheal exudates. The intensive care of tracheotomized animals includes the regular cleaning of the tube itself. Metallic tracheotomy tubes are usually equipped with an inner sleeve which can be withdrawn, cleansed and replaced without interference to the outer tube. Additional tracheal secretions should be aspirated by suction frequently, particularly in the postoperative period when blood may be present. The volume of tracheal exudation increases the longer the tracheotomy tube remains in place, so that cleansing of the implant will become necessary every 15–30 minutes by the third day.

Isolation facilities with barrier nursing should be provided for dogs and cats with suspected contagious diseases. Cats with upper respiratory tract viral infections represent a notable hazard to other hospital patients. They should be accommodated in a separate air space and separate utensils and protective clothing should be provided for the isolation area.

The indications and technique for pharyngostomy intubation for the artificial feeding of dogs and cats is described in detail later in this chapter.

Diet and exercise

Two questions frequently raised by owners when their pets are discharged from hospital treatment are 'what about food?' and 'what about exercise?'. The routine advice to restrict food and fluid intake to small quantities of readily digestible nutrients during the 24 hours following a general anaesthetic is applicable to patients other than those which have been subjected to oropharyngeal and respiratory tract surgery. Dietary advice for these latter patients is, for the most part, dictated by commonsense. Patients with wounds in the oropharynx should not be provided with abrasive foods: not only will these be painful to prehend and swallow but unnecessary trauma to the surgical site will arise. Surgical procedures to the larynx and proximal oesophagus may interfere with normal deglutition and the inhalation of fluids becomes a distinct possibility. The oral intake of fluids for these patients should be restricted to water and although the food component should be non-abrasive, a sloppy consistency, including gravy, is to be avoided. In general, dogs and cats are prone to gingivitis and periodontal disease through a failure to provide adequate dental work. Dietary suggestions to assist the self-cleaning of teeth should be a routine component of the advice given to new pet owners and to those who present their animals for regular check-ups.

Post-surgical oedema will provide a temporary partial obstruction of the upper respiratory tract, for example after soft palate resection or tonsillectomy. Vigorous exercise and excitement should be avoided in these patients until the oedema has resolved approximately 10–14 days after surgery. After laryngeal surgery a longer period of convalescence is often indicated. For example, dogs with laryngeal paralysis which have been subjected to arytenoid lateralization should be permitted only controlled exercise for the first 6 weeks after surgery so that ankylosis of the laryngeal cartilage components can occur. On the other hand, stagnation of air is undesirable within the nasal passages after surgery to this region. Gentle exercise should be encouraged from an early stage after rhinotomy. Head shaking may be stimulated by cold air when dogs and cats are taken outdoors after surgery to the external ear canals. The owners of these patients should be advised that this is a normal reaction and does not usually indicate a complication of the surgery.

PHARYNGOSTOMY INTUBATION (*Fig.* 1.4)

The condition of an animal inevitably deteriorates when it is unable or unwilling to prehend and swallow the nutrients essential for the maintenance and repair of body tissues. Inappetance, particularly when prolonged, is prejudicial to the outcome of medical or surgical treatment and pharyngostomy tubing is an aid to the nursing of anorexic patients. The technique comprises the surgical implantation of a tube extending from the skin surface of the submandibular region, through the lateral pharyngeal wall and thence, by way of the oesophagus, to the stomach (*Fig.* 1.4*a*). The requisite dietary components and medication can be introduced, in liquidized form, directly into the stomach. This technique is not accompanied by the resentment of forced feeding by stomach tubing *per os*, and to some extent may reduce the necessity for tedious parenteral fluid therapy.

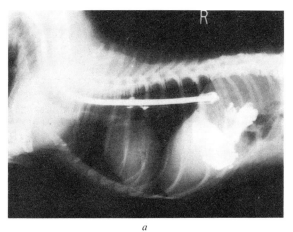

a

Fig. 1.4. Pharyngostomy intubation. (*a*) Radiograph of correctly sited tube.

Indications for pharyngostomy intubation

Road traffic accidents and fights can be the cause of severe injuries to the head and neck. Fractures of the mandible are common in dogs and cats; less frequently fractures of the maxilla and hyoid apparatus, luxation of the temporomandibular joints or soft tissue damage to the larynx and tongue are sustained. After specific treatment for these injuries has been performed, pain and functional interference may result in an inability to eat; pharyngostomy tubing is helpful during the recovery period. The consequences of the inappetance which follows some non-emergency surgical procedures can be reduced by performing a pharyngostomy intubation at the same time. The technique may therefore be indicated when extensive interferences to the nasopharynx and oropharynx, such as cleft palate repair, radical dentistry or tumour ablation, are carried out. Laryngeal surgery may render deglutition painful and on other occasions closure of the glottis may be temporarily impaired; in these circumstances feeding via a pharyngostomy tube prevents inhalation of food material during swallowing. After extensive nasal surgery such as turbinectomy, cats, and to a lesser extent dogs, do not easily tolerate mouth breathing and are unwilling to eat until the nasal packing has been withdrawn. Pharyngostomy intubation has been suggested for the postoperative care of some oesophageal surgical patients, for example following the removal of longstanding foreign bodies, resections and the relief of stenosis. In the postoperative management of gastric volvulus in the dog, nutrients, fluid and medication can be administered through a pharyngostomy tube, which, at the same time, provides a means for gastric decompression.

Veterinary clinicians frequently comment that sick cats 'lose their will to live' and 'give up the fight'. The resultant fatalities can often be ascribed to anorexia as much as to specific primary disease. Cats affected by upper respiratory tract and panleucopenia virus infections are particularly suitable subjects for pharyngostomy tubing. Apart from producing signs referable to the upper respiratory tract, feline calicivirus also produces ulceration in the oropharynx and this exacerbates anorexia. For similar reasons dogs and cats with severe stomatitis, glossitis and gingivitis may find eating painful. Pharyngostomy helps to overcome the effects of inappetance whilst attempts are made to identify and correct the specific causal factors.

Apart from these specific indications, phyaryngostomy tubing is useful in the intensive care of debilitated small animals provided that vomiting is not a feature of the condition. The tube can be left in place and used in preference to forced oral feeding for periods as long as 1 month or 6 weeks. It can therefore be used for severely dyspnoeic patients which are too distressed to interrupt respiration in order to eat and swallow. In this way the complications of anorexia and dehydration can be avoided whilst specific treatment is instituted.

The oral route of fluid administration is usually the method of choice when dealing with a non-vomiting, dehydrated animal. Gut selectivity is less susceptible to error than the judgement of the clinician using parenteral infusions. Pharyngostomy tubing takes full advantage of this selectivity and at the same time tedious dripping procedures can be avoided.

Technique

The apparatus required for pharyngostomy intubation consists of a dental gag, a scalpel, a pair of curved forceps and suitable tubing material. The tube may be made of rubber or polyethylene and should have an external diameter of 8 mm; a cap is required that will fit tightly into the end of the tube. The length of the tube is assessed by measuring the distance from the incision site immediately caudal to the angle of the mandible, via the point of the acromion, to the tenth costochondral junction (*Fig. 1.4b*). The distal end of the tube is rounded so that rough edges will not irritate the gastric mucosa.

When indicated, the procedure is performed at the same time as other surgical interferences. On other occasions restraint may be provided by a short-acting anaesthetic agent such as thiopentone sodium or, for cats, alphaxalone/alphadolone intravenously, or the administration of halothane by mask. Even in a severely debilitated animal it is unwise to attempt the operation under local analgesia.

For the right-handed surgeon, the patient is positioned in right lateral recumbency and the left submandibular area is prepared for surgery. The mouth is held open with a dental gag and the surgeon passes his left index finger into the pharynx to raise the site for implantation of the tube (*Fig. 1.4c*). A pouch, the piriform fossa, can be palpated in the lateral pharyngeal wall; this is bounded by the stylohyoid, epihyoid, keratohyoid and thyrohyoid bones. The ideal position for the tube lies immediately posterior to the articulation between the stylohyoid and the epihyoid (*Fig. 1.4d*). This site, on a level with the cranial oesophageal opening, is sufficiently anterior to avoid important structures (submandibular gland, carotid and maxillary arteries and veins and hypoglossal nerve) and is not so close to the mandible as to produce excessive lateral deviation of the tube when it is in place.

After the site has been elevated, a 1 cm skin incision is made before curved forceps are pushed bluntly through panniculus muscle, connective tissue and the tough lateral pharyngeal wall (*Fig. 1.4e*). The cranial end of the tubing is then withdrawn with the forceps, through the skin incision (*Fig. 1.4f*), until the distal end can be re-directed, *per os*, into the proximal oesophagus (*Fig. 1.4g*). The tubing is then eased back through the incision until the distal end lies 2–5 cm beyond the cardia. At this stage, if the surgeon has any doubts concerning the position of the tube, a check radiograph should be taken. The tube is held in position by sutures and a butterfly attachment formed by two layers of adhesive bandage placed on either side of the tube (*Fig. 1.4h*). The procedure should take no longer than 5 minutes to perform.

Management of a patient with a pharyngostomy tube

Correctly sited tubes are well accepted by both dogs and cats. Tubes of incorrect length, particularly those that are too long, are occasionally rejected by vomiting. To a small degree, leakage around the tube at the

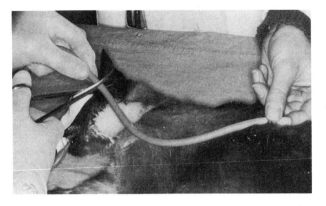

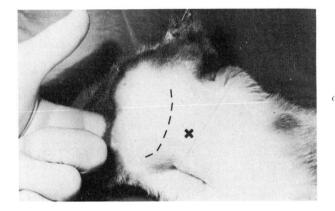

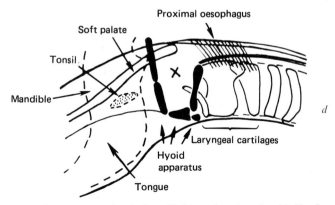

Fig. 1.4. Pharyngostomy intubation. (*b*) Measuring the tube. (*c*) Site for skin incision. (*d*) Anatomical landmarks to locate piriform fossa.

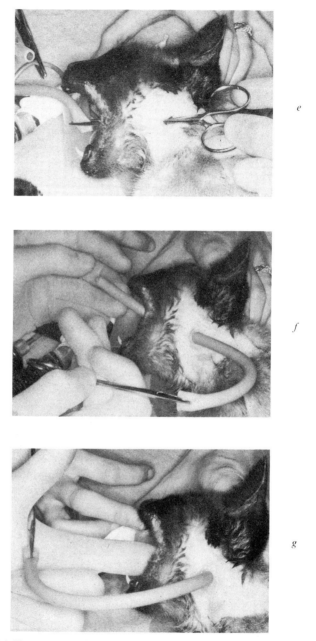

Fig. 1.4. Pharyngostomy intubation. (*e*) Forceps penetrate pharynx. (*f*) Retrieval of external end of tube. (*g*) Redirection of gastric end into oesophagus.

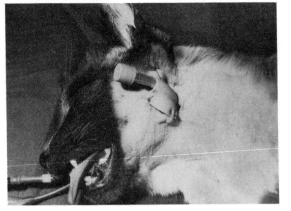

h

Fig. 1.4. Pharyngostomy intubation. (*h*) Attachment of tube by plaster 'butterfly'.

incision invariably occurs. Most patients pay little attention to the attachment site provided that this is regularly cleaned; the cap must be used between feeds to prevent soiling by the return of food through the tube.

All dietary components must be reduced to a fluid consistency prior to feeding. Convalescent diets and baby foods are suitable in the early stages but, later, tinned meats and carbohydrates can be liquidized into a soup. Mineral and vitamin supplementation can be made as necessary. Fluid medicines can be administered through the tube—paediatric drops are convenient in some instances.

Each meal is freshly prepared and ministered by the attachment of a syringe to the pharyngostomy tube; 20–100 ml, depending on the size of the patient, may be given on each occasion. Between four and eight of these meals daily may be required to fulfil the nutritional requirements of the animal. After suitable instruction, and in selected cases, owners can undertake the nursing of a pet with a pharyngostomy tube at home.

At the appropriate time, the sutures are removed and the tube is withdrawn. Healing by second intention takes place within 6 days; cleaning of the site may be indicated during the first 24 hours.

SUPPLEMENTARY READING

Bohning R. H., Dehoff W. D., McElhinney A. et al. (1970) Pharyngostomy for the maintenance of the anorectic animal. *J. Am. Vet. Med. Assoc.* **156**, 611–15.

Gibbs C. (1976) Radiological refresher. The head—Part I: Traumatic lesions of the skull. *J. Small Anim. Pract.* **17**, 551–4.

Gibbs C. (1977) Radiological refresher. The head—Part II: Traumatic lesions of the mandible. *J. Small Anim. Pract.* **18**, 51–4.

Gibbs C. (1978) Radiological refresher. The head—Part III: Ear disease. *J. Small Anim. Pract.* **19**, 539–45.

Gibbs C. (1978) Radiological refresher. The head—Part IV: Dental disease. *J. Small Anim. Pract.* **19**, 701–7.

Harvey C. E. and Venker-Van Haagan A. (1975) Surgical management of pharyngeal and laryngeal airway obstruction in the dog. *Vet. Clin. North Am.* **5**, 515–35.

Kelly D. F., Lucke V. M. and Gaskell C. J. (1982) *Notes on Pathology for Small Animal Clinicians*, Bristol, Wright PSG, pp. 24–5.

Lane J. G. (1977) Pharyngostomy intubation of the dog and cat. In: Grunsell C. S. G. and Hill F. W. G. (ed.) *The Veterinary Annual*, 17th issue. Bristol, Wright–Scientechnica, pp. 164–8.

Chapter 2

Superficial Lesions of the Head and Neck

Although some of the clinical conditions described in this chapter are of small moment to the patients themselves, superficial lesions of the facial regions of dogs and cats are grossly deforming in the eyes of their owners. The head is a primary area of contact between man and his pets, and lesions which would go unnoticed at other sites assume importance because of the disfigurements which they produce. By the same token, the veterinarian has an additional responsibility to provide good cosmetic results with the surgery performed in this area. From the patient's viewpoint, the skin of the facial areas is particularly sensitive and the susceptibility of wounds here to self-trauma has been mentioned in Chapter 1. However, the importance of the use of non-irritant suture materials such as silk bears repetition, as does the value of subcuticular suture patterns.

CONGENITAL ANOMALIES

Harelip (*Fig.* 2.1)

Harelip is the colloquial term for a cleft of the primary palate, so-called because fusion of the premaxilla, cartilaginous septum and lip normally occurs during the primary growth phase of gestation. Clefts of the hard and soft palates (*see* Chapter 10) arise during the secondary growth phase and are defined as clefts of the secondary palate. The traditional view that palatine clefts of both types are due to simple inherited factors has never been proved. Multiple genetic factors may be involved in a small number of cases but dietary, hormonal and teratogenic medication influences should also be considered. Clefts of the primary palate may be uni- or bilateral and may arise in com-

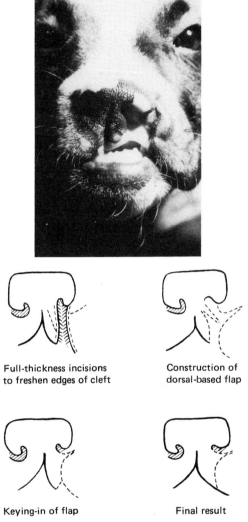

Full-thickness incisions
to freshen edges of cleft

Construction of
dorsal-based flap

Keying-in of flap

Final result

Fig. 2.1. Complete cleft of the primary palate (harelip) in a Boxer puppy and diagrammatic reconstruction of harelip.

bination with a variety of anomalies of the secondary palate. The majority of puppies and kittens with palatine clefts are recognized soon after birth and are destroyed. However, those that survive will require devoted nursing and a strong bond usually develops with the owners, so much so that they will be desperate for surgical corrections to be performed. This surgery can be satisfying for the veterinarian because the painstaking techniques should be rewarded by much-improved patients and delighted owners.

At the initial inspection the depth of the harelip(s) is assessed and the secondary palate is also checked for clefts. Surgery is best staged as late as the health of the puppy will allow (clefts of the primary palate are rare in kittens) so that the risks of anaesthesia and haemorrhage are less daunting; the ideal age for this repair is 10–12 weeks. Superficial defects can be corrected simply by freshening the edges of the cleft and accurate anatomical closure in three layers—oral mucosa, connective tissue and skin, using 3/0 dexon, 4/0 dexon and 3/0 silk respectively. Even with complete clefts, there is not an absolute deficiency of tissue but it will be necessary to construct wide-based flaps to draw the alar cartilage medially into its natural position (*Fig.* 2.1). The edges of the cleft are freshened to the full depth and closure is in three layers as above.

Facial fold dermatitis

Brachycephalic dogs, especially English and French Bulldogs, Pugs and Pekingese, frequently have excessive skin between the eyes and the rhinarium (*Fig.* 2.2). Folds occur over the bridge of the nose and a foul-smelling, suppurative dermatitis will be evident in the crevices. In extreme cases the folds are so marked that a contact keratitis develops from irritation of the cornea by the facial hair. Conservative treatments by antiseptic lavage and regular clipping are often ineffective and tedious.

Surgical treatment is straightforward and consists of a full-thickness skin excision with elongated bielliptical incisions across the bridge of

Fig. 2.2. Facial fold dermatitis in an English Bulldog.

the nose. The strip of skin is incised with a scalpel and then undermined with scissors. Closure is with a continuous buried intradermal pattern using 3/0 monofilament nylon where the knots are secured superficially at the lateral extremities of the wound for easy release after 10 days. Skin sutures are not recommended at this site because of possible abrasion of the cornea.

Labial necrosis (cheilitis) (*Fig.* 2.3)

The lower lip conformation of Cocker Spaniels, Old English Sheepdogs and similar breeds predisposes to the presence of lateral folds which collect stale saliva and degenerate food products. Not only does this cause a foul odour but a severe inflammatory reaction may arise (*Fig.* 2.3*a*). The consequent discomfort provokes the dog to rub the jowl frequently and the inflammation may extend to initiate stomatitis and gingivitis. Local hygiene may be improved by regular bathing with antiseptic solutions such as chlorhexidine or cetrimide. However, cheiloplasty to excise the lip fold is a simple technique which provides a long term cure. A full-thickness skin strip is removed using bielliptical incisions that encompass the necrotic tissue (*Fig.* 2.3*b*) and the wound is closed with 3/0 silk (*Fig.* 2.3*c*). Again, the wound is lubricated with a petroleum gel-based antibiotic ointment until the sutures are removed after 10 days. Although wounds at this site might be expected to become infected and break down, this is not so—lip wounds heal extraordinarily well provided that the anatomical closure is accurate and free of tension.

Pilonidal sinus

Neurectoderm provides the embryological derivative of the spinal cord. The process of cord formation involves the migration of specialized ectodermal elements, the neural plate, into the deeper layers. Occasionally, islets of true dermal tissue become buried in the migration pathway and later act as foci for suppuration (*Fig.* 2.4). Discharging sinuses may appear at the dorsal midline at any point along the back. In dogs, the breed most frequently incriminated is the Rhodesian Ridgeback, and the association with the hair streaming is obvious; the sinuses are usually multiple. Knowledgeable breeders check newborn puppies for the tell-tale tufting of the hair overlying a potential sinus, and for the palpable cord of the sinus tract itself. Treatment necessitates the complete excision of the buried dermal tissues which may lie at any level between the subcutis and the meninges. Pre-surgical radiography using contrast medium to outline the sinus tract is advisable.

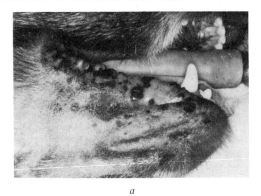

a

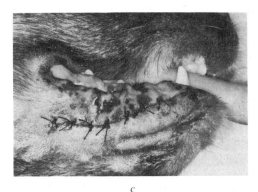

b

c

Fig. 2.3. Labial necrosis. (*a*) Cheilitis in an Irish Setter. (*b*) Cheiloplasty: full-thickness skin incision. (*c*) Cheiloplasty: closure with silk sutures.

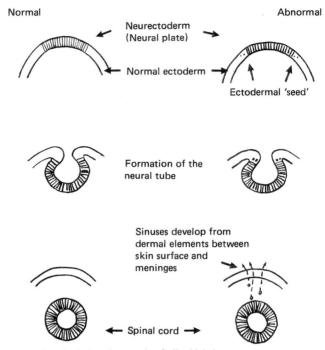

Fig. 2.4. Embryological pathogenesis of pilonidal sinus.

ACQUIRED ADNEXAL DISEASES

Lacerative wounds of the lips

A full-thickness wound of the lip provides an excellent example of the need for local hygiene, débridement and accurate reconstruction—fundamental principles that should be applied to the surgical management of all traumatic wounds. Gross debris such as soil particles should be gently bathed from the depths of the wound and all non-vital tissues are débrided. There is no virtue in the conservation of ischaemic or severely contused tissues within a wound as these are ingredients for dehiscence. When the edges of the wound are freshened for repair note is taken of areas that do not bleed, as probably these have lost their vascular supply and should be discarded. During débridement particular care is taken to identify and preserve important structures such as the parotid duct and external maxillary vessels. Wound closure commences with the reconstruction of the oral mucosa using 3/0 dexon and continues with two layers of continuous sutures through the connective tissue of the lip, taking care not to stenose the parotid duct. The skin is closed with 3/0 silk. Postoperative care may necessitate measures to prevent self-trauma of the wound such as a head bucket, Elizabethan collar or dew claw bindings.

Depigmental and ulcerative lesions of the rhinarium

Apart from ulcerative tumours of the nostrils, which are discussed below, loss of pigment may precede ulceration of the mucous membrane from the nasal vestibule rostrally in response to a persistent discharge. Whenever a dog is presented with ulceration at the angles of the nares and around the entrance to the nasal vestibule, the owner should be questioned as to whether the patient has been sneezing or licking at the nose recently because a discharge may have been undetected. Clearly, further investigations will be required to identify the cause of the discharge (Chapter 3). However, once the intranasal disorder has been controlled and the discharge has ceased, the ulcerated surface epithelizes and pigmentation is restored from the periphery.

Many partly white puppies are born with a partial or total lack of pigment in the rhinarium but this is more often than not made good in puppyhood. 'Pink nose' is a source of great concern where show stock are concerned and many breeders place faith in multivitamin B and iron supplements.

Idiopathic depigmentation is an unusual disorder but it may indicate ultraviolet sensitivity. In some dogs affected by this condition the rhinarium takes on a softer texture. Treatment is difficult and necessitates protection of the nose either by artificial pigmentation— tattooing—or with sun tan lotions, although these tend to be licked away rapidly.

Nasal pyoderma (*Fig.* 2.5)

The appearance of a concentrated area of pustule formation and exudation immediately caudal to the rhinarium in a German Shepherd is almost diagnostic of nasal pyoderma (*Fig.* 2.5*a*). A similar disease may be seen in Collie types. In the first instance treatment aims to improve local hygiene by dislodging the encrustations with a débriding agent such as Dermisol (Beecham Animal Health) before the application of combined antibiotic and corticosteroid cream. A vigorous systemic course of an appropriate antibiotic, chosen after culture and sensitivity tests, is essential. In refractory cases fungal culture for *Trichophyton mentagrophytes* should be performed and only if this is negative should more drastic techniques such as cryotherapy be considered. When cryosurgery is used, the ultrafreezing should be restricted to the surface layers only because underlying bone may be

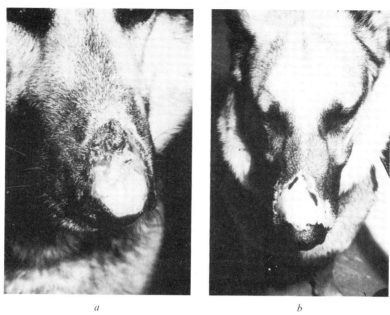

a   *b*

Fig. 2.5. Nasal pyoderma in a German Shepherd. (*a*) Before treatment. (*b*) After cryosurgery: note the unpigmented skin.

damaged and healing will be prolonged. Although this technique produces an unsightly area of unpigmented and hairless skin, the microbial infection should be controlled (*Fig.* 2.5*b*). A postoperative course of potentiated sulphonamide is indicated during the period of cryonecrosis.

Pemphigoid mucocutaneous disease

It is highly unlikely that the lesions of this autoimmune disorder will be confined to the superficial tissues of the head and neck. When a diagnosis of pemphigus is suspected other sites of predilection should be inspected—the lip and eyelid margins, the oral mucosa, the vulval, preputial and anal mucocutaneous junctions, the ears and the feet. The condition may arise in any breed and dogs of all ages are susceptible. The diagnosis is confirmed first by the discovery of pathognomonic clefts in full-thickness biopsies from the skin/mucosal junction and secondly by immunofluorescent antibody testing.

Treatment aims to suppress the autoimmune response and oral prednisolone is often effective. Up to $14\,\mathrm{mg\,kg^{-1}\,d^{-1}}$ in divided doses may be used initially, but this must be tailed off gradually at the end of the course. Recurrences are possible.

Eosinophilic granuloma complex of cats (*Fig.* 2.6)

The so-called 'rodent ulcer' of the upper lip margin is the most common form of this syndrome. An erosion with a firm yellow/grey surface arises at the mucocutaneous junction approximately at the level of the canine tooth. It spreads towards the midline philtrum of the upper lip and sometimes lesions are bilateral. Lesions do not involve the nares themselves—ulceration here is suggestive of a squamous cell carcinoma (*see below*). The cause of eosinophilic lip granuloma is not known and therefore specific treatments cannot be applied. Oral prednisolone, intra-lesional corticosteroids, oral lincocillin or megoestrol acetate have all proved to be empirically helpful in some cases but by no means all. Simple surgical excision is often impracticable and, even in early cases, rarely successful. Cryosurgery is effective in approximately 60 per cent of cases but provokes a deficiency of the upper lip.

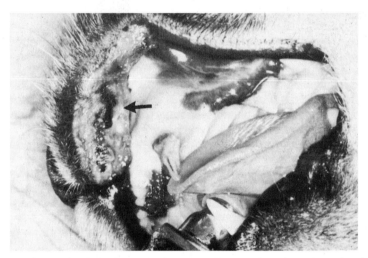

Fig. 2.6. Eosinophilic ulcer on the lip margin of a cat (rodent ulcer). (Reproduced from Kelly D. F., Lucke V. M. and Gaskell C. J. (1982) *Notes on Pathology for Small Animal Clinicians.* Bristol, Wright PSG.)

The other sites where cats may be afflicted by eosinophilic granulomas are the tongue and palate, axilla and ventral abdomen (plaque form), and the limbs (linear form).

NEOPLASIA

General considerations

The head and neck is a region where superficial neoplasms arise frequently in small animals and, at this stage, it may be pertinent to make observations which apply to the management of neoplasia irrespective of the site involved. A series of questions should be asked in each case:

1. Is the lesion in fact a tumour? In many cases the appearance of the lesion will leave no doubt of this but, in the mouth for example, proliferative inflammatory lesions are common. Biopsy is the only sure method of confirmation. The technique and submission of biopsy samples were discussed in Chapter 1.

2. Does the site and appearance of the lesion provide any clues to the diagnosis? Sometimes it is a helpful practice to make a written description of the lesion as this may trigger the grey cells to the correct solution!

3. Does the breed, age, sex or colour of the patient provide any further pointers to the definitive diagnosis?

4. What tissue types are represented at the site in question from which a tumour could have arisen?

5. Is there any evidence of metastasis or multicentric primary tumour involvement? In the first instance local lymph nodes should be palpated. Almost all tumours of the head and neck region which metastasize do so via the lymphatic system. Therefore, if there is no local lymphadenopathy, there is little virtue in taking radiographs to check for chest metastases. Thyroid adenocarcinomas are exceptional in this respect as they spread via the venous system. Lymphadenopathy is not necessarily proof of metastasis because an infected lesion may precipitate local lymph node hyperplasia. Again, biopsy is the only certain method of confirmation.

6. Is there any other evidence of malignancy? Radiographs of the lesions may show areas of destruction or proliferation of underlying bone.

The answers to these questions together with a knowledge of the biological behaviour of tumours should make it possible to give an owner a tentative diagnosis and prognosis pending the biopsy result. A course of action, treatment or euthanasia, may be taken without a biopsy, but wherever there is an element of doubt, the owner and the animal are entitled to have that doubt explored by an experienced histopathologist. After a specific diagnosis has been established a more accurate prognosis can be given and the best method of treatment can be instituted.

Squamous cell carcinoma of the nares in cats

This tumour occurs in cats with white noses and, in common with the similar tumour on the pinna and eyelids, it is probably triggered by the carcinogenic effect of ultraviolet light. The condition presents as a chronic, bleeding ulcer of the external nares and of the skin immediately above the rhinarium (*Fig.* 2.7*a*). The tumour may not be particularly proliferative and much of the rhinarium may be destroyed if the tumour is not treated early. The lesion tends to spread into the anterior nasal chambers and via the lacrimal duct to involve the conjunctiva. Metastasis of this tumour is not rapid but takes place via the local lymph nodes.

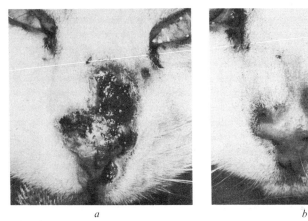

a   *b*

Fig. 2.7. Squamous cell carcinoma of nares of a cat. (*a*) Before treatment: note that this lesion is erosive rather than proliferative. (*b*) After cryosurgery.

Treatment by excision is not usually practicable. Cryosurgery offers an effective method of therapy and a good cosmetic result can be expected (*Fig.* 2.7*b*).

Squamous cell carcinoma of the pinna of cats is described in Chapter 13.

Squamous cell carcinoma of the nares of dogs

Squamous cell carcinoma may arise in the nasal vestibule of elderly dogs and it usually appears as an ulcerated but only slightly proliferative area with a peripheral zone of depigmentation. Dogs afflicted by this tumour frequently sneeze and a bloody discharge may be evident. Metastasis of this tumour is slow and effective treatment may be achieved by ultrafreezing although access to the tumour may require improvement by a lateral rhinotomy incision. Untreated tumours expand by infiltration caudally, medially through the midline septum and contralateral rhinarium and laterally into the alar folds. The treatment of advanced tumours may necessitate extensive cryodestruction of the rhinarium and the cosmetic result may be unacceptable to the owner. This tumour is also sensitive to irradiation.

Histiocytoma

The histiocytoma is a benign skin tumour of young dogs (under 3 years of age) and frequently appears as an isolated unpigmented proliferation on the muzzle or ears. It usually has a raised, hairless nodular appearance and is slow-growing. Some histiocytomas resolve spontaneously. Treatment by excision is effective but may distort the facial appearance of the patient. Cryosurgery is effective but the result may also be slightly unsatisfactory if there is hairlessness or if the hair which regrows is white.

Mast cell tumour

This is the most common malignant skin tumour of the dog and it occasionally occurs in cats. Although the lesion most frequently arises on the trunk, approximately 20 per cent occur on the head region. The tumour seldom occurs in dogs under 5 years of age and its rate of growth and degree of differentiation are variable. Poorly defined tumours metastasize readily and therefore biopsy is helpful for prognosis. The lesion appears as a raised plaque which becomes hairless; there is frequently a zone of erythema at the periphery and the site may ulcerate. Mast cell tumours may show local metastasis and frequently secondary neoplasia occurs to the lung fields. Although excision and cryosurgery may be effective in the treatment of isolated mast cell tumours, a pessimistic prognosis is always advisable.

Other skin tumours

Simple papillomas frequently afflict elderly dogs. Other benign skin tumours include the fibroma and naevus. The fibrosarcoma is no respector of youth because young dogs and cats may be afflicted; the lesion frequently recurs after local excision but metastasis is uncommon. Malignant melanomas may arise at the lip margins and rhinarium; again there is a tendency for local recurrence after excision and metastasis via the lymphatic system is common.

Neurofibroma

As the superficial branches of the trigeminal and facial nerves cross the cheek region they are vulnerable to trauma and this may explain the predisposition to neurofibroma at this site. These tumours are very dense and irregular in outline, but they are generally elongated, corresponding to the nerve trunk involved. Surgical excision is often difficult and local recurrence is a frequent sequel.

Primary bone tumours

Osteoma (*Fig. 2.8*) and osteosarcoma (*Fig. 2.9*) of the skull can produce horrifying appearances. Either of these tumours may develop from the

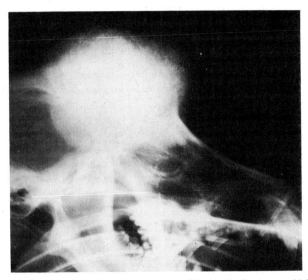

Fig. 2.8. Radiograph of an inoperable osteoma of the skull of a 1 year-old Spaniel.

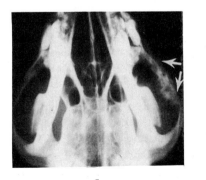   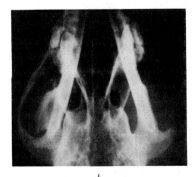

a   *b*

Fig. 2.9. Osteosarcoma of the zygomatic arch of an 8-year-old Labrador. (*a*) Before treatment. (*b*) After resection of the arch. The patient has survived for 18 months so far without recurrence.

cranium, zygoma and mandible. In one series over 20 per cent of osteosarcomas arose in the skull and mandible. The radiographic features are normally sufficient to justify a positive diagnosis, but where there is doubt, biopsy may be necessary. Each of these tumours may be treated on its merits.

Primary intranasal tumours

The breakout of a primary intranasal neoplasm is likely to cause an obvious superficial facial swelling. The most frequent site for such a mass is at the dorsal midline on the level of the medial canthi but these tumours occasionally invade the medial wall of the orbit and proptosis follows. The possibility of an intranasal tumour should be investigated, particularly by radiography, whenever a supranasal swelling appears on a dog. Attempts to biopsy the mass may be misleading because in some cases emergence of a soft tissue mass is preceded by that of a mucus retention cyst.

SURGICAL TECHNIQUES

Lateral rhinotomy (*Fig.* 2.10)

Exploration of the nasal vestibule and anterior nasal chambers or the need to improve surgical access to this region are the indications for a

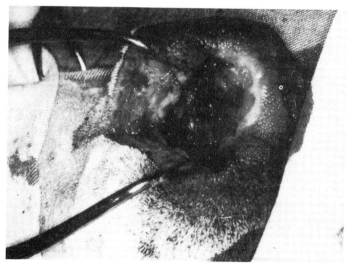

Fig. 2.10. Lateral rhinotomy in a Labrador to expose an erosive squamous cell carcinoma.

lateral rhinotomy. A full-thickness incision is made from the angle of the rhinarium dorsocaudally towards the nasomaxillary notch. This incision aims to divide between the dorsal and ventral parietal cartilages but the accessory cartilage is invariably sectioned. Self-retaining retractors dilate the incision during the exploration or surgical treatment. Closure of the surgical wound is in three layers: first the nasal mucous membrane, using 3/0 catgut; secondly the connective tissue, also with 3/0 catgut; finally the skin, using 2/0 silk. The application of a petroleum gel-based antibiotic ointment is advocated until the sutures are removed after 10 days.

Cryosurgery

The indications for cryosurgery in the head and neck region are confined to superficial lesions thus far, and they may be listed as follows:

Papilloma
Histiocytoma
Fibroma
Squamous cell carcinoma of the nares and pinna
Eyelid tumours—most are suitable
Eosinophilic granulomas in cats
Oral tumours—selected cases
Tonsillectomy—in conjunction with conventional techniques

The usual function of cryosurgery is the local destruction of undesirable tissues, but there is the additional benefit that moistened tissue surfaces adhere to cooled metallic probes and this provides a method for atraumatic manipulation. Cryodestruction is produced by the lethal extraction of heat from living tissues by the precise application of a refrigerant either directly as a spray or within a closed metallic probe. The techniques and equipment used in cryotherapy have been described extensively in the literature. In general, there is a requirement for greater accuracy for cryosurgery of the facial region and within the mouth. Thus, the use of liquid nitrogen as a free spray may not be advisable in these areas. Enclosed cryoprobes are safer and they may be cooled by liquid nitrogen, liquid or gaseous nitrous oxide or freon.

The following criteria should be met if cryosurgery is to be effective in the ablation of living tissues:

1. The target tissues should be frozen to $-20\,°C$ or below.

2. Freezing cycles should consist of a rapid lowering of tissue temperature followed by a slow thaw.

3. The freeze/thaw cycle should be repeated at least once. For malignant tumours, especially those derived from connective tissue, two repeated cycles should be regarded as the minimum.

4. A margin for error should be allowed at the periphery of the frozen lesion but the extent of this will be dictated by the site and the presence of adjacent vital structures.

5. As far as possible, healthy tissue should be preserved.

Unlike irradiation, cryosurgery requires no special facilities to ensure the safety of both the patient and the clinician, and it is repeatable. The attraction of cryotherapy for most veterinarians is that it provides a modality for tissue destruction which is entirely practicable. Given a basic understanding of the equipment and of tissue responses to ultrafreezing, cryosurgery can be performed with competence and precision. In the postoperative phase cryolesions produce minimal discomfort and, therefore, in animals there is little tendency to self-inflicted injury at the site. Cryolesions are also remarkable through the rarity of secondary infection and reactionary haemorrhage, and yet the destruction of tissues depends upon necrosis. Once the necrotic tissue has been shed, the sites heal by neoepithelization across a bed of healthy granulation tissue. There is surprisingly little cicatrization and thus cryosurgery is particularly suitable in sites where fibrosis is undesirable, such as the eyelids and facial areas. On the other hand, the slough process may be unsightly and after intra-oral treatments halitosis may be marked. Owners must be warned of these changes and they should also be informed that the skin at sites treated by cryosurgery may lose its pigment and those hairs that return may be white.

SUPPLEMENTARY READING

Bennett D., Lauder I. M., Kirkham D. et al. (1980) Bullous auto-immune skin disease in the dog. *Vet. Rec.* **106**, 497–503.

Hamer D. L. and Sacks M. (1975) The palate. In: Bojrab M. J. (ed.) *Current Technics in Small Animal Surgery*. Philadelphia, Lea & Febiger, pp. 75–84.

Lane J. G. (1974) Practical cryosurgery—an introduction for small animal clinicians. *J. Small Anim. Pract.* **15**, 715–25.

Scott D. W. (1975) Observations on the eosinophilic granuloma complex of cats. *J. Am. Anim. Hosp. Assoc.* **11**, 261–70.

Withrow S. J. (ed.) (1980) Cryosurgery. *Vet. Clin. North Am.* **10**, No. 4.

Chapter 3

Canine Nasal Disorders

When the respiratory mucous membranes are irritated or damaged the patient reacts in two ways. First, there are attempts to dislodge the irritant by forceful air movements, i.e. *sneezing* from the nose and coughing from the lower airways. Secondly, increased *production of mucus* attempts to wash the irritant away. Thus, sneezing and the presence of a mucus-based discharge at the nostrils are signs common to most nasal diseases of all animals. However, if the flow of air through the nose is obstructed, sneezing becomes a reflex action to clear the passages and by the same token, in intranasal disease, the cause of the obstruction is frequently the discharge itself. A self-perpetuating cycle of events may be initiated in this manner and sometimes the objective of treatment is to break this cycle. The presence of a discharge in the nasopharynx may provoke gagging and coughing, but if the nasal obstruction is severe and bilateral the dog may be forced to revert to mouth breathing. Intranasal structures are highly vascular and therefore nasal diseases are frequently accompanied by episodes of *epistaxis*. Veterinary attention is sought in cases of nasal disease, because the dog is in a distressed condition and because a nasal discharge, especially when bloody, can be unacceptable in the home. Less frequently, a dog may be presented because of facial deformity or pain when the supporting bones of the nose are touched.

ANATOMICAL CONSIDERATIONS

The limits of the nasal cavity are provided by the septum medially, the cribriform plate caudally, the hard palate ventrally and the maxilla, frontal and lacrimal bones dorsally and laterally (*Fig.* 3.1) The posterior nares open into the nasopharynx and these two structures are

41

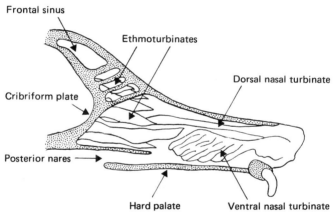

Fig. 3.1. Longitudinal section of canine nose to show the distribution of the turbinates.

divided from the buccal cavity by the soft palate. On dorsoventral radiographs the nasal septum gives a false impression of a continuous bony structure (*Fig.* 3.2). Caudally, the septum sits on the vomer bone and anteriorly it consists of a cartilaginous sheet which is ossified only at its junction with the palate. Provided that this line of ossification remains intact, quite large defects may exist in the cartilaginous portion which would not be apparent on radiographs.

The nasal chambers are occupied by the turbinate bones (*Fig.* 3.1) which are arranged compactly such that any discharge, generalized thickening or local swelling interferes with air flow. The dorsal and ventral nasal turbinate bones occupy the middle segment of each

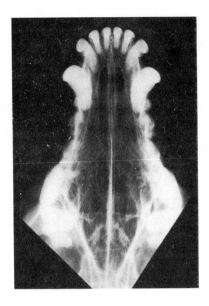

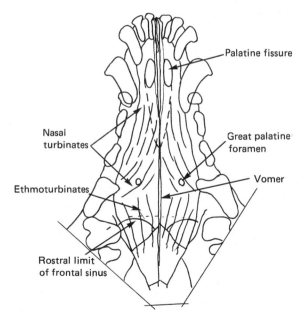

Fig. 3.2. Occlusal dorsoventral radiograph of normal canine nose with diagram to show major anatomical features.

chamber; both arise from the maxilla. The posterior segment is occupied by the ethmoturbinate scrolls which arise from the cribriform plate. The two dovetail and at the overlap zone it is not uncommon to see asymmetry on dorsoventral radiographs even in normal dogs (*Fig. 3.2*). The delicate scrolls of the turbinate bones and their equally fine air interspaces make for good contrast so that radiography is an important aid to the diagnosis of nasal diseases in dogs.

The frontal sinuses drain through narrow ostia which open between the ethmoturbinate scrolls. These openings become obstructed when the turbinates are diseased and mucus accumulates within the sinus cavities. This retained mucus (sinus retention mucocele is the correct term) is usually sterile but it often leads to a mistaken diagnosis of primary sinusitis.

The structures of the nasal chambers and frontal sinuses are covered by a secretory lining. This is highly vascular and, apart from goblet cells in the ciliated epithelium, there are many mucous and serous glands in the stroma. It is estimated that the human nasal mucosae secrete in excess of one pint of fluid per day and dogs must produce rather more. Much of this fluid is lost by evaporation but the remainder is moved caudally to the nasopharynx by the action of cilia. It can be appreciated that if this flow is obstructed by any disease process, there will be major consequences. Stagnant mucus and poor ventilation create conditions ideal for bacterial infections and the flow of secretions will be reversed to some extent to appear at the nostrils as a discharge.

CANINE NASAL PATHOLOGY

Acute rhinitis

During the past decade, a wide range of viruses have been incriminated as the primary pathogens initiating inflammation of the upper respiratory tract of dogs. Adenovirus, herpesvirus, reovirus and influenza virus have all been recovered from clinical cases of acute rhinitis; rhinitis has always been recognized as one of the major features of generalized distemper infection. However, respiratory disease in which distemper virus is involved may occur in the absence of alimentary and nervous signs, particularly in vaccinated dogs. Most upper respiratory tract viruses are epitheliotropic, producing focal areas of necrosis in the nasal, tracheal and bronchial mucosa. Viral infections are accompanied by a variable febrile response together with relatively mild clinical signs referable to the nasal chambers. There is a rapid onset of sneezing and production of a bilateral mucoserous discharge, except in cases of distemper where the discharge is purulent. In addition, it appears that some bacteria, such as *Bordetella bronchiseptica*, can also act as primary pathogens of the canine upper airways. However, the secondary opportunist damage by bacteria, mycoplasma and fungi plays a major role in acute rhinitis. Tissue responses include hyperaemia and engorgement of the mucosa, lymphoid hyperplasia, neutrophil infiltration and, later, mononuclear cell permeation. The degree of destruction of the underlying turbinate bone depends upon the dominant organisms present. Necrotic epithelial elements and pus may be shed into the mucoid discharge. Ulceration of highly vascular tissue can lead to epistaxis but this is a rare sign of bacterial or mycoplasma rhinitis.

External trauma to the nose with or without fractures of the supporting bones can precipitate serious disruption of the delicate turbinate structures and epistaxis follows. Although most of the blood will be removed by sneezing and swallowing, that which remains forms an ideal substrate for bacterial growth. Secondary rhinitis may be a sequel to trauma unless preventive measures are taken.

Foreign bodies, particularly grass seeds, awns and food particles, cause considerable nasal irritation, a purulent discharge and constant attempts to dislodge the offending matter by sneezing. Disturbances of normal deglutition may lead to food being forced into the nasal chambers. Congenital defects of the hard and soft palates, oronasal fistulas, pharyngeal paralysis, oropharyngeal neoplasia, cricopharyngeal achalasia and megaloesophagus are all conditions where secondary rhinitis can be expected.

Parasites within the nasal chambers will provoke rhinitis. It has become traditional when discussing nasal diseases of the dog to mention *Linguatula serrata* infestation. However, as the dog and the herbivorous intermediate host have been separated by improved slaughterhouse hygiene, this condition has become very rare.

Chronic hyperplastic rhinitis

Prolonged irritation and stimulation of the nasal mucous membranes occur when microbial infection remains uncontrolled, when intranasal foreign material is not eliminated and in the presence of neoplasia. Hyperplastic changes of the epithelium, particularly of the mucous gland elements and stroma, follow. The copious mucous discharge inhibits normal ventilation and secondary infections follow; the signs of rhinitis will persist as long as there is mucous hypersecretion. Dachshunds and Whippets seem particularly prone to this disease. The hyperplastic changes are often present throughout the conducting airways and therefore signs of a productive tracheobronchitis may also be present. These consist of a productive cough with radiographic changes of bronchopneumonia; it is not unusual to see a marked rise in total white cell count.

Polyps are localized protuberances of chronic inflammatory change; these are not common in dogs, but when they arise, it is most often in the German Shepherd. Polyps tend to become pedunculated and the length of the attachments may permit them to appear at the external nares or to extend posteriorly to the nasopharynx. In either case dyspnoea will be evident.

Irish Wolfhound rhinitis is a breed-specific condition characterized by chronic hyperplastic reactions of the nasal, tracheal and bronchial mucosae, but the nasal signs may be predominant. Although a viral aetiology has been suggested, it seems more likely that an incompetence of the immune system predisposes to repeated opportunist infections. Wolfhound puppies are infected soon after birth and those that survive show chronic signs of a bilateral mucopurulent nasal discharge and persistent productive coughing.

Nasal mycoses

It is unusual for fungal infections to be primary pathogens of the respiratory system. They are more likely to become established during periods of immuno-incompetence or where tissue damage by other microbial infections, trauma or neoplasia provides a suitable substrate for their growth or provokes poor local ventilation. In human patients, where primary pulmonary diseases are more common than in dogs, mycotic lung lesions are correspondingly more frequent. Also, mycotic infections represent a major hazard to human transplant patients who are treated with high doses of immunosuppressant drugs to prevent rejection.

Aspergillus fumigatus is the most frequent cause of fungal rhinitis in dogs. Penicillium spp. and *Cryptococcus neoformans* are rarely isolated from the sinuses and nasal cavities of this species. Once *A. fumigatus* infection is established, the fine trabecular structures of the turbinate bones are destroyed as the mycelium advances. Reproductive hyphae produced by the mycelium may form a mat with the macroscopic appearance of white jam mould (*Fig.* 3.3). Initially, a purulent unilateral discharge is produced but, as destruction advances, epistaxis may be provoked. The infection usually commences in the posterior region of the ventral nasoturbinate scroll and advances from that site anteriorly. Destruction of the midline septum and extension of the infection into the contralateral nasal chamber will lead to a bilateral discharge. The mycotic infection may extend into the paranasal sinuses, or alternatively the natural drainage ostia may become occluded and a retention mucocoele develops. Infiltration of the supporting bones of the nose may be responsible for a painful reaction on palpation. Facial and palatine fistulas are unusual consequences of nasal mycoses.

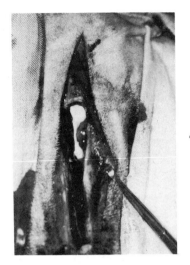

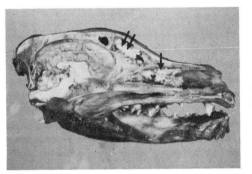

Fig. 3.3. (*a*) *A. fumigatus* colonies *in situ* on the turbinates of an Afghan Hound, exposed by rhinotomy. (*b*) Post-mortem specimen with *A. fumigatus* colonies on the posterior nasal turbinates (single arrow) and within the frontal sinus (double arrows).

Similarly, the infection rarely crosses the cribriform plate but in these circumstances signs such as epileptiform seizures would be expected.

The dolichocephalic and mesocephalic breeds appear most susceptible to nasal aspergillosis and although dogs of any age may be infected, younger patients are most commonly involved (*Fig.* 3.4).

Sequestration of nasal bone fragments

The maxilla, nasal, incisive and frontal bones are prone to fractures during trauma. It is usually possible to manage such depression

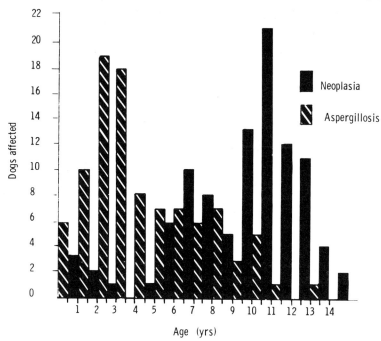

Fig. 3.4. Comparison of the age incidence of canine nasal aspergillosis with nasal neoplasia—100 consecutive cases of each at the University of Bristol.

fractures conservatively without complication. Sometimes, however, fragments of dead bone remain in the frontal sinus or lateral wall of the nasal cavity. A typical sequestration process will follow, leading to suppuration through a superficial sinus or through the nasal airways.

Extension of dental disease into the nasal chambers

Each of the maxillary teeth of the dog is separated from the nasal chamber or maxillary recess by a thin layer of supporting alveolar bone and it is surprising that periapical abscesses are rarely the cause of a nasal discharge. Maxillary dental (malar) abscessation is a well-recognized specific entity of dogs that present with a discharging sinus below the eye. The focus of suppuration is usually, but not always, in the periapical tissues of the upper carnassial tooth. Nevertheless, periapical abscesses of other teeth, most typically the canine and incisors, may cause suppuration directly into the nasal chamber with a consequent nasal discharge (*Fig.* 3.5).

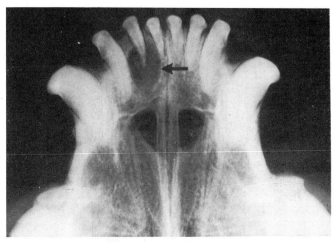

Fig. 3.5. Dorsoventral radiograph from a Boxer with a scanty unilateral nasal discharge. Note the tooth root abscess (arrowed).

Intranasal neoplasia

Neoplasms arising from structures within the nasal chambers account for the majority of dogs presented with persistent epistaxis, for some patients with a chronic non-haemorrhagic nasal discharge and for a small number of cases of persistent non-productive sneezing or nasopharyngeal obstructive dyspnoea. Similar signs may result from the spread of invasive tumours of adjacent organs, particularly of the oropharynx.

A wide range of tumours have been reported from the nasal cavities of dogs but it is more convenient to classify them as (*a*) carcinomas, (*b*) sarcomas and (*c*) other rare types. The behaviour of primary nasal tumours is similar. Medium and medium–large breeds (20–40 kg) are most susceptible whilst giant and miniature types are seldom affected; brachycephalic dogs and patients under 6 years old are rarely involved (*Fig.* 3.4). Males and females are equally represented. The most frequent site of origin of intranasal neoplasia appears to be the ethmoturbinate region (*Fig.* 3.6). Expansion of the soft tissue mass takes place in parallel with destruction of normal structures. The tumour may occupy much of the nasal cavity on the side of origin before breaking through the medial septum or overlying nasal bone; this latter produces a facial swelling. Infrequent lines of expansion are through the cribriform plate, through the medial wall of the orbit (producing proptosis) or through the hard palate. Primary intranasal tumours are locally malignant and show little tendency to metastasize

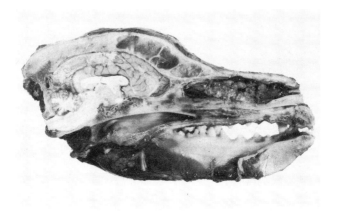

Fig. 3.6. Intranasal sarcoma in a Labrador. The mass has arisen in the ethmoid region and expanded to displace the nasal turbinates.

either to local lymph nodes or to distant sites. They show a high tendency to recur following surgery, presumably because the site of origin makes complete extirpation impracticable.

Sinusitis

Primary sinus diseases are rare in dogs. Those conditions which are labelled as primary sinusitis are almost invariably extensions of disease from adjacent tissues and this may explain why so-called sinusitis can be difficult to treat! It is most likely that infections reach the frontal sinuses by spread from the turbinate structures or, in the case of the maxillary recess, from a tooth root abscess. Intranasal tumours may expand into the sinuses. It has already been suggested that the roof of the frontal sinus may be subjected to trauma but bony tumours may arise from the walls of the paranasal sinuses.

DIAGNOSIS (*Table* 3.1)

A routine should be adopted for the investigation of cases of nasal disease. The owner's estimation of the degree of dyspnoea shown, and of the characteristics and progress of any nasal discharge, are noted. For example, a history of sudden onset of frenzied sneezing with a unilateral purulent discharge is highly suggestive of an intranasal foreign body.

During the general clinical inspection the attitude and overall bodily condition of the patient is noted. Attention is paid to any nasal discharge, facial deformity or ulceration at the angles of the rhinarium.

Table 3.1. *Differential diagnosis of chronic nasal disease of the dog*

	Nature of discharge						Other features			Radiography					Specific techniques			
	Mucoid	Purulent	Epistaxis	Food material	Unilateral	Bilateral	Facial deformity	Pain on nasal bone	Cough	Bone destruction	Periapical rarefaction	Increased soft tissue density	Sequestrum	Lung changes	Serology	Culture	Histopathology	Exploratory rhinotomy
Intranasal neoplasia	*	*	XX		X →	*	*			X		X					X	X
Chronic hyperplastic rhinitis (including Irish Wolfhound syndrome)	X		*		*	X			*			X		*			X	X
A. fumigatus infection		X			X →	*		*		X					X	X	X	X
Dysphagia		X		X		X										X	X	
Intranasal parasitism	*	X	*		X	*												
Dental periapical abscess		X			X						X							X
Post-traumatic sequestrum		X			X								X					

x Frequent positive finding; * Occasional positive finding.
This table is intended as a general guide to diagnosis. Case exceptions have a habit of proving clinical rules of thumb.

This ulceration may be excoriation resulting from persistent licking of a nasal discharge. The presence of an ocular discharge may suggest interference with normal tear flow through the nasolacrimal duct. Temperature, pulse and respiratory function are assessed. In a patient with symptoms of short duration, a febrile reaction suggests an acute infection. Observations on the dyspnoea may help to localize the intranasal lesion. When sneezing is the dominant sign the lesion is likely to be in the anterior area of the nasal chamber; on the other hand, where snorting and gagging predominate the lesion probably lies posteriorly. A tendency to mouth-breathe suggests a severe, possibly bilateral, nasal obstruction. A simple assessment and comparison of airflow through the nasal passages can be made by holding a wisp of cotton wool at each nostril. Palpation of the nasal bones may reveal asymmetry or swellings as well as areas of softening or pain. At this stage a preliminary inspection of the oropharynx is made.

The patient is anaesthetized for more detailed investigations. *The possibility of inhalation of discharges or other fluids makes it imperative to utilize a cuffed endotracheal tube.* The examination of the oropharynx includes inspection of the dental crowns, hard and soft palates, tonsils and oropharynx. The nasopharynx is viewed by drawing the soft palate forward before introducing an illuminated dental mirror. Anterior rhinoscopy is performed by introducing an auriscope or 5 mm fibre-scope into the nasal vestibule. Although this endoscopic procedure is usually frustrated by the presence of a discharge, it is occasionally possible to identify a foreign body, fungal colony or neoplasm.

Forced flushing of the nasal passages by saline may be helpful for diagnosis or treatment. In addition to the cuffed endotracheal tube, a known number of swabs are placed in the nasopharynx for this procedure. The saline is introduced either through a plastic cannula or through a blunt-ended (Spreull) needle. For this procedure the patient is best placed in lateral recumbency on an inclined surface with the nose downwards and the end of the table protruding over a suitable receptacle. Forced nasal flushing may dislodge a suspected foreign body or may be useful for the retrieval of specimens for direct smear or cytological investigations. It is not uncommon for slight epistaxis to be provoked by this procedure.

The following projections are used in the radiography of the nasal chambers:
  1. Dorsoventral occlusal (film in mouth).
  2. Straight lateral.
  3. Tilted ventrodorsal (open-mouth).
  4. Anteroposterior (frontal sinus view) (*Fig.* 3.7).
  5. Lateral oblique (maxillary dental arcade view).

The occlusal view is the single most useful projection but a lateral view should be taken in all cases to provide an accurate three-

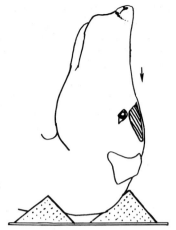

Fig. 3.7. Radiographic projection to skyline the frontal sinuses.

dimensional location of any lesion (*Fig.* 3.8). The tilted open-mouth
and anteroposterior projections are reserved for those cases where there
is suspected sinus disease. This should be apparent from loss of the air
shadow on the plain lateral view (*Fig.* 3.8). The anteroposterior
projection skylines the frontal sinuses and is particularly useful where
depression fractures or other lesions of the roof of the sinus are
suspected (*Fig.* 3.9). In the open-mouth projection the tilted beam leads

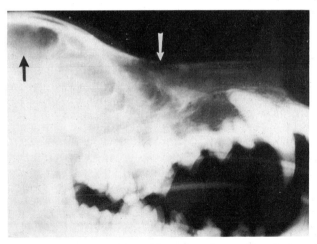

Fig. 3.8. Lateral radiograph of dog with nasal carcinoma. Note the loss of air
shadow in the frontal sinus (black arrow) and the destruction of the overlying
bone (white arrow). There is an increased radiodensity of the ethmoidal area.

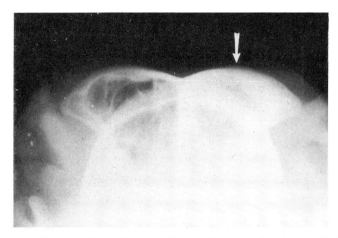

Fig. 3.9. Skyline projection showing unilateral thickening of the bony wall of the frontal sinus with reduction of the air shadow due to empyema or mucus retention.

to significant foreshortening of the nasal turbinates but it brings the sinuses forward from the cranial vault.

The radiologist relies on subtle changes in the contrast between the delicate turbinate trabecular bone, soft tissue and air in the interspaces when reading films of nasal chambers (*Fig.* 3.10). Optimum definition is obtained by the use of slow double-wrapped films or cassettes with high definition screens.

Before inspection of the turbinate trabecular pattern, the supporting bones and the midline septum should be examined for evidence of distortion, destruction or proliferation. Any evidence of rarefaction around the tooth roots should be noted and correlated with abnormalities of the clinical dental crowns. Radiological interpretations of the turbinate trabecular pattern, as seen on the occlusal view, can be categorized into four groups:

1. Normal: the fine turbinate trabecular pattern is seen against the contrasting background of air throughout both nasal chambers. It is not uncommon to see slight asymmetry in the pattern at the level of the anterior roots of the carnassial tooth. This corresponds to the area of overlap of the nasal- and ethmoturbinates.

2. Increased soft tissue shadow: the fine turbinate pattern is still visible throughout, but air contrast is reduced as the interspaces have become filled by soft tissue, e.g. chronic hyperplastic rhinitis.

3. Turbinate destruction without increased soft tissue shadow (*Fig.* 3.10): lakes of negative (air) contrast are visible but the trabecular pattern is absent in part, e.g. the destructive rhinitis of *A. fumigatus*

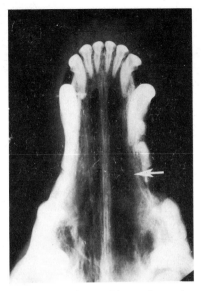

Fig. 3.10. Occlusal view showing turbinate destruction typical of nasal aspergillosis.

infection. In the early stages of this infection the destructive changes are most likely to be seen in the posterior nasal turbinates.

4. Turbinate destruction with increased soft tissue shadow (*Fig.* 3.11): the trabecular pattern is absent and in its place the soft tissue shadow eliminates any contrasting air. This ground glass appearance is typical of intranasal neoplasia. Tumours are most likely to commence in the posterior section of the nasal chamber corresponding to the ethmoturbinate region.

Although a diagnosis of nasal aspergillosis may be confirmed either by direct smear or by culture of the nasal discharge, these tests are highly unreliable as they are likely to produce false negative results. Smears should be stained with methylene blue to demonstrate fungal hyphae and spores. Selective culture media for fungi, such as Sabouraud's medium, may produce *A. fumigatus* colonies but they are more likely to be overgrown by bacterial species such as Proteus which are secondary invaders within the nasal cavities. In general terms, culture and sensitivity testing of swabs from the nasal passages of dogs do not make a useful contribution to diagnosis or treatment and in fact the results obtained may be confusing. The most accurate diagnostic method for intranasal aspergillosis is the agar gel double diffusion test to confirm the presence of antibodies in serum. Blood from suspected patients should be collected into glass containers and allowed to clot.

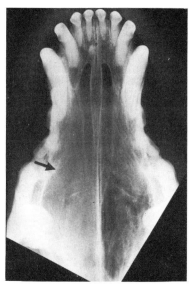

Fig. 3.11. Occlusal view showing ground glass appearançe indicative of unilateral intranasal neoplasia.

As the clot retracts against the glass container, serum becomes easy to collect. This is then tested on an agar gel plate against commercially available *A. fumigatus* antigen. Precipitation at the junction between the antibody and antigen wells on the agar plate is indicative of a positive reaction. This test is extremely reliable.

Haematological parameters may give further evidence to support a diagnosis of aspergillosis. A total white cell count raised above $15 \times 10^9/l$ with a shift to the left and depressed absolute lymphocyte count support this diagnosis. Nevertheless a raised WBC can be expected in the prolonged presence of an intranasal foreign body. Mycotic rhinitis due to Penicillium spp. infection shows many features similar to those of aspergillosis. The possibility of this rare infection might be considered if destructive rhinitis is discovered on radiographs in the absence of a positive diffusion test for aspergillosis. A similar immunological test is available for the diagnosis of penicillosis and there is a good argument for using antigens to both Penicillium spp. and Aspergillus when a mycotic rhinitis is suspected.

In some patients with nasal disorders a definitive diagnosis is not possible without resort to exploratory surgery. When there is reason to suspect intranasal neoplasia, polyps, nasal mycosis, nasal parasitism or the presence of a persistent foreign body, exploratory rhinotomy is justified. In such cases, the macroscopic appearance of the nasal contents is usually sufficient to make a diagnosis prior to carrying out the appropriate treatment. Excised material should always be submitted for histopathological evaluation so that an accurate diagnosis and prognosis can be given.

TREATMENT

Acute rhinitis

Therapy is directed towards the elimination of the initiating factors when possible but, more frequently, towards the prevention of chronic sequelae, particularly by controlling secondary bacterial invasion. Acute viral infections are therefore treated using a broad spectrum antibiotic cover, provided, for example, by ampicillin, oxytetracycline or potentiated sulphonamides, for a period of 15–30 days depending on the severity of the signs at the outset. Antihistamines should be avoided since they lead to drying up of the discharges and crusting of the nostrils. Corticosteroids retard the healing processes and suppress the natural immune mechanisms; they are therefore contraindicated.

Nasal trauma

Conservative management should include a course of antibacterial medication. In the short term, post-traumatic epistaxis can usually be controlled by the application of cold compresses to the external surfaces of the nose. Only rarely is intranasal packing necessary to arrest the haemorrhage.

Fractures

Fractures of the supporting bones of the nasal chambers and frontal sinuses do not usually require open reduction. Many are of the depression type and spontaneous resolution takes place with minimal disfigurement. When there is significant displacement with over-riding fragments, reduction may be achieved with levers and fixation with simple wire sutures is adequate. Severe fractures of the maxilla may require half-pin splintage.

Foreign bodies

Foreign bodies can often be removed under direct vision through an auriscope using alligator forceps. Other, possibly hidden, foreign bodies may be dislodged from the nasal meati into the nasopharynx by forced flushing of saline solutions through the nostrils. This procedure should be carried out under general anaesthesia taking routine precautions to prevent inhalation. Swab packing in the pharynx soaks up the irrigation fluid as well as collecting the offending matter. Although it may not be possible to demonstrate the foreign body at the time of irrigation, in some cases the patient will void the material at a later stage; presumably it is loosened by the flushing procedure. In all cases a short period of antibiotic cover should be provided afterwards but the symptoms can be expected to continue for a few days even after the successful retrieval of a foreign body.

Chronic hyperplastic rhinitis

Treatment aims to break the cycle of chronic inflammation, mucus overproduction and secondary infection. Corticosteroids may be prescribed at the beginning of treatment but for the most part therapy consists of a combination of a broad spectrum antibiotic and a mucolytic agent such as bromhexine hydrochloride. However, the condition may remain intractable even in the face of vigorous polypharmacy, presumably because the mucous glands have increased irreversibly in size and number. Occasionally, when changes are localized within the nasal chambers, rhinotomy and total turbinectomy may be considered.

Intranasal aspergillosis

It is unusual for this mycosis to be controlled by medical therapy alone. Certainly, conventional anti-fungal drugs such as nystatin and amphotericin B are rarely of any use. Most cases require rhinotomy with curettage of the fungal colonies and diseased tissues at some stage. The author's preferred régime in the management of this disease is to provide a 6-week course of oral thiabendazole prior to rhinotomy. In exceptional cases, complete resolution may be obtained with the thiabendazole therapy alone, but it is more likely that following this treatment the extent of the mycosis will be reduced to the point where rhinotomy serves to remove a few residual colonies and fragments of sequestrated bone. Thus, the preliminary medication reduces the severity of the subsequent surgery. Oral administration of the thiabendazole commences at $10\,mg\,kg^{-1}\,d^{-1}$ in two equal doses for the first week and this is increased to $20\,mg\,kg^{-1}d^{-1}$ until the end of the sixth week. Thiabendazole is claimed to be non-toxic to dogs at these dosages but occasional patients show lassitude and intermittent vomiting towards the end of the course of treatment: a return to normality can be expected within 24 hours of withdrawal of the drug. At the time of rhinotomy the nasal chambers are packed with bandage inpregnated with iodoform paste and this is withdrawn 5 days later. A 10-day course of broad spectrum postoperative antibiotic is combined with a further 14 days of thiabendazole therapy. Unless the infection is exceptionally active, a cautiously optimistic prognosis can be given for cases of intranasal aspergillosis in dogs.

Neoplasia

Intranasal tumours only rarely lend themselves to successful surgery. Rhinotomy and turbinectomy may be performed in those few cases where there is a realistic prospect of total extirpation of the neoplastic tissue, e.g. where localized lesions are confined to the middle or anterior segments. After surgery of nasal tumours there is almost invariably an early recurrence and thus, for the majority of confirmed canine nasal neoplasms, rhinotomy and excision cannot be justified and euthanasia should be advised. At the time of writing, the value of irradiation, chemotherapy and cryosurgery, either singly or in combination, remains to be established.

RHINOTOMY

The indications for exploratory rhinotomy have already been mentioned, as has the role of rhinotomy in the treatment of intranasal *A. fumigatus* infection. Apart from these occasions, rhinotomy may be used to remove discrete polyps and for the extirpation of other localized chronically diseased tissues such as sequestra and hyperplastic mucosa. For the most part, rhinotomy and radical turbinectomy is unlikely to contribute to a significant extension of life in cases of intranasal neoplasia. However, one occasionally encounters intranasal tumours that are well circumscribed and sited in the middle and anterior portions of the nose; these may be successfully extirpated.

Although rhinotomy is surprisingly well tolerated by dogs, it should be performed only after a full haematological and biochemical evaluation. Whole blood transfusion is indicated for anaemic dogs and, if possible, rhinotomy should be postponed in dogs showing intercurrent disease such as nephritis.

The operation is performed with the patient in ventral recumbency (*Fig.* 3.12*a*); anaesthesia is maintained through a cuffed endotracheal tube and the pharynx is packed with gauze swabs. A dorsal midline skin incision is made from the rhinarium to a point 4 cm posterior to a line joining the supraorbital processes (*Fig.* 3.12*b*). The subcutis and periostcum are elevated and reflected laterally from the midline on the affected side. As a preliminary measure, the frontal sinus should always be trephined and this is achieved using a 6·5 mm drill at a site midway between the midline and the supraorbital process (*Fig.* 3.12*c*); the contents are inspected and any stagnant mucus or pus is removed by suction. If necessary, the trephine hole may be enlarged with a rongeur

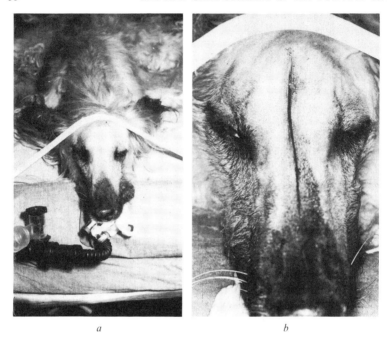

a   b

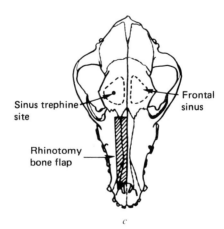

c

Fig. 3.12. Rhinotomy. (*a*) Position of patient for rhinotomy. (*b*) Extent of the skin incision. (*c*) Extent of the bone flap and site to trephine the frontal sinus. (*d*) Creating the bone flap. (*e*) Exposure of the nasal content. (*f*) Closure of the skin using a running subcuticular cosmetic pattern of monofilament nylon.

d

e

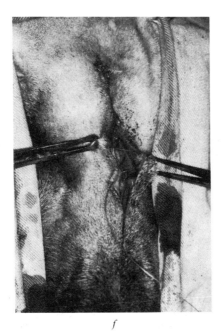

f

to permit thorough curettage of the contents of the sinus. A bone flap is made (*Fig. 3.12d*) to expose the contents of the nasal chamber for exploration (*Fig. 3.12e*). The flap is fashioned with a hand-held or oscillating saw; it remains attached anteriorly by the dorsal nasal ligament which joins the nasal bone to the rhinarium. Thus, a hinge is provided which allows the flap to be elevated forwards and if the edges are bevelled, replacement at the conclusion of the procedure is facilitated. Diseased turbinate tissue is removed using a Volkmann spoon, and infected bone may be broken away with the rongeur; specimens are submitted for histopathology. Drainage of a sinus retention mucocoele may be improved by enlargement of the normal ostium. When bilateral exposure of the nasal chambers is required, a unilateral rhinotomy followed by ablation of the nasal septum affords an adequate exposure except in small breeds where a second rhinotomy flap may be necessary. Throughout the procedure, haemostasis is achieved by intermittent pressure packing of the cavity; suction is invaluable for maintaining visibility. By the time thorough excision of the diseased contents of the nasal chamber has been completed, haemorrhage has usually reduced to a slight venous ooze. Only in those dogs where significant bleeding continues is a pressure bandage pack left in place for 48 hours prior to withdrawal through the nostrils. However, a bandage pack can be a useful vehicle for postoperative topical medication, such as iodoform installation in the treatment of nasal mycoses. For medication purposes, the bandage packing may be left in place for as long as 5 days. Withdrawal of the bandage is best performed under a short-acting general anaesthetic and a brief episode of epistaxis is to be expected. Postoperative irrigation of the frontal sinus and nasal cavity following rhinotomy may be provided by the implantation of a circle polythene tissue-drainage tube. This is introduced through the sinus trephine site and passes through the exposed nasal cavity via the sinunasal ostium and out through the nostrils. The circle is completed by tying the ends of the tubing together.

Closure of the rhinotomy begins by replacement of the bone flap if this has not been excised. The flap is held in position by the coaption of the overlying periosteal and areolar connective tissue layers with absorbable suture material. For the best cosmetic result skin sutures are avoided and a continuous subcuticular monofilament nylon pattern is suggested (*Fig. 3.12f*). The knots remain exposed at each end of the incision and the suture is removed on the tenth postoperative day. The use of such a cosmetic suture prevents an unsightly ridged appearance in the months following surgery.

Postoperative care consists of broad spectrum antibiotic cover for 10 days and, if a circle drain has been implanted, twice-daily flushing with saline to remove debris. The provision of an alternative airway by tracheotomy intubation is rarely necessary, although facility for this procedure should always be on hand during anaesthetic recovery. Postoperative emphysema is encountered from time to time but usually resolves spontaneously. During the months following rhinotomy and turbinectomy occasional opportunist bacterial infections may be encountered. *Staphylococcus aureus* and Pseudomonas are the bacterial types usually involved and appropriate topical antibiotic therapy by intranasal drops may be required on a tactical basis. In general, the more radical the turbinectomy procedure and surgical trauma caused by scraping of the lining of the nasal passages, the greater is the frequency of secondary infection. Radical scraping of the nasal chambers precipitates major reactions in the tissues, including periostitis and squamous metaplasia. Naturally, such changes are undesirable and demand that unnecessary surgical insults are avoided at the time of rhinotomy. It is the prevention of these chronic sequelae of rhinotomy which provides the rationale for the less radical treatment régime for intranasal aspergillosis described above.

PROGNOSIS

Uneventful resolution can be expected in cases of acute viral rhinitis provided that broad spectrum antibiotic cover is provided. Control of chronic hyperplastic rhinitis may be tedious but when the changes are localized within the nasal passages complete excision can be helpful. The majority of dogs with intranasal aspergillosis can be cured with a combined medical and surgical protocol. Long term studies of dogs with intranasal tumours confirm that excision alone is followed by a very high rate of local recurrence. The occasional long term success is achieved when the tumour arises from, and primarily involves, the nasal turbinates, lending itself to thorough ablation. The tumour type does not seem to influence the rate of recurrence. Owners of dogs with nasal tumours should be advised that the prognosis is poor and that surgery is likely to produce palliation for a short period only. Although rhinotomy is well tolerated by dogs, the consequences of unnecessarily vigorous currettage of the nasal passages may precipitate changes which are just as serious as the original disease.

SUPPLEMENTARY READING

Bradley P. A. and Harvey C. E. (1973) Intranasal tumours in the dog: an evaluation of prognosis. *J. Small Anim. Pract.* **14**, 459–67.
Gibbs C., Lane J. G. and Denny H. R. (1979). Radiological features of intranasal lesions in the dog: a review of 100 cases. *J. Small Anim. Pract.* **20**, 515–35.
Lane J. G., Bedford P. G. C., Harvey C. E. et al. (1982) Observations on the incidence and diagnosis of canine nasal *Aspergillosis fumigatus* infections. *J. Small Anim. Pract.* **22**, (In the press.)

Lane J. G. and Warnock D. W. (1977) The diagnosis of *Aspergillus fumigatus* infection of the nasal chambers of the dog with particular reference to the double diffusion test. *J. Small Anim. Pract.* **18**, 169–77.

Morgan J. P., Suter P. F., O'Brien T. R. et al. (1972) Tumours in the nasal cavity of the dog: a radiographic study. *J. Am. Vet. Radiol. Soc.* **13**, 18–26.

Withrow S. J. (1977) The diagnostic and therapeutic nasal flush in small animals. *J. Am. Anim. Hosp. Assoc.* **13**, 704–7.

Chapter 4

Feline Nasal Disorders

Although the presenting signs of rhinitis and sinusitis in the cat are essentially similar to those exhibited by the dog, they are usually more severe and occur with far greater frequency. The emphasis when considering feline nasal disease is on acute viral infections and their chronic consequences. Tumours of the nasal chambers and paranasal sinuses are uncommon in the cat while fungal and parasitic infestations of this region are also unusual. Primary sinusitis is a term which is often misused in cats when an underlying rhinitis is present.

ANATOMICAL CONSIDERATIONS

The anatomical features of the feline nasal chambers are similar to those of the dog. The obvious difference is that in the cat the nasal turbinates are reduced in size and the ethmoturbinates are proportionally enlarged. *Fig.* 4.1 shows the onion-like appearance of the ethmoids on lateral projection. The location of the frontal sinuses can also be appreciated and these drain through small ostia which are closely related to the ethmoturbinate scrolls. The drainage ducts are vulnerable to obstruction by the thickening which occurs during acute viral rhinitis and the proliferative changes in the turbinate tissues which occur in the regenerative phase. A secondary stagnation of mucus occurs in the sinuses irrespective of whether they themselves are involved in an infectious process. The narrow nasal bridge limits the surgical approach to the feline nose.

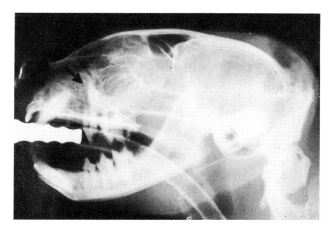

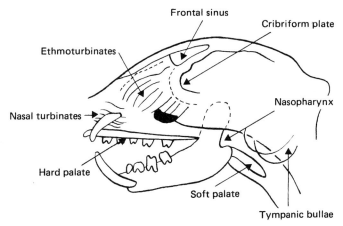

Frontal sinus

Cribriform plate

Ethmoturbinates

Nasopharynx

Nasal turbinates →

Hard palate

Soft palate

Tympanic bullae

Fig. 4.1. Radiographic anatomy of feline nasal chambers: lateral view. Note the ventral ethmoidal density (arrowed) which is a normal feature and should not be mistaken for a sequestrum or foreign body.

FELINE NASAL PATHOLOGY

Acute rhinitis

The two viruses, feline viral rhinotracheitis (FVR) virus and feline calicivirus (FCD) are the primary pathogens responsible for the majority of upper respiratory tract infections in cats. These viruses have a world-wide distribution and have been isolated in approximately equal frequency from clinical cases. FVR virus usually provokes severe clinical signs, especially in young susceptible cats. The signs in calicivirus disease (FCD) tend to be similar to, but milder than, those of FVR. Although the signs of FVR may be variable, they develop within 2–10 days of contact with the infection. Paroxysms of sneezing are accompanied by production of a clear mucoid nasal discharge which becomes copious and mucopurulent within a few days. Sometimes conjunctivitis with a marked ocular discharge is the first sign seen and on occasions this may even be unilateral. Severe debilitation and depression with total anorexia may occur; mouth breathing may be adopted and coughing can add to the distress. A febrile response in excess of 104 °F is not uncommon and leucocytosis with a shift to the left parallels the temperature elevation. Unlike other viral infections leucopenia is not observed. Occasionally with FVR but more frequently with FCD, ulceration of the lingual and buccopharyngeal mucous membranes develops. During the early stages the forepaws become soiled by oculo-nasal discharges transferred by natural feline cleansing activity. Later this lavage behaviour reduces, leaving the nares encrusted and the eyelids may be held partly closed by a tenacious exudate; contact keratitis may develop. Failure to eat and drink precipitates dehydration. The common causes of fatalities are anorexia, dehydration and secondary bacterial infection which may extend to produce pneumonia and pleurisy. Older and partly immune cats are less severely affected, exhibiting a mild conjunctivitis and rhinitis, yet still retaining a normal appetite. Some FCD strains may cause an upper respiratory disease which is clinically indistinguishable from FVR. However, it is more usual for FCD to produce a milder disease in which oral ulceration may be the only sign. FVR produces its most marked effects on the turbinate tissues, provoking an intense inflammatory reaction with necrosis and ulceration of the mucosa. In the growing cat, there is also a severe osteolytic response, with resorption of turbinate bone. Excessive mucus production, fibrin exudation, suppuration and the shedding of necrotic debris contribute to the oculonasal discharges. In the regenerative phase of the disease squamous metaplasia and mucous gland hyperplasia occur, so that in many cats recovering from the acute phase areas of permanently damaged nasal mucosa remain which are prone to recurrent microbial infection. FCD produces, at worst, a similar necrotizing rhinitis but there is a lesser tendency to secondary bacterial invasion.

Rhinitis initiated by virus infections is often prolonged and exacerbated by organisms such as streptococci, staphylococci, pasteurellae and coliforms. Apart from intensifying the acute condition, bacterial opportunist invasion increases the likelihood of chronic, irreversible changes.

Chronic rhinitis and secondary sinusitis

Epithelial hyperplasia and submucosal proliferation contribute to the thickening of the turbinate tissues which takes place during the acute phase of rhinitis. In a significant number of affected cats this response does not subsequently regress and areas of damaged tissue provide nidi for recurrent opportunist infection.

It has not yet been established whether the spread of viral particles from the nasal chambers contributes to the aetiology of frontal sinusitis. However, it is clear that the acute and chronic inflammatory changes which take place in the mucosa obstruct the normal ventilation and drainage of the sinuses through their small nasal openings. A suitable environment thereby exists for secondary bacterial infection, but the accumulation of secretions is more important in the precipitation of a sinus mucocoele. Prolonged build-up of inspissated secretions within the frontal sinuses may lead to softening of the thin overlying bone producing a facial distortion.

Cats afflicted by chronic rhinitis are sometimes designated 'snufflers'. These animals exhibit intermittent bouts of sneezing and a purulent discharge which is occasionally bloodstained. The general attitude of the cat fluctuates in parallel with the nasal symptoms and there is a tendency to unthriftiness. Inappetance and constant mouth breathing are signs of a severely affected patient.

Foreign bodies

Cats are, by nature, more discriminating than dogs and this may explain the relatively low incidence of intranasal foreign bodies in this species. Nevertheless, if a foreign body lodges in the nasal chambers of a cat, a typical suppurative reaction will develop with a unilateral purulent nasal discharge. The surrounding turbinate structures may be distorted by the intranasal abscess (see Fig. 4.4).

Nasal mycoses

Mycotic infections of the feline nasal chambers are rare. *Cryptococcus neoformans* is the most frequent fungal agent to be involved and although this may affect other organs, it shows a predilection for the upper respiratory tract. The presenting signs of nasal cryptococcosis are similar to those of severe chronic rhinitis with persistent sneezing and an intractable mucopurulent nasal discharge. Granulomatous lesions develop in one or both nasal passages and these lesions may extend to produce destruction of the facial bones and the development of a swelling. There is no evidence that transmission of cryptococcosis takes place from infected cats to human contacts. Although isolated cases of feline nasal aspergillosis and pencillosis have been reported, these are very rare indeed. The destructive changes in the turbinate scrolls are similar to those that occur in dogs with these mycoses.

Intranasal neoplasia

Although nasal tumours are common in dogs, they seldom occur in cats. Feline nasal tumours are divided into two groups: carcinomas, which behave like canine nasal tumours, and lymphosarcomas, which are usually localized manifestations of a multicentric condition. Lymphosarcomas account for the majority of feline nasal tumours. The presence of a soft tissue mass in the nasal chamber obstructs airflow and dyspnoea will be evident. Poor ventilation in the nasal passages allows secondary bacterial infection to become established so that the dominant sign of intranasal neoplasia in this species is a purulent nasal discharge. Epistaxis is less frequently encountered but a facial distortion can be a feature in the later stages.

Nasopharyngeal polyps

Polypoid lesions which arise in the middle ear may expand in two ways; first, to the external ear canal and secondly, via the eustachian tube to the nasopharynx. Cats with nasopharyngeal polyps present with two major signs—respiratory obstruction and a purulent nasal discharge. The lesions may attain a considerable size to fill the nasopharynx and cause depression of the soft palate. A nasal discharge arises because normal aeration is inhibited and the natural flow of mucus through the nasal passages is obstructed (*see* Chapter 5).

DIAGNOSIS

Acute FVR and FCD can be diagnosed from the presenting signs described above; a marked leucocytosis provides further diagnostic evidence. Virus recovery and identification is unnecessary unless advice is to be given on the control of carrier cats in a cattery or breeding colony. In this respect FVR and FCD show differing characteristics; approximately 80 per cent of cats infected by FVR become carriers, half of which are epidemiologically important as they shed viral particles, particularly during periods of stress. These carrier cats may or may not show clinical signs during periods of shedding. The carrier status of FCD-infected cats tends to be self-limiting but a few patients remain life-long shedders and represent a threat to susceptible cats. Screening by virus isolation from oropharyngeal swabs is of limited value as it can only help identify cats in the acute stage of infection or those which are shedding virus at the time of sampling. In any event the advent of live intranasal FCD vaccines adds further confusion to the role of viral isolation. The non-pathogenic strains of calicivirus behave similarly to those that cause disease and will also be recoverable on swabs. Trial therapy by parenteral use of a broad spectrum antibiotic will temporarily resolve most cases of chronic rhinitis, but failure to respond is an indication to consider other rarer diagnoses. Such suspicions are particularly justified if the nasal discharge has been *unilateral*. Direct smears of the nasal discharge are taken for the identification of *C. neoformans* which can also be identified on biopsy samples of granulomatous lesions. Bacterial and fungal growth media are used in the culture and sensitivity testing of swab samples in cases of persistent nasal discharge. The most valuable swab material is obtained from within the nasal chambers, after the nares have been cleansed with antiseptic solution. Swabs from a trephined sinus mucocoele are unlikely to be helpful as they do not provide a representative sample of the organisms that are perpetuating the underlying rhinitis. In many instances sinus swabs are sterile on culture.

The narrow nasal vestibules render anterior rhinoscopy a useless diagnostic technique in cats. When proliferative tissue is apparent at the external nares, for example in some cases of fungal granuloma or intranasal neoplasia, a biopsy sample should be taken for histopathology. Posterior rhinoscopy using an illuminated dental mirror is a routine procedure in cats with nasopharyngeal dyspnoea and by this means polyps are identified (*see Fig. 5.6*).

In cats radiography contributes less towards the definitive diagnosis of intranasal diseases than in the dog. The following projections are used in the radiography of the feline nasal chambers:

1. Dorsoventral occlusal (film in mouth).
2. Whole skull, ventrodorsal.
3. Straight lateral.

In the occlusal view the anterior areas of the nasal cavities and particularly the nasal turbinates are projected but the frontal sinuses cannot be included. On the other hand, on the ventrodorsal projection, the posterior nasal chambers and frontal sinuses can be viewed while the anterior areas are obscured by the overlying mandible (*Fig. 4.2*). The skull conformation of the cat is unsuitable for skylining the frontal sinuses using an anteroposterior view. The lateral view is helpful, not only for the identification of filling of the frontal sinuses, but also in suspected cases of polyps where the nasopharynx becomes filled by a soft tissue mass.

Radiographs may demonstrate serious disruption of the fine turbinate pattern as a result of FVR virus osteoclasis. Destruction of the turbinate pattern is to be expected in cases of intranasal neoplasia and fungal granuloma. Breakdown of the supporting bones of the nose

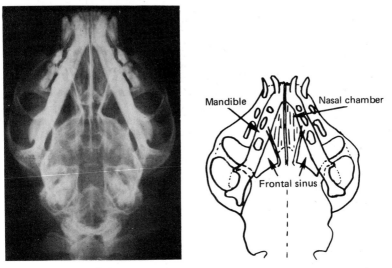

Fig. 4.2. Radiographic anatomy of feline nasal chambers: dorsoventral view.

occurs in the later stages of neoplastic and granulomatous proliferation and, at the same time, there is increased soft tissue density within the chambers. Dorsoventral views are helpful to determine whether there is symmetrical involvement of the nasal chambers and frontal sinuses (*Figs.* 4.3–4.5). Rare dental anomalies and sequestra may also be discovered on radiographs.

In cases of chronic feline nasal disease, where neoplasia or fungal granuloma are suspected, an accurate diagnosis can be reached only by biopsy sampling and histopathological investigation of intranasal

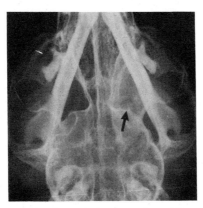

Fig. 4.3. Dorsoventral radiograph showing unilateral frontal sinus density.

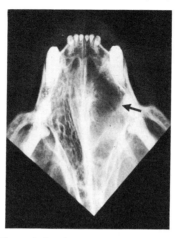

Fig. 4.4. Occlusal radiograph showing unilateral turbinate disruption caused by a grass seed abscess.

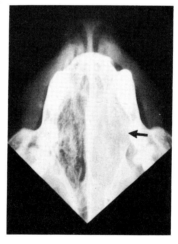

Fig. 4.5. Occlusal radiograph showing unilateral increased turbinate density caused by nasal lymphosarcoma.

tissues. A sample can be obtained by introducing a fine curette through the nasal vestibule and the haemorrhage which accompanies this biopsy collection is usually slight and of short duration. However, the procedure is best carried out under general anaesthesia with a cuffed endotracheal tube in position. Alternatively, exploratory rhinotomy may be considered.

It has already been noted that the most frequent nasal tumour in cats is the lymphosarcoma, and if this is suspected, a careful inspection of other organs should be made to identify other centres of activity. Ocular and renal lymphosarcomas are common sites in multicentric involvement.

TREATMENT

Acute rhinitis

At present there are no suitable antiviral drugs for the treatment of acute feline viral rhinitis although 5-iododeoxyuridine (IUdR) has been recommended in cases of ulcerative keratitis associated with FVR. The management of infected cats consists of special nursing and medication to eliminate secondary bacterial infection. The veterinarian is placed in an invidious position because of the risks to other hospital patients when a cat with a highly contagious infection is admitted. On the one hand intensive care is required, but on the other, the scrupulous hygiene which is necessary to prevent cross-infection makes demands which some clinics cannot meet. Outpatient nursing by the owners should be employed if at all possible. On the hospital premises it is irresponsible to permit infected animals to mix with other patients, for example in the waiting area; they should be admitted directly to the treatment room. Afterwards, infected surfaces and utensils should be treated with a cationic surface-acting agent such as cetrimide, or they should be discarded.

A dirty cat is a dejected cat; the patient with acute rhinitis should be provided with a clean, warm and well-ventilated environment, and at the same time it should be assisted with its cleaning activities. Regular, gentle bathing to remove encrusted discharges from around the eyes and nares contributes to the comfort of the cat. A bland ointment is applied to these areas to prevent excoriation. Attention should be paid to thorough grooming which the cat with lingual ulceration may be reluctant to carry out for itself. Most cats resent the restraint which is necessary for the application of nasal drops and this method of administering decongestant inhalants is not recommended. Nebulizers and steam inhalations are well tolerated and can help to reduce the tenacity of nasal discharges and maintain clear airways. A simple technique which is applicable to home nursing consists of holding a cup with TCP diluted in a small quantity of boiling water to the face of the cat. Antihistamines should be avoided since they lead to drying up of the discharges which then become difficult to dislodge. Corticosteroids are also contraindicated because they retard the healing processes and may potentiate the virus infection. Cats afflicted with acute FVR and FCD infections may reject their normal diet through lack of olfactory stimulation; they often find strongly tasting foods, such as pilchards, tinned salmon, sardines or anchovies, more attractive. These aromatic foods are provided in a liquidized form which makes swallowing less painful as well as increasing fluid intake. If necessary, food is liquidized to a suitable consistency for feeding through a disposable syringe. It is always correct to prevent dehydration before it commences; the oral administration of fluids should begin as soon as voluntary drinking ceases. Owners should be advised to observe their cats carefully because some will sit over their drinking bowls appearing to drink but swallowing nothing. The target for oral administration of fluids should be 200 ml per day.

Severe URT infections in cats represent an obvious indication for pharyngostomy intubation (*see* Chapter 1). This technique should be considered when a patient has remained totally inappetent for longer than 4 days and it affords a humane and convenient route for forced feeding, fluid therapy and medication.

A broad spectrum antibiotic cover is provided for 14 days, but may be continued for a further 10 days in severe cases. Tablets are avoided because they are painful to swallow; for oral administration paediatric syrups are suitable. A loading dose of antibiotic is provided parenterally at the outset of treatment. The following choice of antibiotics together with dose rates is suggested:

1. Ampicillin: loading dose, 7 mg/kg subcutaneously, followed by 10 mg/kg orally twice daily.

2. Potentiated sulphonamide: maintenance dose, 4 mg/kg orally twice daily.

3. Spiromycin (not to be administered by injection to cats): maintenance dose, 50 mg/kg orally once daily.

4. Tylosin: loading dose, 10 mg/kg intramuscularly, followed by 40 mg/kg orally three times daily.

Supportive vitamin therapy is helpful because:

1. Vitamin A (1000 i.u. per day) is said to be important in assisting the regeneration of damaged mucosa.

2. Vitamin B complex preparations may stimulate the return of appetite. Vitamin B12 (250 mg daily) has a marked euphoric effect on depressed cats.

3. Vitamin C (up to 100 mg daily) may shorten the recovery period. Abidec drops (Parke–Davis) are suitable for oral use and, with the exception of B12, provide the required levels of the vitamins mentioned.

Dehydration must be corrected and, in cats, fluid is best administered subcutaneously. However, when there is severe dehydration, the shut-down of the peripheral circulation can lead to poor absorption of fluids from this site; the intravenous route is then indicated. A useful rule of thumb is that if the cat is sufficiently depressed to lie still for administration, the i.v. route is used, but if there is resentment and non-cooperation, s.c. injection will be satisfactory. The objective of fluid therapy of cats with acute rhinitis is the correction of water depletion rather than of ionic imbalance. Therefore 0·18 per cent saline with 4·3 per cent dextrose is a suitable solution: concentrations of dextrose in excess of 5 per cent are irritant and are not used.

Each case of acute rhinitis should be reappraised 1 week after the start of treatment. Failure to control the secondary bacterial infection may be due to the choice of the wrong antibiotic or to inadequate concentrations of antibiotic reaching the nasal chambers. Swab cultures and sensitivity tests are performed and the therapy is amended if necessary. Lack of response to parenteral or oral antibiotic therapy while rhinitis is in the acute phase is an indication to consider local administration through the frontal sinuses. Dye tests have shown that infusions made through the sinuses reach all areas of the nasal chambers. The procedure is performed under general anaesthesia with a cuffed endotracheal tube in place. The sinus trephine site depends upon the age of the patient. In cats under 5 months of age where the sinuses are still small the sites lie on either side of the midline on a line joining the lateral canthi (*Fig.* 4.6). In adult cats the points are more caudal, again on either side of the midline, but on a line joining the supraorbital processes (*Fig.* 4.7). Stab skin incisions are made and the sinuses are entered using a 2·5 mm drill or intramedullary pin. Infusions are made through a closely fitted blunted needle (Spreull type). The sinuses, sinus ostia and nasal chambers are flushed clear of pus and debris with saline before the appropriate antibiotic is instilled. Indwelling tubes are not well tolerated by cats and irrigation through the

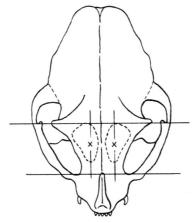

Fig. 4.6. Frontal sinus trephine sites for young cats. The sites lie on either side of the midline on a line joining the lateral canthi.

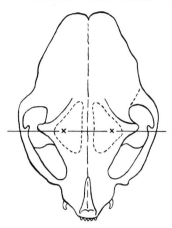

Fig. 4.7. Frontal sinus trephine sites for mature cats. *The sites lie on either side of the midline on the line joining the supraorbital processes.*

sinuses when conscious causes great distress and in the author's view is contraindicated. Although each incision may be closed using a single mattress suture of monofilament nylon, the irrigation procedure may be repeated under a general anaesthetic through the original trephine sites on alternate days until the infection is brought under control.

Chronic rhinitis

This condition is characterized by the presence of irreversibly damaged tissues within the nasal passages. There are two fundamental approaches to treatment: first, conservative methods whereby the recurrent opportunist infections are tactically controlled for short periods and, secondly, a more radical surgical excision of the diseased tissues.

The conservative methods are as follows:

1. Prolonged courses of oral antibiotic therapy based on culture and sensitivity testing of nasal swabs. The choice of drugs and dose rates are similar to those advised for the acute phase of rhinitis and a similar course of supportive vitamin therapy is also recommended.

2. Local infusion of antibiotics through the frontal sinuses. In the chronic phase, sinus irrigation provides temporary relief but appears to have no advantages over other conservative methods. Again it must be stated that the implantation of a drainage tube and the conscious irrigation of the nasal chambers is contraindicated in cats on the grounds of the considerable distress which is inflicted. There can be no justification for a method which is inhumane and fails to effect a permanent relief.

3. Autogenous vaccines prepared from cultures of nasal swabs provide only temporary relief.

Rhinotomy and turbinectomy to extirpate the chronically diseased tissues cannot be undertaken lightly in cats. The technique is not as well tolerated in this species as in dogs and patients should be carefully selected when conservative treatments produce minimal improvement of the chronic rhinitis and when repeated antibiotic therapy is unacceptable to the owners. Rhinotomy may also be performed on an exploratory basis, for example where a foreign body is suspected, and rarely, the excision of a localized intranasal tumour may be attempted. The surgical procedure for rhinotomy in the cat is similar to that in the dog except that the nasal chambers are entered by creating a double bone flap, the caudal limit of which is 0·5 cm posterior of the line joining the medial canthi (*Fig.* 4.8). The sinuses are trephined as

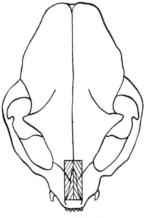

Fig. 4.8. Feline rhinotomy: the extent of the bone flap. The caudal limit of the rhinotomy flap lies 0·5 cm posterior to the line joining the medial canthi.

mentioned above and the sinunasal ostia are enlarged to facilitate drainage. Care is taken to extirpate all the remnants of turbinate and nasal mucous membrane. Fluid and supportive therapy is imperative pre- and postoperatively. After rhinotomy feline patients do not easily adapt to mouth breathing and during anaesthetic recovery the provision of an alternative airway by tracheotomy intubation may be necessary. Pharyngostomy feeding is routinely used until normal appetite returns. Sinus irrigation is performed under a general anaesthetic on the fifth and tenth postoperative days; this serves to flush away blood clots and necrotic debris as well as providing a means of local medication.

Nasal mycoses

The treatment of *C. neoformans* infection may be attempted using amphotericin B. Prolonged courses of therapy may be required using intravenous infusions at a dose rate of 0·5 mg/kg in dextrose saline three times weekly for several months. Throughout the period of treatment blood urea nitrogen should be monitored because amphotericin B produces renal toxicity. Evidence of renal failure usually disappears if the drug is withdrawn promptly.

Imidazole preparations are toxic to cats and therefore a treatment regimen similar to that suggested for aspergillosis in dogs is not applicable to this species. Under those rare circumstances where infection due to Aspergillus spp. or Penicillium spp. are encountered, rhinotomy and curettage of the affected nasal chamber(s) is indicated.

Intranasal neoplasia

Feline intranasal neoplasms are usually advanced when the diagnosis is confirmed, and surgical excision is rarely attempted. Furthermore, there is little justification for surgery because carcinomas show a high tendency to recur and lymphosarcomas may be part of a disseminated condition.

PROGNOSIS

Provided that attention is sought and treatment is instituted at the earliest sign of acute infection, careful nursing combined with intensive medical therapy should lead to resolution of most cases of FVR and FCD. Cats that are neglected by their owners or inadequately treated may develop chronic rhinitis. Nevertheless, even some of those that are intensively treated may become chronic 'snufflers'. The owners of cats with chronic rhinitis must be advised that the condition arises through persistent infection of irreversibly damaged tissues. At present, there is no satisfactory method of treatment as conservative medication or surgical interferences to the frontal sinuses bring only temporary amelioration. The more radical approach of rhinotomy with extirpation of the diseased structures from the nasal cavities should provide a solution but this procedure carries significant risks with occasional fatalities and many owners may prefer to continue with tactical medical therapy.

The potential hazards to susceptible young cats which are posed by carriers have already been mentioned. Carriers act as a reservoir for further cat-to-cat transmission of infection in breeding catteries and other colonies. The continuous excretion of virus by an FCD carrier constantly boosts immunity within the group and keeps clinical disease at a low level until new stock is introduced. However, excretion of virus by the FVR carrier is intermittent and immunity within the colony may fluctuate so that irregular outbreaks of disease can be expected. Young kittens whose passive immunity is falling are most vulnerable where virus infections are endemic.

Prevention and control of URT virus infections are best approached through a combination of management and vaccination. Vaccination is relatively successful in the prevention of disease provided that individual cats are boosted annually and that they are protected from excessive contact with the virus. Extra boosters should be given when stress situations and contact with other cats are unavoidable, for example, prior to admission to veterinary hospitals or boarding catteries. Breeding queens should be boosted before mating and kittens should receive their initial vaccination soon after weaning when their levels of maternal antibody have fallen, i.e. at between 8 and 10 weeks of age.

SUPPLEMENTARY READING

Barrett R. E. and Scott D. W. (1975) Treatment of feline cryptococcosis. *J. Am. Anim. Hosp. Assoc.* **11**, 511–18.

Gaskell C. G. and Gaskell R. M. (1980) Respiratory diseases of cats. *In Practice* **2**, No. 6, 5–14.

Gaskell R. M. (1981) An assessment of the use of feline respiratory virus vaccines. In: Grunsell C. S. and Hill F. W. G. (ed.) *The Veterinary Annual,* 21st issue. Bristol, Wright–Scientechnica, pp. 267–74.

Lane J. G., Orr C. M., Lucke V. M. et al. (1981) Nasopharyngeal polyps arising in the middle ear of the cat. *J. Small Anim. Pract.* **22**, 511–22.

Winstanley E. W. (1974) Trephining frontal sinuses in the treatment of rhinitis and sinusitis in the cat. *Vet. Rec.* **95**, 289–92.

Chapter 5

Differential Diagnosis of Obstructions of the Upper Respiratory Tract

The causes of respiratory distress can be grouped under four headings:

1. Obstructive dyspnoea: the conducting airways are restricted and do not permit an adequate flow to and from the tissues where gas exchanges occur.

2. Reduced thoracic volume: normal respiratory function is compromised because the lungs are unable to expand to fill the pleural cavities. Examples: ruptured diaphragm, pneumothorax, haemothorax, chylothorax and mediastinal neoplasia.

3. Primary pulmonary diseases: the pulmonary tissues are diseased and the alveoli are incapable of adequate gas exchange. Examples: pneumonia, emphysema and paraquat poisoning.

4. Physiological dyspnoea: although the conducting airways permit normal flow and normal gas exchange is possible at the alveolar interface, the utilization of the available oxygen is inhibited. Examples: anaemia, carbon monoxide poisoning, circulatory failure and shock. Metabolic acidosis may give a false impression of dyspnoea because of an increased respiratory rate and effort.

Irrespective of the cause, some clinical signs are common to all forms of dyspnoea. These include an increase in respiratory effort, exercise intolerance and a tendency to cyanosis of mucous membranes and eventual collapse. Although the work of respiration may be increased in obstructive dyspnoea, this group may differ from other forms in that an increase in respiratory rate (tachypnoea) may not be evident. In fact, for reasons which are explained below, in severe cases of respiratory obstruction the rate is slow and accompanied by great thoracic effort. Another clinical sign which typifies obstructive dyspnoea is that respirations are noisy and the stridor is especially marked during the inspiratory phase.

ANATOMICAL CONCEPTS

The function of the conducting airways, which extend from the nares to the small bronchioles, is that of a semi-rigid tube which permits the free passage of inspired and expired gases. During the inspiratory phase the pressure within the airway is lower than that in the surrounding tissues, and conversely during expiration it is greater. Thus the conducting airways are constructed to offer minimal resistance to airflow and at the same time to resist the collapsing forces of inspiration and the expansive forces of expiration. In this context a drinking straw makes a suitable analogy: suction of fluid through the straw depresses the pressure in its lumen compared with that in the surrounding atmosphere and it is a common observation that the straw will collapse if it is at all defective. Other observations may be made by those who attempt to drink through such a damaged utensil:

1. Drinking requires considerable effort.
2. The process may be very noisy.
3. To blow out through the straw requires less effort than suction.
4. Slow, steady drinking is more productive than short, sharp efforts.
5. The straw will tend to collapse proximal to the site of initial damage during suction.

Each of these points is borne out by the clinical signs and natural progression of obstructive dyspnoea.

In the healthy animal the airways are constructed so that they will not collapse or rupture when the intraluminal pressures are lower or higher than those in the surrounding tissues. The stability of the system depends upon several anatomical features, the most important of which is the rigid framework provided by bone and cartilage for a closely adherent mucous membrane. For example, cartilage helps to maintain the patency at the nares, trachea and bronchi whilst the turbinate bones provide rigidity through the nasal passages. In other sites active muscular effort is required to prevent collapse of soft tissues into the tract. Thus, at the nares, in addition to the support given by the alar cartilages, active muscular effort is required to dilate the nares and to reduce airway resistance during forced inspiration. Similarly, active abduction by the arytenoid cartilages produces dilatation of the larynx and, for mouth-breathing (i.e. panting in the dog), the epiglottic cartilage is actively depressed by the hyoepiglotticus muscle. Occlusion of the airway by soft tissue structures such as the palatine arch and laryngeal ventricles is prevented by stability of position. In the healthy larynx the laryngeal ventricles are sandwiched between the vocalis and ventricularis muscles; the ventricular openings become narrowed during laryngeal dilatation.

Obstructive dyspnoea arises when the airway is narrowed by external compression, defects or distortions of the tubular wall or obstructions which arise within the airway itself. Space-occupying lesions such as abscesses or thyroid and mediastinal tumours can provide external pressure which narrows the airway. Structural and functional defects such as stenotic nares, soft palate hyperplasia, laryngeal collapse, laryngeal paralysis or tracheal collapse will provoke considerable obstruction to air flow. Intraluminal obstructions arise from intranasal neoplasia, foreign bodies, eversion of the laryngeal ventricles or endotracheal parasitism. When the upper airway is obstructed, the collapsing forces of inspiration become exaggerated in the caudal portions of the tube and the system will tend to yield at other sites of weakness. In this way laryngeal collapse and eversion of the ventricles may be consequences of soft palate hyperplasia.

When the laminar flow of air through the tubular airways becomes disturbed, turbulence occurs, which may produce an audible sound. Similarly unstable structures vibrate within the tube and a noise is provoked. Thus, stridor is a frequent feature of obstructive dyspnoea.

SPECIFIC ANATOMICAL CONSIDERATIONS

The nares

The rhinarium has a similar structure in both dog and cat and it is supported by a pair of alar cartilages which are in contact at the midline. The alar cartilages are covered by hairless keratinized skin on the outside and by mucous membrane internally. Ligamentous attachments hold the rhinarium to the nasal bones and in most adult dogs and many cats the skin of the rhinarium is pigmented. The semi-rigid configuration of the parietal cartilages maintains the patency of the nasal vestibule.

Soft palate and nasopharynx

Unlike the horse, the dog is not an obligatory nose-breathing animal. Stability of the equine upper airway both at rest and at vigorous exercise is maintained by the firm engagement of the larynx into the nasopharynx. In this species, the arch formed by the free border of the soft palate encircles the epiglottis and arytenoid cartilages to provide an airtight seal for the intranarial larynx. Although normal dogs have a soft palatine arch which is structurally similar to that of the horse, nose or mouth breathing is optional in this species (*Fig. 5.1*). At rest, many dogs nose breathe and under these circumstances it is usual for the larynx to occupy an intranarial position with the arch of the soft palate lying ventral to the epiglottis. At the other extreme, for athletic

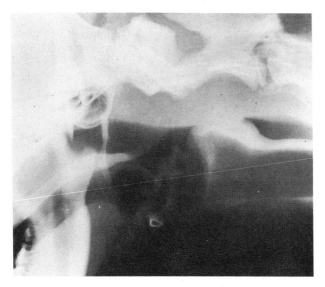

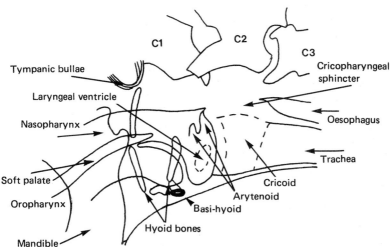

Fig. 5.1. Lateral radiograph and explanatory drawing of the pharynx and larynx of a mesocephalic dog.

performance such as racing in the Greyhound, breathing through the nasal chambers and nasopharynx offers excessive resistance and an inadequate airway. Mouth breathing provides the dog with the option of an efficient airway with minimal resistance. This is achieved by active elevation of the palatine arch and depression of the epiglottis by the hyoepiglotticus muscles. Whenever an animal attempts nose or mouth breathing with a flaccid soft palate lying dorsal to the epiglottis, snoring results.

The pharynx is a muscular tube lined by mucous membrane. The patency of the airway is maintained by the activity of this musculature which has attachments to the base of the skull and hyoid apparatus. In healthy dogs of the dolichocephalic or mesocephalic breeds, the soft palate and pharyngeal walls are relatively thin with little connective tissue or interstitial fat deposits.

Larynx

The larynx is a box suspended from the hyoid apparatus and comprising four cartilaginous components—the thyroid, cricoid and paired arytenoids (*Figs.* 5.2–5.4). Anteriorly, the ventral and lateral sides of the box are formed by the thyroid and the roof is occupied by the arytenoids which are joined by a midline sesamoid band and from which the true vocal folds are suspended. The cords attach ventrally to the thyroid at the midline. Caudally, the box is open-ended to the trachea but is encircled by the complete ring of the cricoid. This overlaps the thyroid medially and dorsally and on either side there is a cricothyroid articulation. The gap in the floor of the box is closed by the cricothyroid ligament. The rostral end of the box is variably open where the rimaglottis can be covered by a transverse sheet of cartilage, the epiglottis, when the tip folds back during deglutition. Of greater importance in the regulation of the glottic opening are the arytenoid cartilages and true vocal cords. In the resting animal the glottis actively opens during inspiration and passively reduces during expiration. During periods of exertion the glottis is actively opened during all phases of the respiratory cycle. For swallowing, the arytenoids and vocal folds are tightly closed. Folds of mucous membrane join the epiglottis to the arytenoids on either side; posteriorly these form a band—the false vocal cord. The true and false vocal folds lie parallel and between them the openings of paired blind pockets of mucosa, the laryngeal ventricles, are sited.

The innervation of the larynx is derived entirely from the vagus. On either side a direct branch, the cranial laryngeal nerve, is given off. Slightly caudal to this another nerve originates, but this reaches the larynx by a circuitous route. It passes the length of the neck in the carotid sheath and enters the anterior thorax before returning to the larynx: this is the recurrent nerve. Sensation to the larynx is mediated through both cranial and recurrent nerves. The intrinsic laryngeal muscles which control the diameter of the rimaglottis have a specific motor innervation. All the abductors (openers) and all bar one of the adductors (closers) are supplied by the recurrent nerve; only the

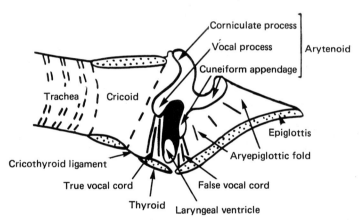

Fig. 5.2. Longitudinal section of canine larynx with anatomical explanations.

cricothyroid muscle, an adductor, receives its motor supply through the cranial branch.

The larynx serves three primary functions.

1. To protect the lower conducting airways from the consequences of inhalation of foreign materials, particularly during swallowing.

2. To regulate the airflow to the lungs such that a minimum of resistance to the passage of air occurs at the times during excercise when demands are greatest.

3. To produce noise.

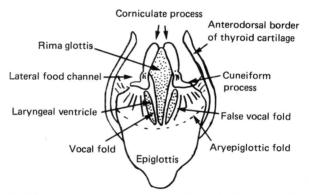

Fig. 5.3. Cranial view of canine larynx with anatomical explanations.

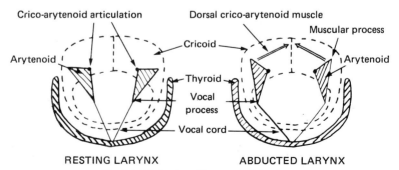

Fig. 5.4. Mechanics of laryngeal abduction.

The most important intrinsic muscle that abducts the vocal fold is the dorsal cricoarytenoid. *Fig.* 5.4 illustrates the fulcrum mechanism by which this muscle achieves abduction.

Trachea

The canine and feline trachea is composed of between 30 and 40 cartilaginous rings which are usually almost circular in cross-section, but may be U-shaped. The rings are held together by a thick fibro-elastic membrane. The rings are not complete dorsally but the tubular structure is completed by the dorsal tracheal ligament which is composed of smooth muscle and fibrous connective tissue.

AETIOLOGY OF OBSTRUCTIVE DYSPNOEA

Stenotic nares

In this condition the external nares of some short-nosed dogs are restricted by a congenital deformity of the alar cartilages and the nasal meati are restricted to small clefts (*Fig.* 5.5). This anomaly is the first component of a series of disorders which may be collectively termed the 'brachycephalic obstruction syndrome' (BOS). The individual components of this syndrome, which also includes soft palate hyperplasia and laryngeal collapse, should never be considered in isolation because afflicted patients show extensive deformities of the head, nasal passages and pharynx which must be blamed upon selective breeding. French

Fig. 5.5. Pekingese with stenosed nares.

and English Bulldogs, Pekingese, Pugs and Boston Terriers are the breeds most frequently involved, but lesser changes may be seen in breeds such as the Boxer, where extreme brachycephalia is unusual. The owners of 'normal' brachycephalic dogs must come to terms with the characteristic nasal and pharyngeal sounds which result from inherently deformed airways.

Nasal neoplasia

Although the more typical signs of intranasal neoplasia include persistent sneezing, epistaxis or a purulent nasal discharge, and facial swellings, some dogs may be presented when respiratory obstruction is the primary complaint. Apart from tumours that arise in the turbinate regions, tumours of the tonsils and pharyngeal wall may become so extensive that the oro- and nasopharyngeal airways are obstructed.

Nasopharyngeal polyps of cats

A pathological phenomenon, apparently peculiar to cats, may be encountered when inflammatory polyps extend from the middle ear, through the eustachian tube, to occupy the nasopharynx. The nasopharyngeal airway may become totally occluded so that affected cats show great respiratory embarrassment, cats being much more reluctant to mouth breathe than dogs. The polypoid lesions may be so extensive that the soft palate is displaced ventrally (*Fig. 5.6*). Poor aeration of the nasal passages provides an ideal climate for secondary bacterial infection and thus cats with nasopharyngeal polyps frequently present with a persistent nasal discharge. The aetiology of these middle ear polyps is not known but it has been conjectured that they arise as the result of prolonged infection within the middle ear which in turn follows an ascending spread from the nasopharynx. Young cats are usually involved.

Soft palate hyperplasia

The gross foreshortening of the upper conducting airways of brachycephalic dogs provokes its most serious consequences in the soft tissues of the pharynx. The pharyngeal airways are restricted by marked thickening, oedema and folding of the pharyngeal walls. The restriction is exacerbated by a relative hyperplasia of the soft palate. In many brachycephalic dogs, the soft palate is too bulky to be accommodated in a normal subepiglottic position for nasal breathing. On the other hand, the organ is too flaccid to be drawn dorsally towards the roof of the nasopharynx to allow noiseless mouth breathing. Thus, an oedematous, thickened and overlong mass of tissues lies passively in the

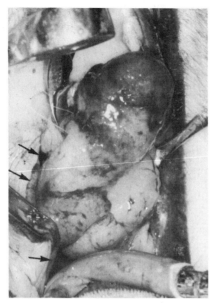

Fig. 5.6. Nasopharyngeal polyp in a cat. Arrows indicate the incised soft palate.

pharynx where it will tend to be drawn caudally towards the laryngeal opening (*Fig.* 5.7). Naturally, the effects of this anomaly will be most marked during periods of increased respiratory effort such as exercise or during hot weather. The secondary oedema of the soft palate

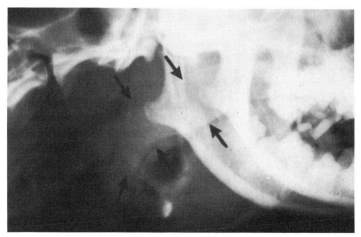

Fig. 5.7. Lateral radiograph of pharynx of a Boxer with soft palate hyperplasia (arrows). Note the overall reduction of air shadow and compare with *Fig.* 5.1.

becomes exaggerated by constant vibration. Persistent mouth breathing may predispose to secondary tonsillitis. It is not uncommon for dogs with soft palate hyperplasia to be afflicted by periods of febrile illness and bronchopneumonia. Eversion of the tonsils from the crypts reduces the oropharyngeal airway still further.

Reverse sneezing

This phenomenon is mentioned here because it represents a differential diagnosis of soft palate hyperplasia. It consists of a behavioural anomaly which depends upon irregular phonation using the soft palate as a sounding board during forceful expiration. The soft palate is positioned dorsal to the epiglottis and vibrates in the expired airstream. The anomaly is thought to be an attention-seeking behaviour and is most common in small lap dogs. Cases are presented suspected to have 'something stuck in the back of the throat'. Although the patient gives a convincing impression of distress, there is no physical obstruction and the performance ceases as the dog is startled, for example, by a clap of the hands. Reverse sneezing does not produce obstructive dyspnoea and may be differentiated from airway obstructions because exercise tolerance is not compromised and for all but the shortest periods the patient behaves normally.

Abnormalities of the epiglottis

The position of the epiglottis is such that if affected by deformity, injury, malposition or neoplasia, severe respiratory embarrassment would ensue; fortunately such anomalies are very rare. In BOS the lateral borders of the epiglottis may fold dorsally towards the midline so that the cartilage becomes tubular. The aryepiglottic folds lie between the margins of the epiglottis and the forward projections of the larynx—the cuneiform appendages—so that a tubular configuration of the epiglottis usually accompanies laryngeal collapse.

The role of the hyoepiglotticus muscle in depression of the epiglottis to facilitate mouth breathing has already been mentioned. Occasionally this muscle is damaged in choke-chain or other injuries so that epiglottic depression is impaired. Dogs with this injury show normal nasal breathing but are distressed if mouth breathing is attempted.

Congenital laryngeal anomalies

Congenital deformities of the laryngeal cartilages have rarely been reported in the dog. An inherited and congenital form of laryngeal paralysis has been recognized in the Bouvier de Flandres; this anomaly shows a sex-linked predisposition to males. The present author has single-case experiences of the condition in a Labrador and an English Setter. Roaring dyspnoea, a muted bark and exercise intolerance are present from an early age. Congenital laryngeal paralysis has also been incriminated as the cause of dyspnoea in English Bull Terriers. Although endoscopy reveals an inability to open the glottis satisfactorily, hyperplasia of the intrinsic musculature suggests that paralysis is not involved but there may be a congenital deformity or tendency to spasm.

Laryngeal oedema and trauma

Rough technique for the intubation of a patient for anaesthesia can provoke ulceration, hyperaemia and oedema within the larynx, particularly around the vocal cords. An endotracheal tube should be chosen which will pass through the larynx easily but which will fit the trachea snugly after inflation. The tube should always be lubricated with a water-soluble gel or an analgesic cream. Intubation should not be attempted until the anaesthetic induction has eliminated the glottic reflex.

The larynx occupies a relatively protected position, posterior to the intermandibular space, and it is rarely vulnerable to trauma in traffic accidents or dog fights. It has been suggested that fractures of the laryngeal cartilages are more likely to occur in older dogs where the structures have lost their elasticity and become calcified. Choke-chains can provoke laryngeal fractures as well as fractures of the hyoid bones. Bite penetrations of the larynx and trachea may cause subcutaneous emphysema which is sometimes a sequel to surgery of this section of the respiratory system. Penetrations of the airway may also provoke the formation of intraluminal granulomas.

Pharyngeal penetrations, which typically arise in dogs that chase sticks, may predispose to severe inflammation of the paralaryngeal tissues as the foreign body passes from the pharynx through the soft tissues of the upper neck. Residual foreign material will act as a focus for suppuration and sinuses may discharge close to the larynx. The oedema and cellulitis which accompany the acute reaction may compress the airway.

Laryngeal spasm

Spasmodic tight adduction of the vocal folds would obviously close the airway and lead to asphyxiation. Although spontaneous laryngeal spasm is not infrequently diagnosed in veterinary practice, the condition appears to be very rare. Laryngeal spasm usually results from stimulation by a trigger factor, such as intubation in the cat and partial laryngeal paralysis or injury in the dog. For example, the author has encountered a case of fracture of the epihyoid bone in a Greyhound which was presented in a cyanosed state with laryngeal spasm.

Laryngeal paralysis

Degeneration or disruption of the recurrent laryngeal nerves deprives the larynx of much of its intrinsic muscular innervation. Motor impulses to all the abductor muscles are inhibited so that active opening of the glottis is prevented. Dogs with laryngeal paralysis show noisy breathing ('roaring'), poor exercise tolerance, a muted bark and occasionally episodes of cyanosis and collapse. The efficiency of the cough reflex is also compromised so that a soft, moist cough is a frequent additional clinical feature. A possible congenital laryngeal paralysis has been mentioned above, but an idiopathic acquired neurogenic atrophy of the laryngeal muscles is also recognized in adult dogs. The condition has been confirmed in a variety of breeds of larger dog, usually over 30 kg bodyweight, and in the United Kingdom the aged working Labrador Retriever is the most commonly represented breed. There is a similar but lesser predisposition in the Afghan Hound. Idiopathic laryngeal paralysis is a well-recognized condition of the horse and may be detrimental to the performance of animals that are used for athletic competition. The condition of the horse is almost invariably left-sided only, but in the dog, clinical cases of paralysis are more commonly bilateral. The majority of acquired cases of laryngeal paralysis are seen in elderly dogs, which show spasmodic stridor at first, but are eventually distressed even at rest. Cases have been encountered in racing Greyhounds but, surprisingly, the respiratory distress is not evident until completion of the race.

Apart from the idiopathic paralysis described above, animals may be affected by a similar disease in which there is a demonstrable cause of damage to the laryngeal innervation. Trauma or surgery to the ventral cervical region may sever the nerve. Space-occupying lesions in the neck or anterior mediastinum (*Fig. 5.8*), such as abscesses, thyroid adenocarcinoma, lymphosarcoma or heart-base tumours, may infiltrate or provoke pressure necrosis of the conducting pathways.

Laryngeal collapse

The arytenoid cartilages of the canine larynx show forward projections, the cuneiform appendages, which are attached by a narrow isthmus. The thyroid, cricoid and arytenoids are composed of hyaline cartilage but the cuneiform appendages, like the epiglottis, are formed by elastic cartilage. In fact, in other species the cuneiforms form an integral part of the epiglottis. The junction between the cuneiforms and the arytenoids represents a point of weakness and in BOS the congenital

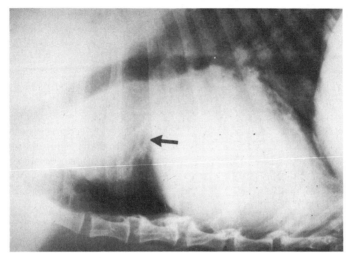

Fig. 5.8. Lateral chest radiograph in an Afghan Hound with laryngeal paralysis. The anterior mediastinal mass (arrowed) has infiltrated the recurrent laryngeal nerves.

anatomical features (e.g. stenotic nares and soft palate hyperplasia) that lead to obstructive dyspnoea may in turn predispose to distortion of the larynx. When the upper airway is obstructed in BOS, the collapsing forces of inspiration are markedly increased and the system will tend to yield at sites of weakness (*Fig.* 5.9). In the larynx this may entail eversion of the lateral ventricles or inversion of the corniculate and cuneiform processes. When a ventricle is everted, the avascular mucous membrane is turned inside out and lies like a bubble across the

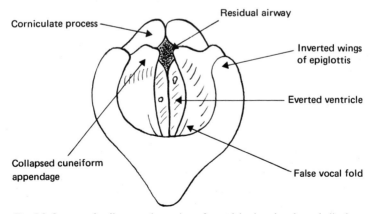

Fig. 5.9. Laryngeal collapse and eversion of ventricles in a brachycephalic dog.

glottic opening. The relatively weak forward projections of the arytenoid cartilages will also tend to collapse to the midline. Severe dyspnoea is present in these patients, which may show episodes of cyanosis and loss of consciousness. Laryngeal collapse is more frequently encountered in hot climates than in the United Kingdom.

Laryngeal neoplasia

Primary neoplasms of the canine larynx are very rare but chondrosarcoma at this site has been reported. Tumour-like granulomas arise within the laryngeal lumen and cause serious respiratory obstructions. These chronic inflammatory lesions are usually the result of traumatic penetrations such as bites but may follow radical laryngeal surgery.

Tracheal collapse

In this condition the lumen of the trachea is reduced in size as a result of the distortion of the normal ring structure. The tracheal lumen becomes narrowed in the dorsoventral plane as the dorsal ligament becomes extended (*Fig.* 5.10). The rings in the middle third of the trachea are most severely affected but in some cases there is an extension of the collapse into the main stem bronchi. Although the condition has been diagnosed occasionally in larger breeds, the high incidence in toy and miniature types suggests that the condition may be associated with miniaturization. The major factor in the development of tracheal collapse is weakness in the tracheal cartilages and the condition is more

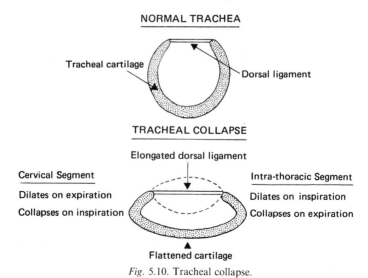

Fig. 5.10. Tracheal collapse.

likely to be acquired in those dogs that have a congenital predisposition to cartilaginous degeneration. Patients do not show clinical signs unless there is a predisposing lower respiratory tract infection or a severe reduction in the size of the tracheal lumen caused by prolapse of the dorsal ligament. Poodles, Pugs, Yorkshire Terriers, Pomeranians and Chihuahuas are particularly susceptible to tracheal collapse. The average age at which clinical signs appear is approximately 7 years but it is unusual to encounter cases under 4 years old. A vibrant inspiratory and expiratory stridor is evident and this is aggravated by excitement, palpation and exercise. It is not unusual for there to be concurrent bronchitis or tonsillitis, often of considerable duration. In severe cases cyanosis may be a feature and the disorder is exacerbated by any tendency to overweight.

Miscellaneous tracheal obstructions

The management of the respiratory emergencies that arise from disruption of the trachea has been described in Chapter 1. However, tracheal trauma may go unsuspected and evidence of localized damage may not become apparent until a fibrous stricture has formed and the patient is presented with respiratory distress.

Extensive submucosal haemorrhage with diffuse narrowing of the trachea is a recognized, if unusual, clinical expression of warfarin poisoning (*Fig. 5.11*). Patients are presented with acute obstructive respiratory distress.

Paroxysms of coughing are the most likely sign of infestation by the parasite *Filaroides osleri*. In occasional instances the granulomas

Fig. 5.11. Lateral cervical radiograph to show tracheal collapse due to submucosal haemorrhage in a case of warfarin poisoning.

caused by this parasite are so numerous and large that the distal trachea and main bronchi become partly occluded. Dyspnoea is more obvious during expiration whenever the intrathoracic airways are obstructed.

Tracheal neoplasms are uncommon but there have been isolated reports of chondrosarcoma and osteosarcoma which have obstructed the airways.

DIAGNOSIS

Presentation and history

In the light of the explanation of the factors that predispose to obstructive dyspnoea, the recognition of the general condition should be straightforward and the breed and age of the patient may provide useful pointers to the specific diagnosis. Inquiries should be made about any previous illnesses or trauma which may be relevant and an assessment of the duration of onset of symptoms is helpful as a sudden onset may imply unknown trauma. Information should be sought regarding any other symptoms referable to the respiratory system, for example, the presence of a nasal discharge or any tendency to sneeze, gag or cough. Notice must also be taken of signs apparently divorced from the respiratory system which may be indicative of a multiple system disease in which the respiratory component is the owner's primary complaint. An owner's observation of a change in tone or volume of the bark may point to a laryngeal disorder. It is helpful to ascertain whether the patient is more comfortable when nose breathing or mouth breathing. *Table* 5.1 sets out a guide to the breed, age and sex predisposition for some of the common causes of obstructive dyspnoea, but as every veterinarian will appreciate, clinical cases show a wicked tendency to provide exceptions for rules.

External examination

Observation of the patient at rest may reveal the site of obstruction. Animals with a nasal or nasopharyngeal obstruction will tend to mouth breathe. Nasal air conduction can be assessed by holding a wisp of cotton wool at each nostril in turn. Alternatively, condensation on a dry glass slide provides evidence of patency. The nares of brachycephalic dogs should be checked for stenosis and if a nasal obstruction is suspected, the supporting bones of the nose should be palpated for swelling or deformity. While the patient is still conscious, a brief inspection of the mouth should be attempted to identify obvious lesions of the oropharynx but the animal should not be provoked to struggle as this may exaggerate the respiratory distress. Evidence of trauma may

Table 5.1 A guide to the diagnosis of obstructive dyspnoea in dogs

	Breed predisposition	Age incidence (yr)	Sex predisposition	Change of bark	Diagnostic techniques				
					Oral inspection	External inspection	Radiography	Endoscopy	Histology
Nasal neoplasia	Dolicocephalics Mesocephalics	>5			*	*	x		x
Stenotic nares	Brachycephalics	<2				x			
Soft palate hyperplasia	Brachycephalics	<2			*		*	x	
Laryngeal collapse	Brachycephalics	<4						x	
Everted ventricles	Brachycephalics	<4						x	
Laryngeal paralysis Congenital	Bouvier de Flandres	<1	M	x				x	x
Acquired	Labrador/ Afghan Hound	>7		x				x	x
Congenital laryngeal spasm	Bull Terrier	<1							
Tracheal collapse	Toy/miniature breeds	>4					x	x	
Tracheal trauma	—					x	x	x	
Nasopharyngeal polyps	Cats	<4			*	x Auriscopy	x	x	x

x Frequent.
* Occasional.

be discovered on palpation: the normal laryngeal and tracheal cartilages are firm and well defined so that swellings will be obvious except
in overweight patients. The throat should be palpated for subcutaneous
emphysema, local lymphadenopathies, abscessation, thyroid gland
enlargement or other soft tissue swellings. A brief period of exercise
should be provided if the patient does not demonstrate the dyspnoea at
rest; this may be helpful to clarify any confusion in the owner's history
regarding the noise. Auscultation is rarely helpful to localize the site of
airway obstruction.

Radiography

Comments have been made elsewhere regarding the suitability of the
respiratory system for diagnostic radiography. There are arguments for
and against the conscious radiography of patients with obstructive
dyspnoea. On the one hand, radiation protection procedures must be
strictly followed and the unnecessary restraint of all patients with
dyspnoea should be avoided because this may lead to a fatal exacerba-
tion of the disease. On the other, radiographs may provide information
that could be invaluable in the preparation of the patient for safe
general anaesthesia and surgery. Preliminary lateral soft tissue views of
the pharynx, larynx, trachea and thorax can usually be obtained safely
so that space-occupying lesions may be identified in the airway or
hyperplasia of the soft palate may be confirmed. Whenever tracheal
collapse is suspected, radiography is best performed on a standing,
conscious patient (*Fig. 5.12*). The exposures must be taken during
inspiration otherwise a false negative diagnosis may be made. Functional studies of the palate, epiglottis and larynx require facilities for
fluoroscopy and they are performed on conscious animals. After the
patient has been anaesthetized, detailed radiographs of the nasal
chambers, pharynx, larynx, trachea and thorax can be taken. The value
of the dorsoventral occlusal projection of the nasal chambers has been
described in Chapter 3, but because the skull and cervical spine overlie
the pharynx, larynx and trachea, only a lateral projection is useful in
most cases. A lateral view of the thorax should always be taken in cases
of suspected laryngeal paralysis so that the anterior mediastinum can
be checked for the presence of a soft tissue mass.

Endoscopy

Inspections of the pharynx, larynx, trachea and main stem bronchi are
made with the patient anaesthetized and placed in sternal recumbency.
The mouth should be held open by a gag and the tongue stabilized with
retractors. A diagnosis of hyperplasia may be confirmed if the soft
palate shows gross enlargement and if it shows extensive overlap of the

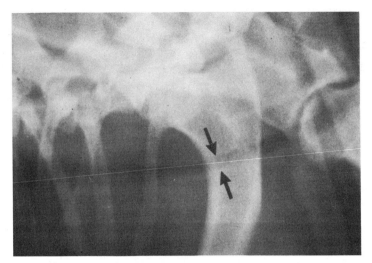

Fig. 5.12. Lateral radiograph to show tracheal collapse in a Chihuahua. Note that the collapse is most marked at the thoracic inlet.

epiglottis. A useful rule of thumb is that if the palate is not obviously thickened and oedematous, then it cannot be hyperplastic and does not warrant resection. The most useful landmarks to assess palatine hyperplasia are the caudal limits of the tonsillar crypts which normally lie at the same level as the cranial border of the palatine arch. Although the soft palate normally overlies the epiglottis by 0·5–1 cm this relationship is distorted when the mouth is open and the tongue is drawn forwards, and it is even more difficult to evaluate in an intubated patient. Palpation of the soft palate should establish the presence of any soft tissue mass in the nasopharynx dorsally. The nasopharynx is inspected with an illuminated dental mirror after the palate has been drawn forward with tissue forceps. Negative endoscopic findings can be expected in cases of 'reverse sneezing'.

The position and conformation of the epiglottis should be obvious and this structure must be depressed to afford a view of the larynx. The usual purpose of laryngoscopy is to assess function. In horses this technique is achieved by the passage of an endoscope through the nasal chambers of a conscious patient. Clearly, this is not possible in dogs, but the best alternative is to make an inspection *per os* under light intravenous thiopentone sodium anaesthesia (*Fig.* 5.13). The dog remains placed in sternal recumbency and the mouth is gagged open with the upper jaw raised by an assistant. It is important that there is no support or distortion at the laryngeal area. The positions of the corniculate and cuneiform cartilages relative to the midline should be

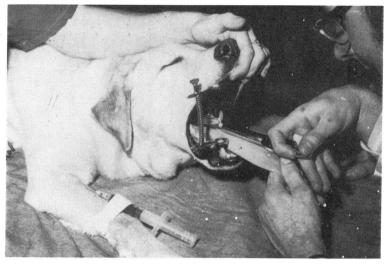

Fig. 5.13. Position and technique for laryngoscopy.

noted. As the plane of anaesthesia lightens symmetrical movements of the arytenoid cartilages and their appendages should be
seen in normal dogs as the tone returns to the vocal cords. Care is
required to correlate the movements observed with the respiratory
cycle. In cases of laryngeal paralysis the vocal cord on the affected
side(s) shows no active movements but is flaccid and passively drawn
towards the midline during inspiration and then pushed away in the
flow of expired air. At this time confirmatory evidence that the larynx is
the site of respiratory obstruction can be obtained if the passage of an
endotracheal tube beyond the larynx relieves the dyspnoea. Direct
laryngoscopy may reveal other changes such as everted laryngeal
ventricles which resemble bubbles in the ventral portion of the glottis
where the vocal cords will be obscured. In brachycephalic types, any
evidence of collapse of the cuneiform cartilages or tendency to tubular
configuration of the epiglottis should be noted. Dogs with laryngeal
obstruction often make a poor recovery from diagnostic endoscopy
and, therefore, corrective surgery should be performed immediately
following confirmation of the diagnosis.

    A rigid bronchoscope or flexible fibrescope is necessary for en-
doscopy of the trachea and main bronchi. The instrument should not
be passed through the larynx unless lubricated and unless the glottic
reflex has been eliminated. Deformities and fractures of the tracheal
rings should be visible and the presence of intraluminal lesions such as
traumatic or parasitic granulomas (*Fig.* 5.14) will be obvious.

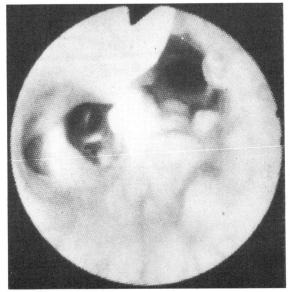

Fig. 5.14. Endoscopic view to show modest infestation by *Filaroides osleri* at the tracheal bifurcation.

Histology

Biopsy samples may be necessary for the differentiation of some neoplastic and inflammatory proliferations. At the same time, tumour typing may be helpful for accurate prognosis. Biopsy of the dorsal cricoarytenoid muscle may be made at the time of surgery to lateralize the arytenoid cartilage. In cases of laryngeal paralysis this muscle will be atrophied, but confirmation of the presence of neurogenic atrophy of the fibres provides retrospective reassurance of a correct diagnosis.

Haematology

Tracheal obstruction as a complication of warfarin poisoning has been mentioned above. The diffuse narrowing of the tracheal lumen is readily demonstrated on lateral radiographs but the diagnosis is confirmed by a prolonged clotting time. Management with whole blood transfusions and intravenous vitamin K produces a steady improvement after 24 hours.

SUPPLEMENTARY READING

Done S. H. and Drew R. A. (1976) Observations on the pathology of tracheal collapse in dogs. *J. Small Anim. Pract.* **17**, 783–91.

Gaskell C. J. (1974) The radiographic anatomy of the pharynx and larynx of the dog. *J. Small Anim. Pract.* **15**, 89–100.

Harvey C. E. and Venker-van-Haagan A. (1975) Surgical management of pharyngeal and laryngeal airway obstruction in the dog. *Vet. Clin. North Am.* **5**, 515–35.

O'Brien J. A. and Harvey C. E. (1975) The upper airway. In: Ettinger S. (ed.) *Textbook of Veterinary Medicine: Diseases of the Dog and Cat.* Philadelphia, Saunders pp. 565–603.

O'Brien J. A., Harvey C. E., Kelly A. M. et al. (1973) Neurogenic atrophy of the laryngeal muscles of the dog. *J. Small Anim. Pract.* **14**, 521–32.

Chapter 6

Surgery of the Conducting Airways

The purpose of this chapter is to describe the surgical procedures which are used in the treatment of obstructive dyspnoea, the aetiology and diagnosis of which have been discussed in Chapter 5. Although the considerations that apply to the anaesthesia of patients for surgery to the respiratory tract have been mentioned in Chapter 1, some of the points made bear repetition here. A primary commitment in all anaesthesia is to establish and maintain an effective airway; this may be critical where dyspnoea already exists. Safe and accurate surgery to the respiratory tract not only requires a patent airway but also a clear view of the surgical field. This may influence the choice of intubation route, for example in pharyngeal and laryngeal surgery, when a bypass tracheotomy approach may be preferred (*Fig.* 6.1). Intubation directly into the trachea provides the anaesthetist with the facility to use gaseous and volatile agents without the anxiety of asphyxiation of the patient by inhaled blood clots during the operation. At the same time the surgeon can make an unobstructed approach to the pharynx and larynx either *per os* or through a ventral incision. It is less satisfactory for balanced anaesthesia to pass the endotracheal tube orally in the normal way and then intermittently to withdraw it into the pharynx whilst surgery is performed within the lumen of the larynx or trachea. Irrespective of the anaesthetic technique employed, every care must be taken to prevent the inhalation of blood, saliva and other debris into the lower respiratory tract. A known number of moist swabs may be packed into the pharynx, around the endotracheal tube, or over the glottis itself when the bypass tracheotomy approach is used. Alternatively, special disposable throat sponges have recently been introduced which have tape attachments to facilitate postoperative retrieval.

There are two phases when particular anaesthetic vigilance is

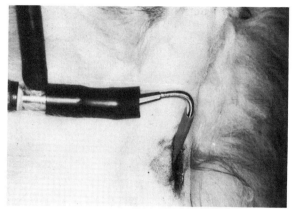

a

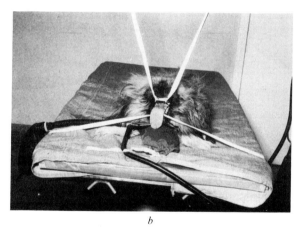

b

Fig. 6.1. Bypass anaesthesia into the trachea permits unobstructed oral access to pharyngeal and laryngeal surgery.

required. First, brachycephalic dogs with the obstruction syndrome are difficult to intubate and therefore are vulnerable to asphyxiation during induction. Secondly, all animals recovering from airway operations should be kept under continuous observation and a patient with a tracheotomy tube must never be left unattended. For these reasons, elective surgery of the upper airway is best performed at the start of the day's operating list. The patient then recovers during the morning and the critical period of intensive observation coincides with normal working hours. The postoperative progress of the patient determines whether continuous attention is necessary during the following night. Surgical procedures to the conducting airways carry significant risks of complications in the immediate postoperative period and therefore they should never be performed on animals on an outpatient basis. Even those animals that are subjected to relatively minor operations should be hospitalized for 24 hours so that the period of immediate danger has passed before the patient returns home. Some degree of post-surgical oedema is inevitable with all operations, even with careful surgical technique and the most gentle handling of tissue. Swelling around the airway due to oedema may precipitate an obstruction equal to, or greater than, that which has been corrected by the operation itself. The equipment for emergency tracheotomy should be close at hand in the intensive care area where animals are recovering from respiratory tract surgery. Furthermore, it should be a standard procedure during the preoperative preparation of these patients to clip the hair from the tracheal area so that there will be no unnecessary delays if an emergency tracheotomy is required. Surgical oedema can be reduced by the parenteral administration of corticosteroids; a course of 1 ml/kg prednisolone i.m. at the time of surgery followed by a similar injection on the following morning is recommended.

RELIEF OF STENOTIC NARES

It is most unlikely that stenosis of the nares will occur in brachycephalic dogs without other concurrent components of the obstruction syndrome. Thus, an operation to improve the patency of the nares is likely to be an adjunct to other surgery such as resection of a hyperplastic soft palate, excision of everted laryngeal ventricles or extirpation of collapsed laryngeal cartilages. A simple method to relieve stenosis of the nares consists of excision of the lateral flap of the dorsal parietal cartilage, but this leaves an open wound which must heal by second intention. There is a risk of infection and necrosis of the cartilage during the healing period.

The most satisfactory technique to improve the nasal airway consists of the excision of a longitudinal wedge from the lateral portion of the dorsal parietal cartilage (*Fig.* 6.2). The skin edges are joined using 5/0 braided silk. At the same time, an elliptical segment may be removed from the junction between the rhinarium and the skin on each lateral border. This latter procedure is not likely to improve the nares significantly if it is performed alone.

CORRECTION OF SOFT PALATE HYPERPLASIA

Resection of the redundant soft palatine tissue is best performed with the patient in sternal recumbency and with the mouth held open by tapes (*see Fig.* 6.1). The presence of a gag between the dental arcades greatly reduces the surgeon's ability to manipulate instruments within

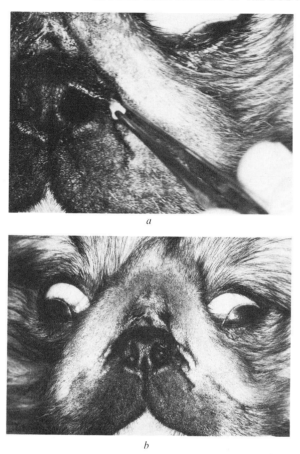

a

b

Fig. 6.2. Correction of stenotic nares in a Pekingese (*see Fig.* 5.5). (*a*) Excision of a wedge of dorsal parietal cartilage. (*b*) Closure with 5/0 silk.

the oral cavity. The caudal border of the palatine arch is grasped by Allis tissue forceps and, before it is drawn forward (*Fig.* 6.3*a*), the degree of hyperplasia is measured against the pharyngeal landmarks, particularly the caudal limit of the tonsillar crypts. Two pairs of curved crushing forceps, or alternatively a single gallbladder clamp, are placed across the palate at the line of resection (*Fig.* 6.3*b*). Tonsillectomy forceps are also suitable for this purpose. If an excessive portion of the soft palate were to be resected, persistent dysphagia with a nasal return of food and fluid might result from inability to close the nasopharynx during swallowing. Fortunately, this complication is most unlikely to arise in brachycephalic dogs with true hyperplasia of the soft palate unless most of the organ were to be excised. However, soft palate *hypoplasia* with nasal reflux during deglutition can be expected if palate resections are performed indiscriminately on dogs that show nasopharyngeal stertor and when an accurate diagnosis is not made. As a simple guide, unless the soft palate is significantly thickened and oedematous, it probably does not require resection. (Readers should not be misled by illustrations in standard textbooks that show various techniques to resect apparently normal soft palates: it is extremely difficult to produce informative photographs during the resection of the palate on a clinical case in a brachycephalic dog!)

Once the crushing forceps are correctly placed, the redundant palatine tissue is excised with curved scissors. A continuous over-and-over suture pattern, using 3/0 Dexon, is placed loosely through the edge of the soft palate but includes the forceps (*Fig. 6.3c*). The suture is not anchored at either end until the forceps have been withdrawn and the line has been tightened (*Fig. 6.3d*). When the palate is markedly thickened, the suture pattern may be doubled back to the starting point. The palate is then released and observed for 5 minutes for signs of haemorrhage before the anaesthetic is concluded. The advantage of this technique lies in its simplicity and in the little tissue reaction and oedema which is provoked. Although resection with an electrosurgical knife dispenses with the need for sutures, significant postoperative oedema is provoked and an unnecessary number of dogs subjected to this technique require temporary tracheotomy. After all soft palate resections it is not possible to assess the level of success until the oedema has subsided. Owners should be advised that the full benefit of the operation may not be apparent until 10 days later. Abrasive foods should be avoided during the first 3 weeks after the resection and exercise can be steadily increased from the tenth day.

Provided that there is no concurrent stenosis of the nares, laryngeal collapse or eversion of the ventricles, soft palate resection carries a good prospect of a successful relief of obstructive dyspnoea. The results of the operation may be improved by simultaneous tonsillectomy in those dogs that show persistent tonsillar eversion.

EPIGLOTTIC SURGERY

Although the indications for partial excision of the epiglottis are rare, experimental and clinical studies have shown that dogs tolerate this surgery without serious complications. It would appear that in the dog the epiglottis is not essential for the protection of the glottis during deglutition. Presumably the tight adduction of the arytenoid cartilages and vocal cords is sufficient to prevent the inhalation of food and fluids. Partial resection of the epiglottis is indicated in those cases where

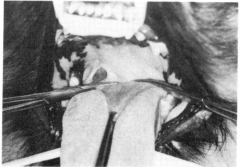

Fig. 6.3. Soft palate resection. (*a*) Palate drawn forwards. (*b*) Curved clamps applied.

malfunction or disease of the cartilage interferes with normal respiration. An attempt should be made to retain the general shape of the cartilage with its central apex.

LARYNGEAL SURGERY

Surgical interferences to the canine larynx are performed on an elective basis to devocalize those dogs whose bark causes nuisance or to relieve laryngeal diseases where obstructive dyspnoea is the usual presenting sign. The decision to perform a debarking operation lies with the individual veterinary surgeon and must be made on the basis of the circumstances of each case. To debark a dog satisfactorily is a serious surgical undertaking which necessitates both short and long term risks

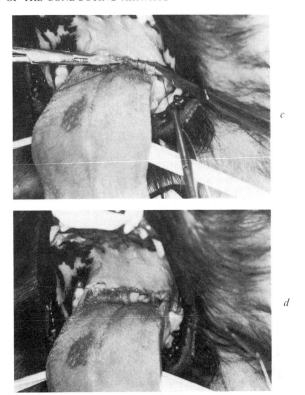

Fig. 6.3. Soft palate resection. (*c*) Palate resected and over-and-over suture commenced. (*d*) Completion of the mucosal suture.

to the life of the patient and it can thus never be justified simply to satisfy the whim of an owner. The author's approach is to resist requests to debark unless the dog is the subject of litigation and/or will otherwise be euthanatized. The usual purpose of surgery performed on the canine larynx is to extirpate those structures that abut on to the glottis and that are producing noise or respiratory obstruction. Thus, partial laryngectomy may be used to debark a dog or alternatively to relieve laryngeal collapse. With the exception of the arytenoid lateralization procedure, canine laryngeal surgery varies only in the quantity of tissue removed and the route by which the operation is performed.

Debarking

A bark is produced during forceful expiration by the flow of air over tensed tissues projecting across the laryngeal lumen. The true and false vocal cords and the ventral processes of the arytenoid cartilages are the principal sources of voice. The aim of debarking operations is to remove all the laryngeal tissues that can emit noise, but even the most radical procedures leave irregularities on the laryngeal walls. Thus it is not possible to devocalize a dog totally, but, in general, the less tissue that is excised, the greater the residual vocal capability. Although excision of the true vocal cords *per os* with long dissection scissors temporarily reduces the volume of bark in most dogs, the return of a subdued bark within 3–4 months can be expected because of a tendency for scar tissue to form at the site of the excised cords. It has been found that simple dissection of the vocal folds can be performed more efficiently by a ventral laryngotomy approach and that the long term results are superior to those of excision of the cords *per os*. However, the best results are obtained by more radical operations to excise the ventral projections of the arytenoid cartilages and the false vocal cord as well as the true vocal fold; this may be performed either by using the oral route or by the laryngo-fissure approach.

For partial laryngectomy by the oral approach, the dog is positioned in dorsal recumbency, the neck is extended, the tongue is drawn forwards and the mouth held open with a gag. Anaesthesia by bypass tracheotomy is essential to this procedure. Simple excision of the vocal folds requires stabilization of the cord by tissue forceps before resection using long scissors. Long-handled biopsy cup forceps are needed for the more radical debarking operation. Bite by bite, the vocal cords, caudal aryepiglottic folds, ventral cuneiform process and vocal process of each arytenoid are extirpated. Each part to be removed is drawn out by tissue forceps and then grasped by the biopsy punch. Haemorrhage is rarely severe in this operation and is controlled by direct pressure using surgical swabs; suction helps to clear blood from the surgical field.

Surgery by ventral laryngotomy (laryngo-fissure) can be more precise, haemostasis is straightforward and the view available is superior to that afforded by the oral route. However, the ventral incision has the disadvantage that adverse reactions by laryngeal tissues are more likely to be provoked. None the less, this is the author's preferred approach to intra-laryngeal surgery in the dog.

The patient is positioned in dorsal recumbency and the neck is tensed by placing a small sandbag behind the poll. A 6–8 cm ventral midline skin incision is made from the level of the hyoid apparatus to the second or third tracheal ring. The larynx is reached by separation of the subcutis and division of the sternohyoideus muscles at their midline raphe. A small vein passing over the larynx will require ligation. The cricoid, cricothyroid ligament and thyroid cartilage are identified before a midline scalpel incision is made through the cricothyroid ligament and the body of the thyroid cartilage (*Fig. 6.4*). Self-retaining

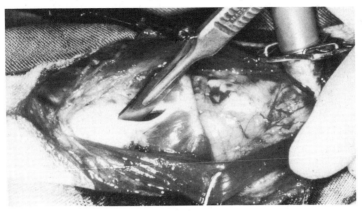

Fig. 6.4. Ventral laryngo-fissure through cricothyroid ligament and body of thyroid. Note the bypass tube for anaesthetic maintenance.

retractors hold the edges of this incision apart. The true and false vocal folds, the vocal process of the arytenoid cartilage and the ventral projection of the cuneiform process are excised by scissors and cup forceps. The ventricular mucous membrane lying against the thyroid lamina is left in place as this will act as a focus for rapid neoepithelization of the laryngeal lumen during the healing process. During the excision, it is inevitable that haemorrhage will arise from the ventricularis and vocalis muscles. This may require specific ligation or alternatively the judicious use of diathermy. Great care must be taken when using diathermy within the larynx that inadvertent cautery of the edges of the laryngotomy incision does not arise and that the lowest setting consistent with haemostasis is employed otherwise suppuration may develop from carbonized tissue deposits. Catgut sutures are used to coapt the edges of the cricothyroid ligament but are not usually needed through the thyroid cartilage itself. The muscle edges, subcutis and skin are closed in the routine manner. In small dogs a tracheotomy tube is used for the first 24 hours after surgery but this is usually not necessary for dogs weighing more than 15 kg.

Excision of everted ventricles

Eversion of the laryngeal ventricles does not occur in isolation but this component of the brachycephalic obstruction syndrome is a consequence of prolonged obstruction, for example by a hyperplastic soft palate. The everted ventricles can be removed *per os* or by laryngofissure, but whichever route is employed, a tracheotomy will be necessary for anaesthesia and aftercare. The mucous membrane is stabilized with tissue forceps or a hook before resection along the anterior border of the true vocal fold.

Laryngeal collapse

Obstruction of the supraglottic laryngeal airway occurs as a result of persistent obstruction of the proximal airways, for example by soft palate hyperplasia. It is not surprising that laryngeal collapse frequently occurs in brachycephalic breeds. Eversion of the ventricles is likely to occur prior to collapse of the corniculate and cuneiform processes. Surgical relief of laryngeal collapse is achieved by resection of the offending cartilage using the oral approach and with a bypass tracheotomy tube in place for general anaesthesia. Most authors agree that treatment is more straightforward, and results are more optimistic, in the larger brachycephalic types, such as Boxers, but with the notable exception of the English Bulldog. English and French Bulldogs, Boston Terriers, Pugs and Pekingese are more difficult to treat because the gross thickening of the pharyngeal tissues makes for poor visibility. For the treatment of laryngeal collapse, the author has adopted the approach proposed by Harvey and Venker van Haagen, which consists of a staged excision of the offending tissues commencing with resection of the hyperplastic soft palate and removal of the everted laryngeal saccules. After this initial procedure the patient is allowed to recover and managed with a tracheotomy tube in place. Four or five days later, when the acute surgical swelling has regressed, the dog is re-anaesthetized and further laryngeal tissue is excised commencing with the vocal cord, medial face of the corniculate cartilage and ventral projection of the cuneiform process. It is possible that this cycle of anaesthesia, re-inspection of the larynx and surgical excision of laryngeal tissues will require repetition on one further occasion. Clearly, such surgery should not be undertaken unless prolonged intensive care can be provided because it is likely that a tracheotomy tube will be in place for 8–10 days.

Complications of laryngectomy

Excessive excision of the aryepiglottic folds or the corniculate processes may lead to a permanent deficiency of the glottic reflex. At best this will leave the patient with a persistent inhalation tracheitis and a chronic cough and, at worst, the dog will succumb to inhalation bronchopneumonia.

Minor fibrosis within the larynx invariably arises as healing occurs after laryngectomy. Fortunately, these 'webs' are rarely sufficient to obstruct the airway significantly but this complication seems more likely to occur when the laryngo-fissure approach has been used.

Similarly, laryngeal 'webs' may form following the relief of laryngeal collapse. The author has abandoned the use of partial laryngectomy for the treatment of idiopathic laryngeal paralysis (*Fig.* 6.5). An unacceptable rate of laryngeal 'web' formation followed this technique, presumably because the deficient glottic reflex in patients with laryngeal paralysis allows the denuded and raw tissues to become contaminated. Infection is then a stimulus for excessive fibrosis. In the event of laryngeal 'web' formation causing a significant obstruction of the airway, resection of the bands of fibrosis is indicated. It is surprising that 'webs' do not reform in all cases following this repeated surgery.

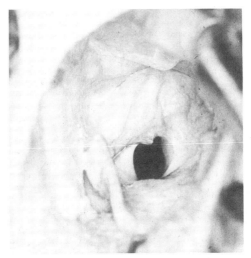

Fig. 6.5. Laryngeal obstruction by fibrosis (webbing) after laryngectomy of a Labrador with paralysis of the vocal cords.

Laryngeal paralysis

The disappointing secondary laryngeal obstructions which arise when paralysis is treated by laryngectomy have been mentioned above. The preferred technique to treat dogs with idiopathic laryngeal paralysis is arytenoid lateralization, sometimes known as a 'tie-back' procedure. The objective of this operation is to provide a modest improvement in the laryngeal airway on one side, even in those dogs that are bilaterally affected, so that these elderly patients can live out their days in relative comfort. The surgery aims to release the left arytenoid cartilage from its cricoarytenoid articulation and its sesamoid attachment to the contralateral arytenoid (*Fig.* 6.6). This allows the left side to be drawn backwards and attached to the wing of the thyroid, and thus the vocal cord is abducted.

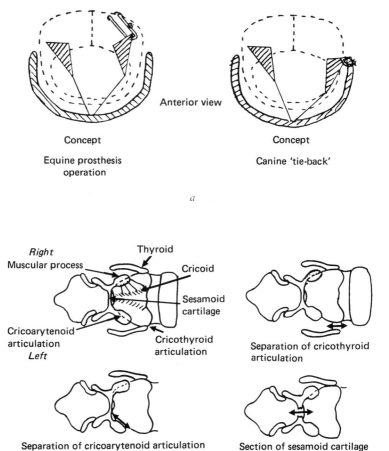

Anterior view

Concept

Equine prosthesis
operation

Concept

Canine 'tie-back'

a

Right
Muscular process   Thyroid

Cricoid

Sesamoid
cartilage

Cricoarytenoid
articulation
Left

Cricothyroid
articulation

Separation of cricothyroid
articulation

Separation of cricoarytenoid articulation

Section of sesamoid cartilage

Placement of 'tie-back' suture

Result of 'tie-back'

b

Fig. 6.6. Arytenoid lateralization ('tie-back'). (*a*) Concept of the technique and comparison with the prosthesis operation used for equine 'roarers' (compare with *Fig.* 5.4). (*b*) Lateralization of the left arytenoid cartilage to relieve laryngeal paralysis (dorsal view).

The 'tie-back' operation is performed with the patient placed in right lateral recumbency and with the neck extended over a small sandbag (*Fig. 6.7a*). The procedure can be completed with an endotracheal tube in place for routine anaesthesia. A 6–8 cm skin incision is made from the level of the vertical ramus of the mandible, ventral to the left external maxillary vein (*Fig. 6.7b*). The panniculus muscle and loose areolar connective tissue are separated so that access is obtained to the dorsal and lateral aspects of the larynx. Useful landmarks to palpate are the hyoid apparatus anteriorly and the trachea caudally; the dorsal margin of the wing of the thyroid cartilage can be flexed through the thyropharyngeus muscle (*Fig. 6.7c*). This muscle is incised at the level of the rim of the thyroid (*Fig. 6.7d*) and a layer of connective tissue on the medial side of the thyroid is penetrated. At its most caudal limit, the thyroid articulates with the cricoid medially. This joint is separated with scissors. Disruption of the cricothyroid articulation is an important stage of the operation because it will permit the arytenoid to.be lateralized to the caudal extremity of the thyroid later in the procedure. At this point the oesophageal mucosa lies dorsal to the larynx and it should be held aside by retractors. The muscular process of the arytenoid cartilage is identified: in cases of idiopathic paralysis, the dorsal cricoarytenoid muscle will be atrophied and thus the muscular process is particularly prominent (*Fig. 6.7e*). Blunt dissection with fine scissors disarticulates the arytenoid from the cricoid immediately beneath the muscular process. Articular cartilage can be readily identified on the cricoid. This articular surface is followed forwards as it curves medially. The sesamoid band which lies between the two arytenoid cartilages is located immediately rostral to the anteromedial limit of the cricoarytenoid articulation. The band, which is approximately 1 mm in diameter, is divided at its midpoint. The left arytenoid cartilage has now been mobilized except for its attachments to the vocal cord and laryngeal mucosa. A mattress suture of 0/0 braided steel is used to secure the muscular process to the medial aspect of the caudal extremity of the wing of the thyroid (*Fig. 6.7f*). Catgut sutures are used to coapt the edges of the thyropharyngeus muscle and the remainder of the wound closure is routine. At the end of the operation the endotracheal tube should be removed and the glottis should be inspected for a satisfactory improvement on the left side. A tracheotomy tube is not normally necessary after this surgery but facilities for this should always be on hand during the recovery phase. The potential short term complications of this operation include haematoma formation and avulsion of the 'tie-back' suture. In either event severe dyspnoea may arise and a tracheotomy tube may be necessary before surgery is repeated.

With experience, arytenoid lateralization is a procedure which can be performed quickly and without complications. The relief of airway

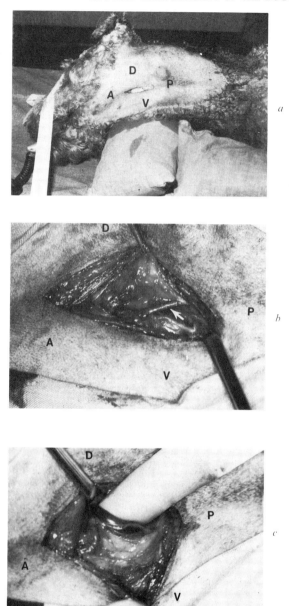

Fig. 6.7. Arytenoid lateralization. (*a*) Position of patient for surgery and site of incision. (*b*) Incision through skin and panniculus muscle: external maxillary vein arrowed. (*c*) Wing of thyroid cartilage palpable through overlying cricopharyngeus muscle.

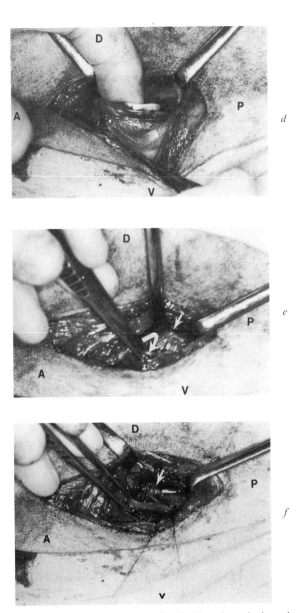

d

e

f

Fig. 6.7. Arytenoid lateralization. (*d*) After incision through thyropharyngeus muscle, cartilage becomes visible. (*e*) Exposure of the dorsolateral aspect of the larynx. The wing of thyroid is held laterally (curved arrow). Muscular process of arytenoid (arrowed) is abnormally prominent because of abductor muscle atrophy due to paralysis. (*f*) Steel suture passing from caudal limit of thyroid, through muscular process (arrowed) and returning through thyroid.

obstruction which is afforded by this technique is permanent once the arytenoid cartilage has ankylosed in its new position and the overall improvement of the patient should be marked. Thus, there is every reason to recommend this procedure even for very old dogs.

Management of dogs after laryngeal surgery

Apart from the course of corticosteroids mentioned previously (p. 105), a 10-day prophylactic course of a broad spectrum antibiotic is recommended.

In many instances, canine laryngeal operations are followed by a short period of adaptation, during which the dog shows discomfort at deglutition, and a temporary glottic impairment which may cause occasional coughing after eating or drinking. Tracheal contamination can be reduced by dietary advice. Milk, an ideal substrate for bacterial growth, should not be offered during the first month after surgery. Abrasive foods should be avoided during this time but sloppy meals are also unsuitable. The dietary consistency should be sufficiently firm for the patient to form discrete boluses for swallowing.

Severe exercise should not be permitted for at least 6 weeks as laryngeal exertion may provoke adverse tissue responses after partial laryngectomy or breakdown of a 'tie-back' operation. Attempts to bark should also be discouraged.

TRACHEAL SURGERY

The indications and technique for tracheotomy have been described in Chapter 1. The remaining indications for tracheal surgery consist of the treatment of tracheal collapse and other congenital deformities, the emergency management of traumatic injuries, the relief of tracheal stenosis, the extirpation of tumours and the treatment of endotracheal parasitism.

The surgical approach to the cervical trachea is straightforward. The patient is placed in dorsal recumbency and the neck is extended over sandbags. It is helpful if the forelimbs are drawn caudally as this will allow access to the lower cervical trachea. A ventral midline skin incision is made and the underlying sternohyoid muscle is divided at its medial raphe. For access to the caudal region the paired sternocephalicus muscles must also be divided. The intrathoracic trachea is best approached by a right-sided thoracotomy through the fourth intercostal space. Thoracotomy by sternal split does not provide easy access to the trachea and is best avoided.

Tracheal collapse

The majority of dogs afflicted with tracheal collapse are best managed conservatively with cage rest, strict diet to reduce weight, corticosteroids and antibiotic cover. However, in a few patients this regimen fails and surgical relief becomes necessary. The objective of surgery is to provide a normal tracheal diameter in the face of gross dorsoventral flattening. Unfortunately, the region of most severe collapse is likely to be at the thoracic inlet where surgical access is most difficult. Nevertheless, the ventral cervical approach combined with judicious traction will permit surgery over a surprising length of the trachea. A wide variety of procedures has been advocated for the reconstruction of collapsed trachea in dogs, including plication of the dorsal tracheal ligament (*Fig. 6.8*), the application of extra-luminal ring prostheses (*Fig. 6.8*), the implantation of intraluminal devices and replacement by total prosthesis.

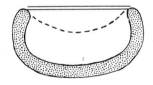

Row of mattress sutures
in dorsal ligament

Sutures draw tracheal
cartilages to the
shape of an external
prosthesis

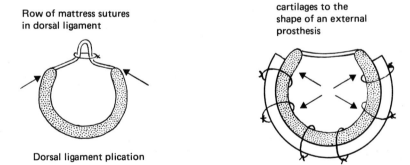

Dorsal ligament plication

Fig. 6.8. The principles of techniques to correct tracheal collapse.

In the first instance, plication of the dorsal tracheal ligament is suggested. This is achieved through the ventral incision as described above, and once the trachea has been exposed it should be isolated from the surrounding soft tissues, particular care being taken to avoid trauma to the recurrent laryngeal nerves. The trachea is then rotated to gain access to the dorsal aspect. Horizontal mattress sutures using 2/0 monofilament nylon are placed at close intervals to provide a continuous tuck which extends as far distally as traction will allow. The coarser suture material is preferred to fine silk because it provokes a tissue reaction which will ensure a lasting effect. The sutures should not penetrate the tracheal cartilage. On completion of the suture pattern the trachea is returned to its natural position and the overlying muscle layers and skin are coapted in the usual manner. A broad spectrum postoperative antibiotic course is provided and exercise is restricted during the first month after surgery. Strict advice should be given to prevent or reverse any tendency to obesity.

For those dogs in which dorsal ligament plication fails to provide a sustained improvement or in dogs that show areas of localized deformity or collapse, the provision of extraluminal prostheses may be considered. Ring prostheses are easily manufactured in general practice from plastic syringes and their cases. The size of ring is assessed by the measurement of normal segments of the trachea on radiographs. In general, each ring should be 5–7 mm wide but on occasions there are indications to use continuous extraluminal prostheses. Holes are drilled through the rings to allow placement of the sutures and the rings are split so that they may be placed around the trachea. The ventral midline approach is used and this procedure also may be performed with an endotracheal tube in position. Again, it is important to identify the recurrent laryngeal nerves and care must be taken not to include these within the ring prostheses. The collapsed trachea is drawn on to the prosthesis by sutures (3/0 silk) which penetrate the full thickness of the tracheal wall and each suture passes around a tracheal cartilage. Sufficient sutures are used to pull the collapsed trachea out to conform to the prosthesis. The number of prosthetic rings required to correct the collapse is dependent on the length of trachea involved. Wound closure is as described above and postoperative radiographs are helpful to assess the improvement obtained. During the postoperative period localized swelling and coughing are to be expected as a result of haemorrhage at the suture penetration sites. The polyethylene material used to manufacture the prostheses is inert and rejection is unlikely.

Tracheal resection

Tracheal resections may become necessary to excise localized strictures or tumours of the tracheal wall. Strictures may be the result of traumatic wounds, tracheotomy intubation or prolonged intubation with an overinflated cuffed tube. In a proportion of cases of stricture the band of fibrosis arises between tracheal cartilages but the dorsal ligament remains relatively unchanged. Under these circumstances complete resection and anastomosis is not necessary because the dorsal ligament should be left intact. The anaesthetic technique for each case should be planned carefully. In most cases the procedure may be commenced with the tube passed *per os* in the routine manner, but during a resection it may become necessary to provide a bypass tube directly into the distal tracheal segment. A return to the oral tube can be made once the anastomosis of the dorsal portion of the trachea has been completed.

Anastomosis following the resection of short segments can be achieved by local isolation and mobilization of the trachea from the surrounding soft tissues. However, larger resections may require extensive mobilization otherwise excessive traction forces will act on the suture lines and, at best, a further stricture will develop. In any event, the placement of tension sutures is recommended for all tracheal anastomoses. Whenever wide mobilization is necessary, care must be taken to preserve the local segmental blood supply through the peri-tracheal tissues. Resection is achieved through healthy annular ligaments above and below the lesion. Sutures (4/0 silk) are laid first around the cartilaginous rings on either side of the resection and, secondly, tension sutures are placed between rings 1–2 cm from the anastomosis.

Endotracheal procedures

The parasitic nodules of *Filaroides osleri* are best treated by the oral administration of levamisole or fenbendazole. This latter anthelminthic (Panacur) is administered at a dose rate of 20 mg/kg for 3 weeks. Although this medication is successful in the relief of most cases, a few dogs remain that continue to cough or in which the presence of persistent nodules embarrasses respiration. The blunt extirpation of the lesions by long-handled, crocodile or cup forceps can be achieved under endoscopic vision with little haemorrhage. Although solid fibreoptic endoscopes may be suitable for diagnosis, treatment should be performed through a rigid open-ended endoscope, which will permit unobstructed respiration throughout a procedure that can be time-consuming.

Rigid tubular endoscopes are also suitable for the retrieval of endotracheal foreign bodies. The procedure should be performed with the patient positioned on an inclined surface so that gravity will assist in the movement of the foreign body through the trachea. Longstanding foreign bodies may be difficult to dislodge because of surrounding granulation tissue, and open exploration and retrieval are indicated.

NASOPHARYNGEAL POLYPS

The polypoid lesions that arise in the middle ear of cats and extend to occupy the nasopharynx can be removed by simple traction. The polyps are exposed by drawing the soft palate forwards with Allis forceps, but occasionally very large lesions necessitate splitting the palate on its midline from the caudal border. The stalk of each polyp is grasped by artery forceps as it emerges at the pharyngeal opening of the Eustachian tube and the lesion is avulsed by gentle pressure. The palatine incision is closed in two layers—the nasopharyngeal mucosa with 3/0 chromic catgut and the oropharyngeal mucosa with 3/0 silk sutures. Polyps that have been removed by simple traction are inclined to recur, but the alternative approach of bulla osteotomy to expose the contents of the middle ear is not without hazards.

EXTERNAL LESIONS OF THE AIRWAYS

Space-occupying lesions such as abscesses, cysts and tumours may distort the pharyngeal, laryngeal and tracheal airways. Clearly each of these lesions must be treated on its merits, but in cases of abscess, it is always sound surgical practice to establish drainage before the institution of antibacterial therapy. Although salivary cysts arising from the sublingual glands are more likely to produce fluid-filled distensions in the sublingual or cervical regions, occasional cysts arise in a midway position and these produce a significant restriction of the pharyngeal airway in the region of the tonsillar crypt. In fact, at a casual inspection, this lesion may be confused with a tonsillar carcinoma. The treatment of the condition is similar to that for salivary cysts and includes the extirpation of the sublingual and submandibular salivary systems with drainage of the cyst.

Parapharyngeal masses may be explored by an approach from the ventral aspect of the submandibular region. The dissection is similar to that recommended for bulla osteotomy, and passes from the medial aspect of the mandible through the myelohyoid muscle, between the digastricus and styloglossus muscles, to reach the lateral pharyngeal tissues by blunt dissection. Occasionally, well-circumscribed and benign tumours lend themselves to successful removal from this site.

A ventral midline incision represents the best route to investigate and excise tumour masses from the tissues around the larynx and trachea. Surgeons working in this area must take care not to damage the important nerves which run parallel and close to the trachea. Although the position of the major blood vessels of the neck may be well known, they may be distorted from their normal course by the presence of the soft tissue mass. In general, the longitudinal plane presents the safest line for dissection.

SUPPLEMENTARY READING

Harvey C. E. and Venker van Haagan A. (1975) Surgical management of pharyngeal and laryngeal airway obstructions in the dog. *Vet. Clin. North Am.* **5**, 515–35.

Lane J. G. (1978) Canine laryngeal surgery. In: Grunsell G. S. G. and Hill F. W. G. (ed.), *The Veterinary Annual* 18th issue. Bristol, Wright–Scientechnica, p. 239.

Lane J. G., Orr C. M., Lucke V. M. et al. (1981) Nasopharyngeal polyps arising in the middle ear of the cat. *J. Small Anim. Pract.* **22**, 511–22.

Rubin G. J., Neal T. M. and Bojrab M. J. (1973) Surgical reconstruction for collapsed tracheal rings. *J. Small Anim. Pract.* **14**, 607–17.

Vasseur P. (1979) Surgery of the trachea. *Vet. Clin. North Am.* **9**, 231–43.

Chapter 7

Swallowing and Dysphagia

This chapter will describe the events which occur in normal animals when food is transferred from the mouth to the stomach and will highlight those stages at which swallowing function may be compromised. Prehension and mastication of food constitute the oral or predeglutition stage and this is followed by the oropharyngeal, pharyngo-oesophageal, oesophageal and gastro-oesophageal phases in the sequence of split-second, precisely timed reflexes which are collectively termed deglutition.

FUNCTIONAL ANATOMY OF DEGLUTITION

The oral phase depends upon the voluntary activity of the mandible and tongue to prehend and masticate food before it is collected into boluses. These are transferred to the base of the tongue by a series of anteroposterior lapping movements which propel solids and liquids caudally by compression against the palatine rugae. Although the hyoid apparatus moves in synchrony with the tongue, the nasopharyngeal and laryngeal airways remain open so that breathing can continue until the involuntary stages of deglutition commence.

Reflex deglutition occurs with the mouth closed and when respirations are halted after inspiration. The presence of accumulated food or fluids at the base of the tongue triggers the oropharyngeal phase of deglutition, which is characterized by the propulsion of the ingesta through the pharynx and past the larynx. The tongue fulfils two roles at this stage; first, it forms a seal against the palate and so prevents reflux into the buccal cavity and, secondly, it acts as a ram to drive the bolus caudally. However, the major propulsion is provided by a wave of constriction of pharyngeal muscles. This is sometimes termed the 'stripping wave' because it empties the pharynx very efficiently. The nasopharynx is protected by the contraction of the soft palate (palato-pharyngeal arch) which closes the posterior nares. Aspiration of ingesta into the lower respiratory tract is prevented by closure of the glottis (adduction of the arytenoid cartilages and vocal folds) and retroversion of the epiglottis so that it overlies the larynx. The adduction of the vocal fold opens the piriform recess on either side of the larynx and it is through these lateral food channels that liquid boluses usually travel. Solid boluses, on the other hand, take a midline route over the epiglottis and larynx. The passage of ingesta past the larynx is assisted by re-alignment of the upper airway which kinks slightly at the cricotracheal ligament so that the larynx faces cranio-dorsally. Movements of the tongue, epiglottis and larynx are synchronized because of their attachments to the hyoid apparatus.

At rest the upper oesophagus is actively closed by the action of the cricopharyngeal sphincter. The cricopharyngeus muscle undergoes receptive relaxation to allow each bolus driven caudally through the pharynx to reach the oesophagus. Thus, for firm boluses the sphincter dilates widely whereas for liquids the relaxation is minimal. Clearly, the pharyngo-oesophageal stage of deglutition must coincide with the pharyngeal stripping wave otherwise the transport of the boluses caudally will be obstructed.

Peristalsis usually propels the ingesta throughout the length of the oesophagus in a single coordinated wave of contraction to the gastro-oesophageal junction. Primary oesophageal peristalsis commences with the contraction of the cricopharyngeal sphincter and therefore it is the immediate sequel to deglutition. However, retention of one or two boluses in the proximal oesophagus may occur before a further swallow initiates a wave of primary peristaltic contraction to the stomach. Secondary oesophageal peristalsis arises when the accumulation of several boluses in the proximal region stimulates peristalsis by stretching the oesophageal wall and it occurs in the absence of a preceding swallow. It is unusual for boluses to stall in transit to the stomach but when this occurs the bolus is either swept along by the next bolus or it triggers secondary peristalsis itself.

Although the lower oesophageal sphincter (cardia) is complicated in structure, its function is straightforward. At rest it forms an efficient barrier to the reflux of gastric contents into the oesophagus but in swallowing it relaxes as each bolus arrives, to permit free passage into the stomach. It is not unusual for small quantities of ingesta to reflux into the oesophagus between peristaltic waves and this is cleared by secondary peristalsis, initiated by the refluxed material itself.

FUNCTIONAL DISTURBANCES OF DEGLUTITION

The literal meaning of dysphagia is 'difficulty in eating' but it is generally accepted that the term includes disorders of swallowing as well as those of prehension and mastication.

TMJ disorders

In Chapter 8 the disorders of the temporomandibular joint (TMJ) are discussed and it is sufficient to point out here that a free range of movements by the TMJ is necessary, not only for the prehension and mastication of food, but also because closure of the jaw is a prerequisite of deglutition. Animals with fractures of the mandible, traumatic dislocation of the TMJ, open-jaw locking and dropped-jaw neurapraxia may be difficult to nurse, even by hand-feeding of liquidized nutrients, because they are reluctant to swallow when they cannot close the mouth.

Dyspnoea

The involuntary phases of swallowing necessitate a pause in respirations and, thus, patients with severe dyspnoea may not eat simply because they cannot afford to stop breathing in order to swallow.

Lingual anomalies

Congenital macroglossia, typically seen in the Chihuahua or Papillon, may limit the range of movements by the tongue. Such animals are often poorly developed and show overspill of food and fluids. The diagnosis is made obvious by the constant protrusion of the tongue, which cannot be completely accommodated within the mouth.

Painful lingual lesions caused by wounds, burns, strangulating or buried foreign bodies and abscesses make for reluctance to move the tongue freely and this is prejudicial to normal swallowing. Drooling of saliva and overspill of ingesta at the lips will be features in these patients. Lingual paralysis is a rare entity in domesticated animals and in the author's experience of a small number of cases it is invariably unilateral. In chronic cases the tongue hangs towards the paralysed side due to contraction of the affected muscle (*Fig. 7.1*). The eosinophilic granuloma complex of cats may produce painful lesions on the tongue, at the fauces and on the palatine mucosa as well as the more obvious erosions of the upper labial margins. Calicivirus ulcers on the tongue may also make a cat reluctant to eat and swallow. Neoplasia of the tongue is rare in dogs but cats may be afflicted by squamous cell carcinoma of this structure.

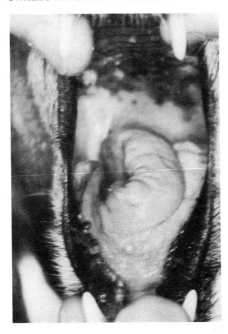

Fig. 7.1. Chronic lingual paralysis: fibrosis of the atrophied muscle distorts the tongue *towards* the paralysed side.

Palatine defects

Congenital clefts of the hard and soft portions of the secondary palate prevent the formation of an efficient seal by the tongue during the voluntary phase of swallowing and by the palato-pharyngeal arch in reflex deglutition. Traumatic clefts are more common in cats than dogs but the presenting signs of nasal return of food and fluids with secondary rhinitis are common to both congenital and acquired clefts (*see* Chapter 10). Although major defects of the palate will be obvious at a preliminary inspection of the mouth, small clefts from the caudal border of the soft palate and other anomalies such as unilateral hypoplasia and pseudo-uvula formation may not be confirmed until the examination is performed under a general anaesthetic. It is not uncommon for foreign bodies, typically sticks and bones, to become wedged across the hard palate between the maxillary dental arcades (*Fig.* 7.2), and the palate is a frequent site of oral neoplasia. Lesions at this site provide physical obstructions to the caudal movement of boluses, but some palatine lesions are so painful that the patient declines from frequent attempts to eat. In other instances the patient may be a messy feeder or shows constant mouthing movements by the tongue after eating.

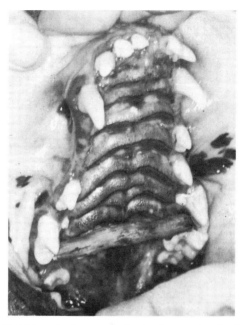

Fig. 7.2. Stick wedged across the hard palate causing dysphagia.

Pharyngeal lesions

Failure of pharyngeal muscular contractions through paralysis or myopathy is a rare cause of dysphagia in small animals when compared with other species such as the horse. Overspill at the lips, nasal return of food and fluids, and aspiration pneumonia are the likely consequences of the uncontrolled distribution of ingesta. Large foreign bodies such as rubber balls may obstruct the pharynx of dogs without being swallowed (*Fig.* 7.3). Not only will the dog show marked dysphagia with persistent gulping and retching episodes but severe dyspnoea may result from occlusion of the pharyngeal airway. There will be an urgent need for treatment, possibly including the use of a temporary tracheotomy tube until the obstruction is relieved. Pharyngeal penetration wounds are most common in dogs that chase sticks and the consequences of this injury are discussed in Chapter 11. In the period immediately following such a wound the patient will be reluctant to eat because deglutition is painful. Air and contaminated ingesta may be aspirated through the defect in the pharyngeal wall. Emphysema in the cervical tissues may be extensive and the degree of cellulitis can range from minimal to severe.

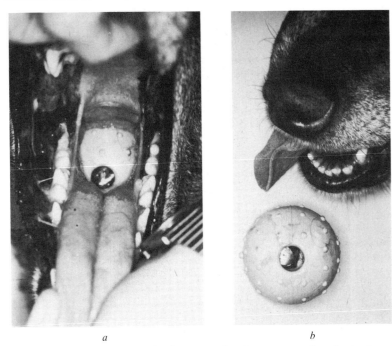

a   *b*

Fig. 7.3. Toy obstruction of the pharynx causing dyspnoea as well as dysphagia.

Acute and chronic tonsillitis produces painful enlargement with or without eversion of the tonsils from their crypts. The role of the tonsils is presumed to be in local defence, and secondary tonsillitis is likely to occur in the face of oral and pharyngeal infections as well as in patients that vomit or cough persistently. A diagnosis of primary tonsillitis is reached by a process of elimination when there are no other predisposing causes of lymphoid hyperplasia. Primary tonsillitis is most frequently encountered in small breeds, typically Toy Poodles, and many of the afflicted dogs are young. Tonsillitis is uncommon in cats. Not only do animals with tonsillitis show a reluctance to eat because of the pain which accompanies the movement of food through the pharynx, but a physical obstruction to its passage may occur if the tonsillar enlargement is severe. During episodes of acute tonsillitis inappetence may be due to febrile illness and general lassitude. Also, it may be difficult to differentiate cause and effect when dogs with tonsillitis show a persistent non-productive cough. Malignant melanoma, squamous cell carcinoma and lymphosarcoma are the common tumours which arise at the tonsils of dogs (*Fig.* 7.4); benign tumours

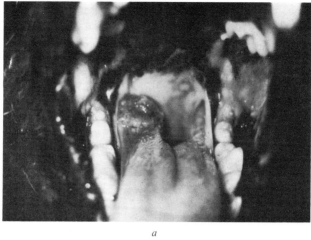

a

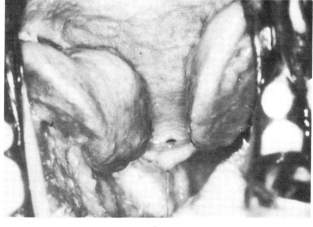

b

Fig. 7.4. Canine tonsillar neoplasia. (*a*) Squamous cell carcinoma. (*b*) Lymphosarcoma: all superficial nodes of this dog were also grossly enlarged.

are rare at this site. Squamous cell carcinomas may be encountered in feline tonsils. The symptoms of tonsillar tumours reflect the patient's response to a physical mass in the oropharynx, with gagging and retching, rather than pain. Nevertheless a cervical swelling due to metastatic spread may be the first sign of tonsillar neoplasia (*see* Chapter 11).

Laryngeal disorders

Efficient laryngeal adduction is required to prevent the inhalation of ingesta, especially fluids, during and after swallowing. When this valvular function is compromised, contaminated material can be expected to provoke an inhalation tracheitis at the least or, more likely, an aspiration pneumonia.

Dogs with laryngeal paralysis show neurogenic atrophy of the adductor as well as abductor muscle groups. Closure of the glottis during deglutition is weak and a moist cough can be one of the major presenting signs. 'Tie-back' surgery (*see* Chapter 6) to relieve the dyspnoea of laryngeal paralysis exacerbates the tendency to aspiration, partly because the glottis is fixed in an open position and partly because the lateral food channel is restricted on the side of surgery. However, most patients appear to adapt in the postoperative period and few are left with a permanent low-grade cough.

The presence of tumours or chronic inflammatory proliferations at the glottis will also inhibit normal function but fortunately these changes are rare in both dogs and cats.

Fractures of the hyoid apparatus are unusual sequels of trauma to the upper neck, brought about by fights or the overzealous use of a choke-chain. As the hyoid bones provide the anatomical link between the tongue and the larnyx and lie partly within the pharyngeal wall, it is not surprising that dysphagia is the predominant sign of this injury.

Whenever ingesta remain within the pharynx, for whatever reason, after the completion of the deglutition sequence, aspiration through the glottis is likely to occur. Thus, the radiographic demonstration of inhalation tracheitis or pneumonia does not necessarily point to a primary laryngeal disorder, in fact, this is seldom the case.

Cricopharyngeal malfunction

Mention has been made above of the split-second timing with which the proximal oesophageal sphincter must relax if the food or fluid boluses, propelled caudally by the pharyngeal stripping waves, are to pass into the cervical oesophagus. Achalasia of the cricopharyngeal muscle exists when it is congenitally strictured or becomes fibrosed through an acquired inflammatory process. Although this entity has been described in the literature, the author has not been able to confirm a diagnosis of cricopharyngeal achalasia in any case by histopathological examination of biopsy material. A functional obstruction at the cricopharynx arises if the sphincter fails to relax at the correct instant to allow the ingesta to pass (*Fig.* 7.5). In the author's experience, cricopharyngeal incoordination has been limited to puppies under 4 months of age and Cocker or Springer Spaniels have usually been

Fig. 7.5. Freeze-frame taken during cine-radiography of deglutition in a dog. Contrast medium is partly arrested in the pharynx cranial to the cricopharynx (arrow). Inhaled material can be seen in the trachea (double arrow).

involved. The clinical signs of structural and functional obstructions at the cricopharynx are indistinguishable. Although the patient attempts to swallow, food and fluids are returned immediately around the tongue base into the mouth and also through the nasal chambers. Apart from a marked tendency to cough when eating and drinking, a moist pharyngeal rattle may be present for much of the time. It is not surprising that these puppies are unthrifty and bouts of bronchopneumonia contribute further to their poor bodily condition.

Retropharyngeal lesions

Space-occupying masses in the tissues surrounding the pharynx may provide an obstruction to swallowing. In cases of abscess at this site pharyngeal contractions and movements of the hyoid apparatus and larynx are painful and the patient is disinclined to eat.

Oesophageal disorders

It is not the intention of this section to enter into a detailed discussion of thoracic surgery, but oesophageal diseases constitute an important differential diagnosis in cases of dysphagia. There is a misguided tendency for veterinarians to consider oesophageal anomalies only when there is overt regurgitation of ingesta shortly after meals.

However, the symptoms may also include chronic respiratory infections, an intermittent productive cough with or without a pharyngeal rattle, tonsillitis, pseudoptyalism and marked discomfort during and after meals.

1. Neuromuscular diseases of the oesophagus produce dilatations which may be localized or generalized, developmental or acquired. The most frequent form of megoesophagus afflicts young dogs from weaning to early adulthood. However, some may not be presented for examination until middle age, perhaps with an owner's complaint of chronic respiratory disease or unthriftiness; the question must be asked whether such patients are suffering from a recently acquired oesophageal dilatation or whether it has been present since puppyhood. There is strong circumstantial evidence that idiopathic megoesophagus is an inherited trait, and in the United Kingdom the Irish Setter is over-represented; elsewhere the Newfoundland and Schnauzer have been incriminated. In affected dogs there is a failure of myenteric function, particularly in the thoracic oesophagus, and primary and secondary peristaltic waves are weak or non-existent. The pressure gradient in the distal section is not sufficient to stimulate relaxation of the gastro-oesophageal junction and pooling of food and fluid occurs in the thoracic oesophagus prior to regurgitation (*Fig.* 7.6). Occasionally the cervical oesophagus is palpably distended. Idiopathic megoesophagus may show spontaneous improvement to the point of resolution of symptoms and efficient peristalsis, in spite of or because of dietary management. This consists of frequent feeding (10–12 meals per day)

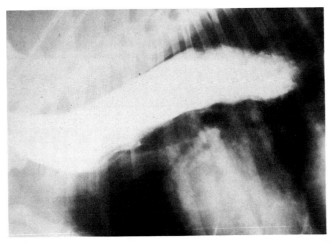

Fig. 7.6. Idiopathic megoesophagus in an Irish Setter. There is generalized dilatation of the thoracic oesophagus.

on an inclined plane, the diet consisting of firm foods which provoke secondary peristalsis more effectively than gruel.

Acquired achalasia is a disorder of mature dogs without previous history of oesophageal disease. Unlike idiopathic megoesophagus, acquired achalasia seldom undergoes spontaneous resolution, although many of the other clinical features are indistinguishable. In both conditions malfunction of the lower oesophageal sphincter may contribute to the failure of oesophageal transport but in achalasia only is cardioplasty indicated to weaken the resistance of the sphincter.

Congenital anomalies of the great vessels may interfere with oesophageal function to cause a constriction at the level of the base of the heart. The clinical signs of a vascular ring stricture are similar to those of idiopathic megoesophagus, although puppies with a patent ductus arteriosus may show additional signs of cardiovascular insufficiency. The stricture produced by a vascular ring provokes an oesophageal dilatation proximal to the heart base (*Fig.* 7.7)

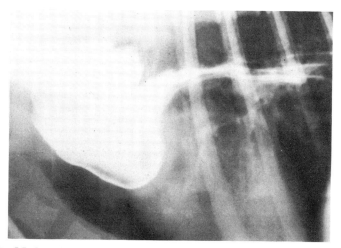

Fig. 7.7. Oesophageal dilatation cranial to the heart: vascular ring stricture.

The results of simple surgical section of the vascular ring are often disappointing because the oesophageal pouch remains and peristaltic function is poor. The symptoms of regurgitation sometimes continue unaltered after surgery.

Acquired oesophageal dilatation with the familiar symptoms of regurgitation or inhalation pneumonia may be a feature of other neuromuscular disorders such as myasthenia gravis and the giant axonal neuropathy of German Shepherd dogs.

Idiopathic megoesophagus is rarely recorded in cats and there have been isolated reports of vascular ring strictures. However, megoesophagus may be a secondary feature in cats, often Siamese, afflicted with pyloric stenosis. The clinical signs of projectile vomiting up to 8 hours after eating point to pyloric dysfunction rather than to the oesophagus.

2. Oesophageal strictures may occur in the absence of external compression and they may be congenital or acquired. The symptoms include choking and regurgitation and the disease is differentiated from other causes of oesophageal dilatation by endoscopy and contrast radiography. Acquired cases may arise at the site of an arrested foreign body or of an oesophagotomy.

3. Foreign body obstruction should be considered in all cases in which a dog suddenly shows vomiting within moments of eating. However, if the obstruction is longstanding, the patient becomes inappetent and vomiting ceases so that the diagnosis is less obvious. The typical sites where foreign bodies become lodged are at the thoracic inlet (*Fig.* 7.8), anterior to the base of the heart and between the heart and the diaphragm. West Highland and Cairn Terriers seem particularly prone to the error of judgement that leads to this condition. Cats on the other hand are discriminating in their eating habits and obstructive oesophageal foreign bodies are unusual in this species.

4. Oesophageal diverticula cause regurgitation, gagging, discomfort or coughing after meals and general depression. Some may be a sequel to foreign body obstructions but there is evidence that most are congenital. In fact, the diverticulum may act as a trap for solid boluses

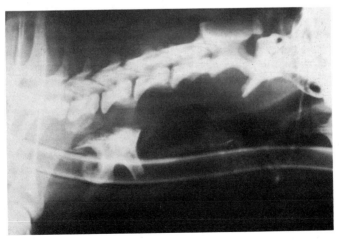

Fig. 7.8. Bony foreign body arrested at thoracic inlet.

in transit and it may not be clear whether a bony foreign body is the chicken or the egg. Broncho-oesophageal fistulas may accompany the diverticula. Dogs with oesophageal diverticula do not respond well to surgical treatments.

5. Reflux oesophagitis and stricture formation is a rare but recognized complication of general anaesthesia in the dog and cat. The major clinical signs are of dysphagia and regurgitation which commence immediately on recovery or within a few days of a general anaesthetic. The length of oesophagus which is diseased can be considerable and in one recorded case the severe inflammatory reaction extended to the pharynx and larynx. Localized strictures are better treated by repeated dilatation than by surgical excision.

Reflux oesophagitis may occur without stricture formation and the patients show marked discomfort, particularly after meals, as well as vomiting.

6. Oesophageal neoplasia is uncommon in both dogs and cats. The sarcomatous lesions stimulated by *Spirocerca lupi* should be considered as a cause of oesophageal dysfunction in dogs that reside or have been resident in climates where this parasite is endemic. In spite of reports of the frequency of oesophageal squamous cell carcinoma in cats, in clinical practice this is a very rare entity.

7. External masses such as abscesses and tumours may cause functional obstructions of the oesophagus (*Fig.* 7.9). In the neck such lesions would be obvious at palpation but radiography is necessary to

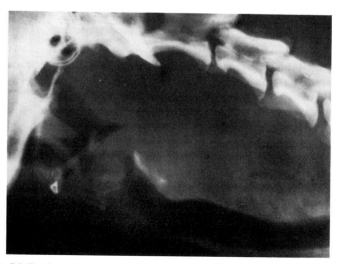

Fig. 7.9. Trachea distorted by a large retropharyngeal mass which also compresses the oesophagus to cause dysphagia.

eliminate this possible cause of dysfunction in the thorax. Anterior mediastinal lesions, including thymic lymphosarcoma in cats, will be readily seen on lateral projections.

DIAGNOSTIC PROCEDURE

Although a careful history may produce useful pointers to the likely diagnosis in cases of dysphagia, owners may have difficulty in providing an accurate description of their pet's dilemma. In due course there may be no alternative but to observe the animal closely when it is offered food and fluid.

Reluctance to swallow and drooling are cardinal signs of rabies. At the very beginning of the consultation, and most certainly before coming to grips with the patient, this possibility should be explored until it has been safely discounted.

After a general clinical examination, the neck is palpated for untoward swellings. An inspection of the mouth takes note of the mandibular position and movements, the health of the teeth and gums, the hard palate and tongue. The tongue must be depressed to examine the tonsils and soft palate and the wisdom of this procedure is dependent on the temperament of the patient.

The anal sacs should be checked for the presence of impaction or sacculitis in cases of intractible tonsillitis and appropriate steps are taken to eliminate this potential source of recurrent infection.

Before the patient is anaesthetized plain lateral radiographs of the neck and chest should be made as many oesophageal disorders, including foreign body obstructions and megoesophagus, can be confirmed at this stage. A decision to continue with the radiographic studies, including the use of contrast media and fluoroscopy, or simply to observe the deglutition performance of the animal, may be made on the basis of the plain films and case history. Some diagnoses can be confirmed only by contrast fluoroscopy, and these include pharyngeal paralysis and cricopharyngeal achalasia or incoordination (*Fig. 7.5*). Contrast material is sometimes necessary to outline those foreign bodies that are not radio-opaque. On no account should contrast material be force-fed in large amounts to dogs or cats that have abnormal swallowing function as this is very likely to provoke a severe inhalation reaction. Whenever a diagnosis of a thoracic oesophageal foreign body has been made, both dorsoventral and lateral views should be inspected for evidence of mediastinitis, which is in turn indicative of penetration of the oesophageal wall. The signs of inhalation pneumonia seen on radiographs include a diffuse parenchymal density, especially in the dependent cardiac and apical lobes.

Air bronchograms crossing the heart shadow confirm that the cardiac lobe is collapsed.

General anaesthesia permits a more detailed examination of the palates, and foreign bodies wedged between or across the dental arcades can be removed. The tonsils can be inspected for neoplastic involvement and it should be noted that a tiny primary tumour may precede an extensive metastatic lymphadenopathy and also that tonsillar neoplasia is sometimes bilateral. The tongue is manipulated so that buried or strangulating foreign material can be detected. Infarction of the anterior section of the tongue invariably points to strangulation, often by a thread. A needle may be attached but this could be as far distant as the stomach, if the free thread is long. The pharynx is checked for intraluminal foreign bodies with a laryngoscope and this may also be used to evaluate laryngeal function. A rigid oesophago-scope or flexible gastroscope is essential to establish the presence of strictures, reflux oesophagitis, broncho-oesophageal fistula and wounds inflicted by foreign bodies.

Buried foreign bodies, such as needles in the soft tissues of the pharynx, require radiographs in two planes to pin-point their exact location (*Fig.* 7.10).

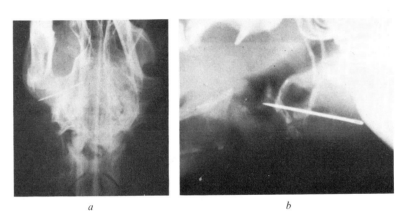

a   *b*

Fig. 7.10. Dorsoventral (*a*) and lateral (*b*) projections accurately locate a needle buried in the pharyngeal wall.

Biopsy samples should be taken from oropharyngeal tumours in order that a useful prognosis can be given. Material for histopatho-logical examination may be more difficult to obtain from deeper sites such as the oesophageal wall, but, fortunately, the indications are infrequent.

SPECIFIC SURGICAL PROCEDURES

Tonsillectomy (*Fig.* 7.11)

The indications for tonsillectomy include chronic, non-responsive tonsillar enlargement where no exciting factor can be identified and neoplasia. Considerable reservations are held concerning the value of the procedure and owners should not be misled to believe that it is always successful. Tonsillar tumours frequently metastasize, first to the local lymph nodes and later to the lung fields. The submandibular region should be checked for palpable metastasis and chest radiographs should be obtained before embarking on tonsillectomy. Primary tonsillar neoplasms are often broadly based with infiltration of the lateral pharyngeal wall, fauces and tongue base. In these circumstances simple surgical excision is not practicable and other techniques such as cryosurgery or irradiation may be considered.

The objective of tonsillectomy is to excise the entire body of each pharyngeal tonsil, including the lesser submucosal portion which is located at the anterior pole. This is seen when the main body of the tonsil is everted with forceps. The surgical technique must produce haemostasis of the tonsillar vessels which enter through the middle and caudal segments of the peduncle, but it must not provoke tissue reaction or oedema that could obstruct respirations. Thus, the choice of technique differs in meso- and dolicocephalic dogs from that used in brachycephalic breeds, where diathermy and cryosurgery should be avoided. Whichever method is used, the patient should be placed in sternal recumbency and the mouth held open with tapes rather than with a gag, which is an unnecessary encumbrance to the surgery. Local infiltration with adrenaline (epinephrine) solution has the disadvantage that it may give a false impression of effective haemostasis. The tonsillar body is everted carefully and curved forceps are applied to the tonsillar fold throughout its length (*Fig.* 7.11*b*), but making sure that the lesser tonsillar tissue at the anterior pole is included. Whenever there is the possibility of significant airway obstruction, a simple continuous lockstitch pattern of 3/0 Dexon is applied across the tonsillar attachments and the tonsillar tissue is excised with scissors before the forceps are removed.

In those animals that have a normal airway, a more elaborate technique is used which provokes appreciable oedema and swelling but which reduces the possibility of secondary tonsillar development from the lymphoid elements which are generously deposited in the tonsillar crypts. The main body of the tonsil plus the accessory anterior component are excised by diathermy before the curved forceps are released and haemostasis checked (*Fig.* 7.11*c*). A cryoprobe is introduced into the crypt and the tissues are frozen to a depth of 3 mm using a double freeze-thaw cycle (*Fig.* 7.11*d*). The addition of this

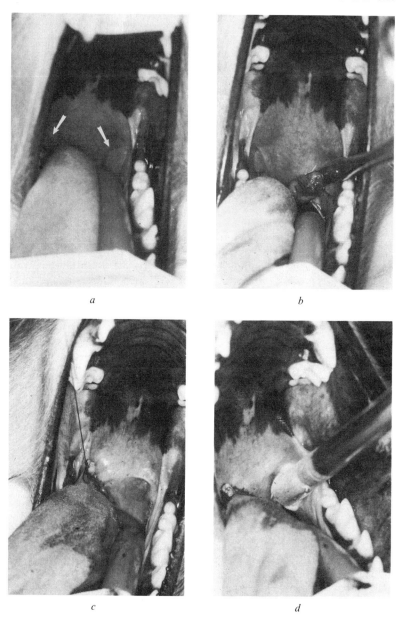

Fig. 7.11. Tonsillectomy. (*a*) Chronic tonsillar enlargement—tonsils everted from crypts. (*b*) Application of tonsil forceps. (*c*) Tonsillectomy by oversewing pedicle. (*d*) Cryosurgery to destroy lymphoid remnants in tonsillar crypt.

cryosurgical innovation has greatly improved the author's tonsillectomy results. Again, it is stressed that patients must be carefully
selected and the technique is not advocated for brachycephalic types.
Whichever method of tonsillectomy is used, the patient should not be
allowed to recover from the anaesthetic until complete haemostasis has
been achieved. Systemic corticosteroids are provided for 24 hours and
broad spectrum antibiotics are dispensed for 10 days when cryosurgery
is included. Solids are withheld for the first 72 hours and abrasive foods
are avoided during the first 2 weeks after surgery.

Cricopharyngeal myotomy

Section of the cricopharyngeal muscle is indicated to weaken the
proximal oesophageal sphincter in confirmed cases of cricopharyngeal
achalasia or incoordination. A technique which produces a bilateral
section of the muscle is suggested. A ventral midline skin incision from
the level of the hyoid bone to the mid-trachea is made and extended
between the sternohyoid muscles until the larynx can be mobilized and
rotated either way. The pliable wings of the thyroid cartilage can be
palpated and make a useful lever to achieve the laryngeal rotation. The
cricopharyngeal musculature can be identified by its insertion on to the
cricoid cartilage and by the oblique direction of its fibres. All the muscle
fibres are carefully sectioned at the level of the wing of the thyroid so
that the underlying oesophageal mucosa is exposed, but this is
preserved. The procedure is repeated on the opposite side after rotation
of the larynx.

In the postoperative period it is important that the patient receives a
bulky but non-abrasive diet to prevent cicatrization and stenosis at
the site of the myotomy.

Oesophageal foreign body removal

Naturally, it is preferable that foreign body obstructions should be
removed by the mouth rather than by surgery. The procedure is most
easily performed under fluoroscopic vision but in practice conditions
direct vision with an endoscope is satisfactory. The choice of forceps
for the manoeuvre is critical. Long obstetrical forceps or a Becket's
probang are suggested because the leading edges are atraumatic and
they dilate the oesophagus in advance of the foreign body as it is
withdrawn. The forceps or probang are thoroughly lubricated before
passage into the oesophagus. Endoscopy is useful to ensure a good hold
on the object but its main function is to prevent unnecessary trauma to
the oesophageal wall. If the mucosa moves together with the foreign
body it is a sign that the obstruction remains held fast and the forceps
must be re-applied. As soon as the foreign body can be moved without

dragging the mucosa it can be withdrawn safely. Some resistance will be encountered over the base of the heart, at the thoracic inlet and particularly over the larynx. Repeated unsuccessful attempts to dislodge the foreign body from its site of arrest are indications for oesophagotomy.

Cervical oesophagotomy

The usual indication for cervical oesophagotomy is the arrest of a foreign body anterior to the thoracic inlet. Before surgery contaminated saliva proximal to the obstruction is removed from the oesophagus by suction. The patient is placed in dorsal recumbency and a ventral midline skin incision is made from the larynx to the sternum. The paired sternohyoideus and sternocephalicus muscles are divided at their midline raphe. The trachea is exposed by blunt separation of the loose areolar tissue and the oesophagus is identified to the left side. The foreign body is palpated and the oesophagus is mobilized as far as possible before it is packed off with swabs. A longitudinal incision is made into the oesophageal lumen and this must be large enough to permit the withdrawal of the obstruction without tearing the tissues. The oesophageal mucosa is closed with 4/0 silk and the muscularis with 4/0 Dexon or catgut, each with simple interrupted sutures. The site is checked carefully for leakages before the packing is removed; the remainder of the closure is routine. Postoperative care includes broad spectrum antibiotics for 10 days and diet is restricted to glucose–water for 48 hours, thereafter gradually returning to soft foods.

SUPPLEMENTARY READING

Hoffer R. E.,MacCoy D. M., Quick C. B. et al. (1979) Management of acquired achalasia in dogs. *J. Am. Vet. Med. Assoc.* **175**, 814–17.

Pearson H. (1970) Persistent vomiting in the young dog. *J. Small Anim. Pract.* **11**, 403–15.

Pearson H., Darke P. G. G., Gibbs C. et al. (1978) Reflux oesophagitis and stricture formation after anaesthesia. *J. Small Anim. Pract.* **19**, 507–19.

Pearson H., Gaskell C. J., Gibbs C. et al. (1974) Pyloric and oesophageal dysfunction in the cat. *J. Small Anim. Pract.* **15**, 487–501.

Pearson H., Gibbs C. and Kelly D. F. (1978) Oesophageal diverticulum formation in the dog. *J. Small Anim. Pract.* **19**, 341–55.

Rosin E. and Hanlon G. F. (1972) Canine crico-pharyngeal achalasia. *J. Am. Vet. Med. Assoc.* **160**, 1496–9.

Chapter 8

Disorders of the Temporomandibular Joint

Dogs and cats may be afflicted by a number of diseases, not only of the temporomandibular joint (TMJ) itself, but also of the muscles of mastication and their motor innervation. The symptoms of TMJ abnormalities include one or more of the following:

1. Pain on mastication and a reluctance to prehend, chew and swallow food or fluids.
2. Inability to open the jaw.
3. Inability to close the jaw.
4. Pain on palpation of the mandibular or facial regions.
5. Swelling of the jaw or masticatory muscles.
6. Atrophy of the masticatory muscles with or without sinking of the eyeball.

A free range of movement of the components of the TMJ is essential for the prehension and mastication of food and for deglutition.

ANATOMICAL CONSIDERATIONS (*Fig.* 8.1.)

Although the TMJ is a condylar joint which is transversely elongated, it is capable of considerable lateral sliding movements. Within the joint capsule lies a thin meniscus which acts as a cushion between the concave articular surfaces of the temporal bone and the mandibular condyle, which would otherwise correspond poorly with one another. Ventrally, the mandibular fossa of the temporal bone is supported by the post-glenoid process which prevents caudal dislocation of the mandible. The loose joint capsule is reinforced laterally by a fibrous thickening which represents a poorly developed collateral ligament. Mandibular movements are mostly in unison but the synchondrosis at the symphysis allows independent movements of the rami which in turn

143

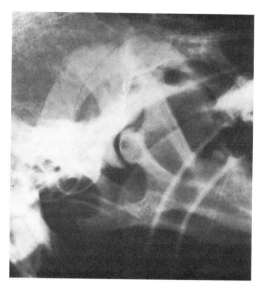

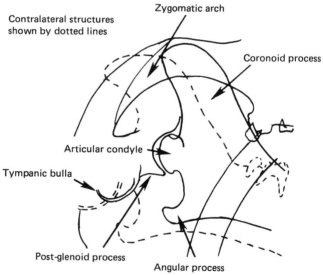

Fig. 8.1. Lateral oblique radiograph of a normal canine TMJ with explanatory line drawing.

permit congenital or traumatic luxations of the TMJ to occur without fracture. Gravity, aided by the digastricus muscles, opens the mouth, and the masseter, temporal and pterygoid muscles are responsible for closure. The muscles of mastication are innervated through the mandibular branch of the trigeminal nerve (V).

During opening of the jaws the coronoid process moves forwards, medial to the zygomatic arch, and the angular process is drawn caudally. When the jaw closes the movements are reversed. Free excursion of the coronoid process is obstructed in the open-jaw locking of TMJ dysplasia and by depression fractures of the zygoma.

DIAGNOSIS

The predominant signs of TMJ disorders have been mentioned above. In the case history, note should be taken of traumatic or painful episodes as well as of any tendency to otitis. A detailed inspection of the head follows the general clinical examination. Patients that are unable to close the jaw tend to drool a mixture of food and saliva and may be difficult to differentiate at first from animals with other swallowing disorders. In this respect the possibility of rabies should be considered and investigated before proceeding. Once this has been eliminated from the differential diagnosis, the mouth may be examined for symmetry or deviation of the bite. In the conscious patient a preliminary assessment of the range of TMJ movements should be made but a more accurate evaluation is deferred until the subject is anaesthetized. Whenever the patient is unable to close the mouth voluntarily, passive closure should be attempted to differentiate firm open-jaw locking, where bony surfaces are abnormally engaged, from neuromuscular disorders. The masticatory muscles should be examined for pain, swelling, atrophy and asymmetry. The masseter face of the mandible and the temporal fossa are the most obvious sites for this investigation, but additional attention should be paid to the position of the eyeball within the orbit. The mandible itself should be palpated for soft tissue or bony swellings as well as asymmetry.

A general anaesthetic will be necessary for detailed manipulative tests, radiography and biopsy. In animals that are unable to open the TMJs anaesthesia is maintained by an intravenous agent or, alternatively, a bypass tracheotomy will be necessary until the jaws can be freed for the normal passage of an endotracheal tube. Open-jaw locking is usually intermittent in dogs and manipulative attempts to recreate the anomaly under anaesthesia should concentrate on each mandible in turn rather than on both in unison. Fractures of the mandible and maxilla are best confirmed by lateral and intra-oral occlusal radiographic projections. The TMJs themselves are investigated by a whole skull, dorsoventral view combined with lateral oblique projections. The oblique views (*Fig.* 8.1*a*) can be difficult to obtain and interpret in general practice and attempts to produce mirror images of the two joints are usually unsuccessful.

Biopsy sampling of the masticatory muscles is helpful to differentiate inflammatory and degenerative processes. The usual site for sampling is the temporal muscle over the temporal fossa. It should be noted that the interscutular muscle crosses the site superficially and the sample should be taken from the deeper muscle layer.

CONGENITAL DISEASE

Dysplasia of the TMJ

Occasionally, intermittent locking of the jaw in an open position is encountered in young Basset Hounds and Irish Setters. Laxity in the TMJ allows the contralateral coronoid process to become locked lateral to the zygomatic arch (*Fig.* 8.2). The breed predisposition implies an inherited disease. Apart from a shallow mandibular fossa, a slack collateral ligament and a joint space which diverges excessively when the mouth is opened, excessive mobility of the mandibular symphysis is required for open-jaw locking. It is not possible to reproduce the disease in skull specimens from confirmed cases if the symphysis has been fixed. Yawning usually precipitates the subluxation, and when the patient is presented simple pressure at the chin fails to close the mouth. The coronoid process can usually be released from the zygoma by opening the jaw still further before applying a

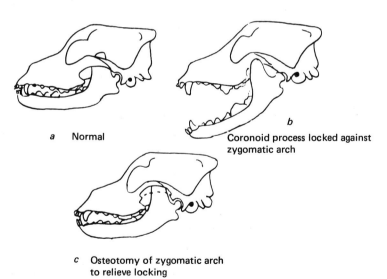

a Normal

b Coronoid process locked against zygomatic arch

c Osteotomy of zygomatic arch to relieve locking

Fig. 8.2. Congenital dysplasia of the TMJ: open-jaw locking. (*After* Robins and Grandage, with permission.)

slight twisting action. Exceptional cases require a general anaesthetic for this manoeuvre but, more frequently, owners acquire the technique in the conscious patient so that treatment is not sought in every case.

A diagnosis of temporomandibular joint dysplasia with open-jaw locking is usually confirmed on the basis of the known breed predisposition and by manipulative tests to recreate the disorder. When the jaw is in the locked position the coronoid process of the contralateral side can be palpated at the lateral aspect of the face where it engages the zygomatic arch. Lateral oblique radiographs of the TMJs can be expected to show shallow mandibular fossae, with a poorly developed anterodorsal surface. There is a tendency to thickening of the post-glenoid process and divergence of the joint space is apparent when the mandible is in the opened position.

Treatment

Although many standard texts refer to the provision of support to the collateral ligaments of the TMJs by the use of screws and steel wire, these techniques have proved ineffective. In theory, it should be possible to prevent open-jaw locking by fixation of the mandibular symphysis with compression screws but there are no authenticated reports of this approach. A simple and effective method to prevent engagement of the coronoid process on the zygomatic arch is to perform an osteotomy of the ventral half of the arch (*Fig.* 8.2). This technique is preferred to complete osteotomy of the zygoma because the facial outline is preserved. The osteotomy site is superficial; a longitudinal incision is made through the skin, subcutis and periosteum before an elongated section of bone is removed. The success of the osteotomy can be assessed during the procedure by attempts to recreate open-jaw locking. Care should be taken to avoid trauma to the major blood vessels, nerves and the infraorbital salivary gland which lie deep to the zygomatic arch. Wound closure is routine.

It can be appreciated that the surgical treatment described aims to correct the consequence of the dysplasia rather than the primary joint anomaly. Nevertheless, the procedure is effective and there seems to be little tendency to subsequent osteoarthritis.

DEVELOPMENTAL ANOMALY

Craniomandibular osteopathy

The breed predisposition of this disorder in West Highland Terriers has led to the synonym 'Westie's disease', although other breeds, such as the Cairn and Scottish Terrier, are susceptible. There are isolated reports of the disease in litters of other breeds. The cause of Westie's disease is not known, but the lesion is essentially a periostitis with new bone formation, typically around the tympanic bullae and ventral borders of the horizontal mandibular rami (*Fig.* 8.3). The symptoms of obvious swelling of the jaws, inappetence, lethargy and febrile illness commence between 3 and 6 months of age. Affected puppies show severe pain when the cranium or mandible is handled and opening of the jaws may be resented and restricted. The condition tends to run an undulant course and, in puppies that survive, it is usual for symptoms to regress at about 1 year of age. Apart from the regression of pain, the proliferative lesions often remodel to leave no more than a slight smooth thickening of the horizontal ramus.

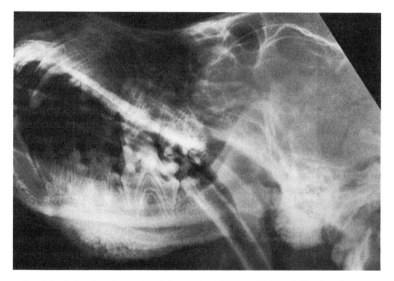

Fig. 8.3. Lateral radiograph of 5-month-old West Highland Terrier showing periostitis of mandible and tympanic bulla: craniomandibular osteopathy.

The known breed and age predisposition should suggest the diagnosis of craniomandibular osteopathy but confirmation is obtained from radiographs, which show extensive new bone depositions on the ventral borders of the mandible and around the tympanic bullae. The range of movements of the TMJs is likely to be restricted by peri-articular periostitis so that affected puppies are often difficult to feed.

Tactical treatment aims to relieve the symptoms, and corticosteroids particularly betamethasone, are usually effective. Nevertheless, in extreme cases euthanasia may be necessary on humane grounds.

ACQUIRED TRAUMATIC DISORDERS

It is not intended that this section should enter into a detailed discussion of techniques for fracture repair as these are more adequately presented in standard orthopaedic texts. Rather, the objective will be to point out those features which may encourage or inhibit normal TMJ function.

Traumatic luxation of the TMJ (*Fig.* 8.4)

Traumatic dislocations invariably occur with the mandibular condyle displaced rostrodorsally. The anatomical features which account for this have already been described. A diagnosis of dislocation should be considered whenever an animal is presented after a traumatic episode with an apparent inability to close the mouth and with deviation of the mandible to one side (*Fig.* 8.5*a*) without evidence of a fracture. The lateral deviation will be slight but dental malocclusion prevents complete closure of the jaws. The major function of radiography is to eliminate a diagnosis of fracture of the horizontal or vertical rami. It is surprisingly difficult to demonstrate a dislocation on a lateral oblique projection but the dorsoventral view (*Fig.* 8.5*b*) establishes the mandibular deviation and will show anterior displacement of the articular condyle.

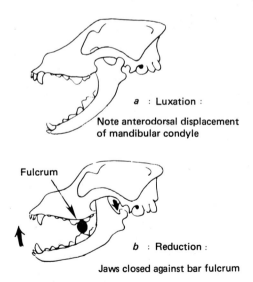

a : Luxation :

Note anterodorsal displacement of mandibular condyle

Fulcrum

b : Reduction :

Jaws closed against bar fulcrum

Fig. 8.4. Diagrammatic illustration of traumatic TMJ luxation and technique for reduction

a

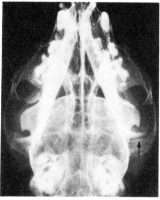

b

Fig. 8.5. Cat unilateral TMJ luxation. (*a*) Mandibular asymmetry: deviation to left means right-sided luxation. (*b*) Dorsoventral radiograph: right mandibular condyle displaced forward (arrowed).

Treatment

Reduction of a TMJ luxation is straightforward under general anaesthesia. It should be noted that the mandible is deviated away from the side of dislocation. A bar is placed between the molar teeth to provide a fulcrum (*Fig.* 8.5*c*) and the jaw is closed against the bar and simultaneously eased caudally until symmetry is restored (*Fig* 8.5*d*).

Mandibular fractures

Separations at the symphysis and fractures of the horizontal rami are more frequent than bony injuries of the articular condyles and vertical

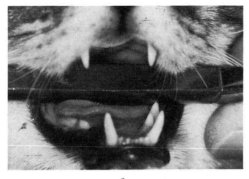

c

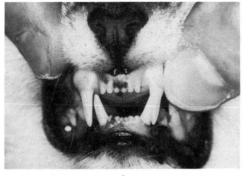

d

Fig. 8.5. Cat unilateral TMJ luxation. (*c*) Fulcrum technique for reduction. (*d*) Symmetry restored after reduction.

rami. These injuries are usually sequelae of a road traffic accident and the patients typically present with sudden onset of pain, mandibular deviation, malocclusion and an inability to eat. Many fractures are obvious on inspection of the rami but radiographs may be helpful to confirm fractures of the caudal components.

Treatment

The objective of the treatment of all jaw fractures is the restoration of normal dental occlusion as well as satisfactory TMJ function. Whenever fixation devices are used they should not be applied until accurate reduction of the fracture or fractures has been achieved. Particular attention is paid to the alignment of the bite.

Simple symphyseal fractures may be repaired by a partially buried wire suture which encircles the mandible caudal to the canine teeth, or by a transfixing screw or pin. Occasionally a combination of wire with a transfixing device maintains the reduction more satisfactorily. Although fractures of the horizontal rami are usually compound, osteomyelitis seldom follows. Whenever a fixation technique is used, be it a bone plate, transfixing pin or half-pin splintage, an attempt should be made to avoid the mandibular canal and the tooth roots. Thus, penetrations through the bone should be sited towards the ventral border of the mandible. Fortunately, most fractures of the coronoid process are accompanied by little displacement of the bone fragments. The masticatory muscles provide adequate splintage and these injuries are best treated conservatively. Occasionally severely comminuted mandibular fractures are encountered which can only be maintained in satisfactory alignment with a normal bite by applying fixation with the mouth in the closed position. For example, a combination of half-pin splintage with a series of wire sutures between the mandible and maxilla may be used. In such cases a pharyngostomy tube should be implanted before the fracture repair is begun and left in place until an adequate bony union has formed to permit the mandible to be released from the maxilla.

Fractures in the region of the mandibular condyles together with fibrosis of the soft tissue around the TMJs may lead to partial immobility. Similar soft tissue inflammatory reactions may follow foreign body penetrations through the region of the fauces. Foreign matter and sequestra should be identified and removed before any attempt is made to break down the periarticular fibrosis to restore function. Excision arthroplasty to remove the mandibular condyle is a last resort which may be used to allow a false joint to form and so to provide improved movement. The decision to remove part or all of the articular surfaces will depend upon the severity of the injury. The TMJ is best approached by a horizontal lateral incision directly over the joint. This is located immediately ventral to the caudal extremity of the zygomatic arch. The overlying soft tissues are cleared and care is taken to retract branches of the facial nerve which may overlie the joint. The mandibular condyle should be excised piecemeal by the judicious use of a chisel. Once the articular surface has been completely removed, the intra-articular meniscus should be identified and withdrawn.

Fractures of the zygomatic arch

When fractures of the zygomatic arch are allowed to heal in a depressed position, the anterior movement of the coronoid process may be inhibited (*Fig. 8.6a*). A dog with a longstanding injury of this sort will be unable to open its mouth to the normal extent. Cats are not prone to this injury because of the wide curvature of the zygomatic arch. Treatment consists of the removal of the offending portion of the arch,

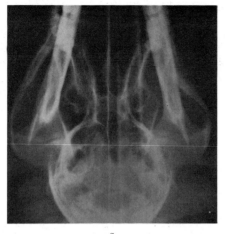

a

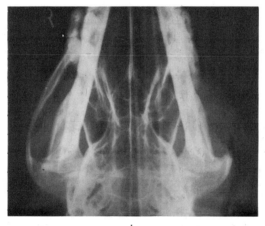

b

Fig. 8.6. (*a*) Dorsoventral radiograph. Labrador unable to open mouth due to depression fracture of right zygomatic arch. (*b*) Relieved by osteotomy of the arch.

which is likely to necessitate a full-thickness osteotomy (*Fig.* 8.6*b*). The principle of the surgical technique is similar to that for the relief of TMJ dysplasia.

Mandibular neurapraxia—dropped jaw

The muscles that articulate the TMJ are innervated by the mandibular branch of the trigeminal nerves. It has been postulated that temporary paralysis of this nerve may arise in dogs that carry heavy objects or attempt to open their mouths excessively, for example, when playing with a football. It is not clear whether this anomaly is the result of ischaemia, compression or overstretching. Patients with mandibular neurapraxia present with an inability to close the mouth completely and show considerable difficulty when eating and drinking. Clinical examination shows that the mouth can be closed by light digital pressure and that the bite is not distorted. There is little pain and the jaws can be opened to the full extent. There will be no significant radiological findings.

Conservative treatment with hand feeding and support for the jaw in a closed position with a muzzle invariably produces resolution within 10–20 days.

OTHER ACQUIRED DISORDERS

Osteoarthritis

The proliferative changes of active osteomyelitis of the tympanic bulla may extend to involve the adjacent TMJ. Osteophyte formation is sometimes very severe and it may surround the articular surfaces of the temporal bone and mandible (*Fig.* 8.7).

It is likely that the case history will include intractable otitis with otorrhoea, but the owner's primary complaint may be that the dog shows pain on mastication, especially when chewing hard objects.

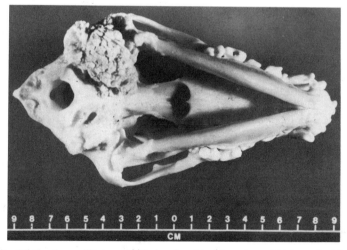

Fig. 8.7. Specimen of 9-year-old Cocker Spaniel with prolonged history of otitis. Finally unable to open mouth due to osteoarthritis of TMJ.

During clinical examination the alignment of the bite will be normal but manipulation of the jaws in the open position will be resented. Irregular, dense, new bone formation will be identified on radiographs of the tympanic bulla and TMJ on the affected side.

Secondary osteoarthritis following primary otitis media carries a poor prospect of resolution by medical or surgical means, except in early cases where bulla osteotomy establishes drainage of infection from the middle ear.

Masticatory myositis

Acute and chronic inflammation of the muscles of mastication occurs occasionally in dogs. The condition is sometimes termed esoinophilic myositis and in its acute form it is characterized by painful swelling in the pterygoid, masseter and temporal muscles, pain on opening the jaw and a reluctance to eat. The inflammatory exudate which is produced during the acute phase of the disorder occasionally contains eosinophils and this explains the derivation of the name; a circulating eosinophilia is rarely present. The subacute and chronic forms of masticatory myositis may occur without a previous acute bout. The chronic form of the disease is characterized by symmetrical atrophy of the masticatory muscles and a progressive inability to open the mouth. Biopsy at this stage will show that the muscle fibres have been replaced by dense fibrous tissue which is directly responsible for the restriction of jaw movement.

Masticatory myositis is said to occur more frequently in German Shepherd dogs but the author has encountered the disease in a wide variety of breeds. Dogs under 3 years of age are most commonly affected. Apart from the presenting signs mentioned above, clinical examination will reveal that the alignment of the jaw is symmetrical, that the masticatory muscles are symmetrically involved by swelling in the acute phase or atrophy in the chronic form, and that opening of the jaw is either resented or firmly restricted. There are no abnormalities to be identified on radiographs. Chronic myositis may be differentiated from neurogenic atrophy on several counts. First, the fibrosis of myositis provides a physical obstruction to jaw movement, and secondly, there is symmetrical involvement. Biopsy of the temporal muscle establishes the diagnosis, but this structure may be difficult to identify in the chronic phase when, grossly, it appears to consist of a layer of fibrous tissue. The cause of masticatory myositis is not known, but preliminary studies suggest the possibility of an autoimmune phenomenon.

The treatment of confirmed cases of myositis consists of the tactical use of corticosteroids, particularly betamethasone, initially at a high dose with a steady reduction over a 4-week period. Steroids are indicated first to reduce the inflammatory reaction and secondly to suppress what may be an autoimmune response. Relapses are not uncommon after the primary attacks. The treatment of the chronic form may require forced opening of the jaws to break down the fibrous tissue deposits; again, steroids must be used in the postoperative period if further fibrosis is to be discouraged. Forced opening of the jaws is unlikely to be possible by manual means alone and a mechanical rib spreader is a suitable aid. However, the overzealous application of such a device could produce a mandibular fracture and therefore it is suggested that jaw opening should be staged as a progressive procedure, performed under general anaesthesia on alternate days until an adequate range of movement has been restored to enable the patient to eat voluntarily.

Neurogenic atrophy of the masticatory muscles

On rare occasions dogs are presented with marked, asymmetrical atrophy of the masticatory muscles. A marked depression at the temporal fossa, possibly with sinking of the eyeball, will be the usual complaint by the owner. Examination will show that a full range of jaw movements is possible and that pain is not present. Biopsy of the temporal muscle fails to show an inflammatory reaction but merely neurogenic atrophy of the muscle fibres. Fortunately, this disorder is likely to be unilateral and therefore TMJ function can be maintained by the muscles on the normal side. The author has encountered a single case of bilateral involvement, which presented with dropped jaw that failed to improve spontaneously. Therefore it differed from the neurapraxia which is described above. The cause of neurogenic atrophy of the masticatory muscles is unknown and there is no effective treatment.

Retrobulbar abscess

Suppuration in the retrobulbar tissues is likely to interfere with normal TMJ articulation, first because a physical swelling will interfere with movements by the coronoid process and secondly because pain in this region deters the patient from moving the jaw voluntarily. The presence of proptosis and painful swelling of the periorbital tissues indicates the site of disease, but differential diagnosis of an abscess from a fulminating tumour or infraorbital salivary cyst may not be straightforward. Many retrobulbar abscesses arise through the presence of a foreign body which penetrates through the pharynx or conjunctival sac. The patient should be examined for the presence of an entry point or a drainage tract. A raised total white cell count with neutrophilia provides additional evidence of an abscess. Drainage of the abscess to the mouth should be established and this usually takes place caudal to the last maxillary molar tooth. The careful introduction of blunt forceps at this site is usually sufficient to establish drainage but the temptation to prescribe broad spectrum antibiotic cover should be resisted until this procedure has been completed.

Tetanus

Tetanus is such an unusual infection in small animals that it does not merit inclusion in many standard texts on internal medicine. It is mentioned here because of the synonym of 'lockjaw', and yet tetanic spasm of the muscles of mastication is not the most obvious feature of tetanus in dogs. Stiffness of gait and spasm of the auricular muscles, giving the patient an anxious facial expression with furrowing of the brow, are more common (*Fig. 8.8*). Trismus and dysphagia may arise in the later stages of infection.

Treatment should aim to identify and cleanse the source of tetanus inoculation and to provide tetanus antitoxin and high dosages of crystalline penicillin. In the author's experience of a small number of

Fig. 8.8. Tetanus in a pedigree Labrador puppy. Spasm of the auricular muscles, which distorts the facial expression, is a more obvious sign of tetanus in dogs than trismus.

canine cases of tetanus the prognosis is favourable, although some would argue that this is in spite of the recommended therapy rather than because of it.

NEOPLASIA

Isolated cases of osteoma and osteosarcoma of the mandible, temporal bone and zygomatic arch may be encountered. The clinical signs will include the physical obstruction of jaw movements, pain on mastication or, simply bony swelling. The diagnosis depends upon the demonstration of the tumour on radiographs (*see Fig.* 2.9) but a comprehensive range of projections may be required. Where doubt exists, a biopsy sample should be taken for histopathological confirmation. Each case must be treated on its merits, as some will lend themselves to complete excision and others may be inoperable.

Soft tissue tumours of the masticatory muscles and retrobulbar tissues arise from time to time, and again the clinical signs are variable. Biopsy sampling may be required to achieve an accurate diagnosis and to provide a reliable prognosis.

SUPPLEMENTARY READING

Bennett D. and Campbell J. R. (1976) Mechanical interference with lower jaw movement as a complication of skull fractures. *J. Small Anim. Pract.* **17**, 747–51.

Hardy W. D., Brodey R. S. and Riser W. H. (1967) Osteosarcoma of the canine skull. *J. Am. Vet. Radiol. Soc.* **8**, 5–16.

Riser W. H., Parkes L. J. and Shirer J. F. (1967) Canine craniomandibular osteopathy. *J. Am. Vet. Radiol. Soc.* **8**, 23–31.

Robins G. M. (1976) Dropped jaw—mandibular neurapraxia in the dog. *J. Small Anim. Pract.* **17**, 753–8.

Robins G. M. and Grandage J. (1977) Temporomandibular joint dysplasia and open mouth jaw locking in the dog. *J. Am. Vet. Med. Assoc.* **171**, 1072–6.

Ticer J. W. and Spencer C. P. (1978) Injury of the feline temporomandibular joint: radiographic signs. *J. Am. Vet. Radiol. Soc.* **19**, 146–56.

Chapter 9

Dentistry and Oral Surgery: I

Dental care and, to a lesser extent, the other diseases of the oral cavity account for a significant proportion of procedures performed under general anaesthesia in small animal practice. Not only are gingival and dental disorders common in dogs and cats, but halitosis, which tends to be the predominant clinical sign, renders these pets less desirable.

DENTISTRY

Diseases of the gingivae and periodontium form the majority of cases presented for dentistry and the remainder constitute anomalies of development and eruption, degenerative conditions of the teeth themselves (e.g. caries and dental fractures), suppurative lesions of the periapical tissues (e.g. maxillary dental abscess) and neoplasia of the soft tissues of the gum margins. For many veterinarians the repertoire of therapy of small animal dental disorders is restricted to a choice between manual scaling to remove calculus and extraction. The purpose of this section is to classify the important dental diseases of dogs and cats and to point out those areas where rational treatment can be applied.

Anatomical considerations (*Fig.* 9.1)

In the erupted tooth the enamel is acellular and, if damaged, it cannot be replaced. Similarly, the cement is acellular, except in the apical region where residual cellular elements are capable of significant cementosis in response to infection. The pulp cavity is lined by odontoblasts which, under normal conditions, continue to lay down dentine throughout the life of the tooth and this leads to a progressive

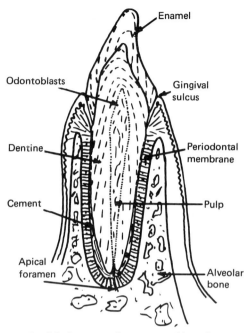

Fig. 9.1. Anatomy of a monocuspid tooth.

restriction of the root canal and pulp cavity with age. The process of secondary dentine deposition may be accelerated if dentinal tubules are exposed in a variety of circumstances including caries, abrasive wear and tooth fracture. However, if the pulp cavity becomes infected, the odontoblasts die and dentinal production ceases.

The periodontal membrane occupies the space between the cement and the alveolar bone. It consists of heavy bundles of collagen fibres which are arranged to form a sling suspension for the tooth. The fibres are embedded at one end in bone and at the other in cement substance. The periodontium is quite vascular and has a generous nerve supply which provides dental tactile sense. The fibres of the periodontal membrane are slightly longer than the shortest distance between the side of the tooth and the wall of the socket. This allows microscopic movements within the socket in a suspensory fashion so that, irrespective of the direction of force applied to the tooth, tension can be taken up in the periodontium to prevent compression of the alveolar bone. Thus, apart from the provision of a firm anchorage for the teeth, the periodontal membrane has important sensory and protective roles. In dogs and cats the periodontium shows major differences from the same structure in man. Not only is the collagen fibre deposition much denser in carnivores, but the mean length of the fibres is significantly shorter, e.g. the periodontium is narrower. This has important consequences for veterinarians undertaking dental extractions.

Diagnosis of dental disease

The presenting signs of dental disease include difficulty when eating hard foods, halitosis and gingival bleeding. Occasionally patients are presented with a discharging sinus in the malar region or at the ventral aspect of the mandible. Abnormalities of oral conformation and dentition are more likely to be noticed by the owners of show animals.

A conscious examination of the oral cavity should enable the surgeon to identify the presence of gingivitis, dental calculus, gingival recession, dental caries, fractured teeth, loose radicles and neoplasia. The value of routine dental check-ups and the importance of prophylactic advice cannot be overstated. Inspection at the time of purchase of a puppy or kitten should include an evaluation of the conformation of the jaws, the absence of congenital anomalies within the mouth and the presence of a full complement of deciduous teeth. The next examination at 7 months of age is timed to check on the normal progress of eruption of the permanent dentition and at the same stage advice can be given on the influence of diet on dental health. Thereafter annual examinations can be made to coincide with vaccination programmes. This protocol should facilitate the identification of calculus and gingivitis before periodontitis develops. Disclosure solutions are helpful to confirm the presence of plaque or calculus and render a convincing demonstration to an owner. At the earliest sign of these conditions, ultrasonic scaling should be performed and dietary advice reiterated.

Radiography is an underrated aid to diagnosis of dental disease. Enamel and dentine are two of the most radiodense tissues in the body and there is good contrast between them and surrounding tissues. This is particularly valuable in the investigation of suspected root sequestra and periapical reactions. On rare occasions information on unerupted teeth is sought and radiographs may be helpful. Although intra-oral occlusal projections are more easily made, oblique views to isolate the arcade in question are of greater diagnostic value.

Developmental anomalies

Veterinary surgeons are occasionally approached, usually by the misguided owners of potential show stock, with a view to the cosmetic correction of congenital dental and oral defects. Inferior and superior prognathism reflect the relative length of the mandible, not the maxilla, and both show an inherited pattern. The most frequent requests for orthodontic interferences arise through malalignment of teeth, especially of the incisor arcades. Again there is a genetic predisposition, especially in working terrier breeds. It is suggested that the correction of congenital inherited defects, dental or otherwise, for cosmetic reasons alone, is totally unethical.

The foreshortened maxilla and mandible in brachycephalic breeds cannot accommodate a full complement of molar and premolar teeth. Thus, partial anodontia is normal in these circumstances. The canine teeth in Siamese cats may also be absent and this should be regarded as an undesirable trait. It is not uncommon for a double row of incisors to be present in brachycephalic dogs and these supernumerary teeth are regarded as normal even in show specimens (*Fig.* 9.2).

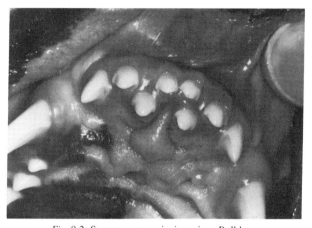

Fig. 9.2. Supernumerary incisors in a Bulldog.

Epitheliotropic viral infections, typically distemper, may damage the developing teeth of young dogs. Because the enamel-forming cells are of epithelial derivation enamel defects of the permanent dentition are a common sequel. In time these 'distemper teeth' become stained and they can be very unsightly. Conservation techniques using enamel etching and adaptic materials can be used to restore the appearance of the affected crowns.

Tetracycline and its derivatives have an affinity for developing bone and teeth, which may become discoloured as a result. When these antibiotics are prescribed to pregnant bitches and queens the temporary dentition of the offspring is afflicted, whereas their use in puppies and kittens mars the permanent teeth. During the early years of life teeth stained by tetracyline derivatives are bright yellow, but with age the colour fades to a dirty brown.

Dental cysts and odontogenic tumours are not common in small animals. Both are anomalies of dental development and therefore young animals will be afflicted. The typical presenting sign is one of mandibular or maxillary swelling and diagnosis depends upon radiographs and biopsy investigation. Localized lesions may lend themselves to extirpation but some odontogenetic tumours are very persistent and others may be highly anaplastic and destructive with a poor prognosis.

Abnormalities of eruption

Serious delay of the eruption of the permanent premolar and incisor teeth, to the extent where absence of these radicles may be suspected, is occasionally reported in breeds such as the Lhasa Apso and Shih Tzu. The temporary dentition of patients with pseudo-anodontia is usually fragmented and probably provides poor stimulation of the eruption pathway. Radiographs reveal that the permanent teeth are present but have failed to cut through the overlying gingivae even at 2 years of age. Pain on mastication may be observed by owners. Treatment consists of gingivectomy to bring the teeth into wear. It is not abnormal to find that the carnassial teeth in a brachycephalic dog have erupted into a position transverse to the remainder of the mandibular or maxillary arcade.

Impactions (obstructed or maldirected eruptions) are unusual in small animals. However, retention of the deciduous incisors and canines frequently occurs in miniature dogs (*Fig.* 9.3). Retained temporary teeth should be extracted to prevent abnormal occlusion by the permanent crowns.

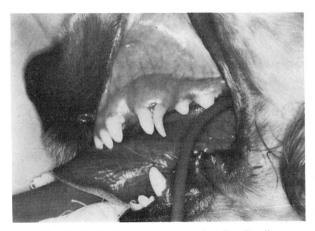

Fig. 9.3. Retained temporary canine in a Toy Poodle.

Abnormalities of wear

Abrasive wear by persistent chewing of hard objects is a common entity in dogs and the canine teeth are particularly vulnerable. Fortunately, apart from cosmetic considerations, this is unlikely to be detrimental to the dog: the pulp cavity is rarely exposed because secondary dentine is produced faster than the tooth is worn down. Nevertheless, the performance of police and guard dogs may deteriorate or stress fractures can occur if abrasive wear is severe (*Fig.* 9.4). There is a place in these patients for capping or crowning of the canine teeth to restore normal function rather than extraction. Other techniques to build up the worn caudal border of the crown have been described, again by the use of etching and composite resins.

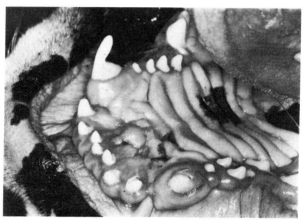

Fig. 9.4. Abrasive wear of the canine teeth by stone chewing. The tooth at the bottom of the picture has fractured.

Diseases of the gingivae and periodontium

The periodontal diseases, including gingivitis, account for a greater loss of human teeth than all other dental disorders collectively, and this is also true of dogs and cats. This complex of diseases is generally divided into two groups: inflammatory, e.g. gingivitis and periodontitis and non-inflammatory, e.g. atrophy and neoplasia.

It is generally agreed that periodontitis, which includes inflammation of the periodontal ligament, alveolar bone and cement, is a sequel of gingivitis (*Fig.* 9.5).

The causes of gingivitis may be attributed to local factors such as micro-organisms, calculus, food impaction, dental malalignment and malocclusion, granulomas and tumours and disuse atrophy. The

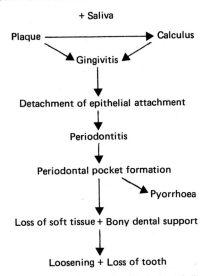

Fig. 9.5. Aetiopathogenesis of periodontal disease.

systemic factors that contribute to gingivitis include nutritional disturbances, hormonal influences and inherited predisposition.

Micro-organisms are invariably present in the mouth and in the
absence of cleaning there is a tendency for a bacterial film—plaque—to
gather on the surfaces of teeth, particularly at the gingival sulcus, in the
interproximal spaces and in the retaining centres of the molar teeth of
the dog. There is good evidence that plaque can be cleared away in the
course of chewing food and that diet is important to the health of the
periodontium. (One study has shown that for Beagles, half an oxtail per
dog per week is sufficient to clean teeth.) Those reservations that have
arisen concerning the feeding of dried cat foods because of a possible
association with the urolithiasis syndrome should be weighed against
the proved benefits of this method of feeding for periodontal hygiene.
The demonstration that antibacterial chlorhexidine paste prevents the
formation of tartar has further confirmed that bacterial plaque is
responsible for calculus deposition.

Dental calculus is mineralized bacterial plaque and the mineral
component, mostly calcium hydroxyapatite, is derived from saliva. It is
therefore not surprising that calculus formation is greatest at sites
adjacent to the openings of the major salivary ducts, on the lateral
aspect of the molars and premolars (*Fig.* 9.6), and at the lingual aspect
of the lower incisors. Calculus lies supragingivally at first, but as
separation of the epithelial attachment and periodontal ligament
progresses, subgingival tartar may be deposited. Calculus becomes

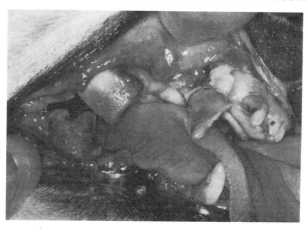

Fig. 9.6. Extensive calculus deposition on the buccal aspect of the premolar teeth.
Note the proximity of the parotid papilla.

firmly adherent to the surface of the tooth and this attachment develops
in one of several ways:

To microscopic irregularities of the enamel surface resulting from the
abrasions of normal wear and tear and of previous dental treatments.

To microscopic irregularities in the cement surface corresponding to
the location where periodontal ligament fibres have detached.

To the matrix of cement following micro-organisms penetration.

To areas of cement resorption, particularly in cats.

Thus it can be seen that in spite of, or because of, veterinary attention
to teeth, an ideal foundation will persist for further calculus deposition.

Calculus is the most important exciting cause of periodontitis in the
dog and cat. It has an overlying mat of micro-organisms which,
together with unmineralized plaque, initiates a mild gingival hyperaemia with oedema and leucocyte infiltration. The epithelial attachment represents a vulnerable focus because it readily detaches and
thereby the way is clear for infection to gain access to the periodontal
ligament (*Fig.* 9.7).

Food impaction at the region of the gingival sulcus and interproximal
spaces provides a suitable substrate for micro-organisms to grow. The
degrading food products themselves may be irritant to the gingival
tissues and impaction of this nature is most likely to occur in pets that
are fed exclusively with soft, non-abrasive foods.

Dental malalignment and malocclusion prevent the normal cleansing
action of eating and exacerbate food impaction at vulnerable sites.
Direct occlusion of opposing teeth on to the gingivae promotes
gingivitis. In some cases the alveolar supporting bone will react by
proliferation, but, more likely, resorption will occur.

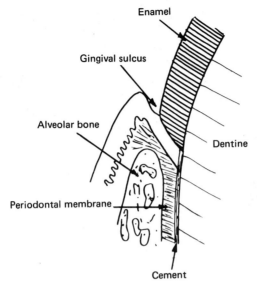

Enamel

Gingival sulcus

Alveolar bone

Dentine

Periodontal membrane

Cement

Fig. 9.7. Epithelial attachment.

Granulomas and tumours may lead to derangement of the epithelial attachment. Although squamous cell carcinomas, fibrosarcomas and malignant melanomas may arise on the gingival tissues, the most common lesion at this site in the dog is epulis, the reactive fibro-granuloma (*see* Chapter 10).

Nutritional disturbances such as deficiencies of vitamins A and D may predispose to gingivitis.

Periodontal atrophy, gingival recession and alveolar bone resorption may all result from disuse atrophy where insufficient dental work is provided. Although these changes are initially free of inflammation, periodontitis may be a sequel. The periodontal ligament requires frequent and varied stress to maintain normal width and function.

Male dogs are more prone to gingivitis, calculus formation and periodontitis than females. Other hormonal changes brought about by diabetes mellitus, hypothyroidism and pregnancy may predispose to gingivitis.

An inherited predisposition to gingivitis may explain the high incidence of periodontal disease in miniature and toy dogs. Although such dogs are frequently fed exclusively on soft foods with minimal cleaning action, a disproportionate number of correctly fed toy dogs are presented for treatment of dental pyorrhoea.

Untreated gingivitis leads to progressive detachment and recession of the soft tissues supporting the teeth at the gum margins. The cleft which is formed by this separation is ideal for the accumulation of degenerate food and bacteria. Periodontitis follows with further regression so that pockets form on the lateral and medial aspects of teeth and later the interproximal crests recede. Macroscopic inflammation with oedema, hyperaemia and suppuration (pyorrhoea) will be evident. At this stage a patient may show pain in mastication and this in turn exacerbates poor dental hygiene. Halitosis will invariably be present and the gingival tissues bleed readily when touched. The condition advances as the pockets increase in size and there is resorption of the supporting alveolar bone. The periodontal ligament, which serves to hold the tooth firmly in place within the alveolar socket, becomes weakened and the tooth progressively loses its support, loosens and finally falls away.

Periodontitis is to some extent reversible in the early stages, but this rarely occurs because re-attachment of the supporting tissues is inhibited by: (*a*) folding over of the gingival epithelium into the periodontal pockets; (*b*) movements of the tooth; (*c*) continued inflammation and pyorrhoea; (*d*) necrosis of the exposed cement.

Although routine prophylactic attention to dental hygiene, typically by ultrasonic cleaning, may help to prevent or postpone the onset of gingivitis, once regression of the gingival tissues has begun, conventional dental treatments can, at best, only slow down the progress of periodontitis. In many instances, short of flap gingivoplasty, loosened teeth and those with extensive root exposure are best extracted as they act as foci for debris accumulation and will be responsible for the unnecessary return of symptoms.

Disorders of the teeth and periapical tissues

Caries

Caries is a chemico-parasitic process which comprises the decalcification of enamel and dentine and the dissolution of the residue. The acid which effects the primary decalcification is derived from the fermentation of starches and sugars lodged in the retaining centres of the teeth. Although resorption of tissues around the neck of feline teeth has been reported as a sequel of periodontal disease, this species is not prone to true caries because feline teeth have no retaining centres.

In the dog, caries is often present in the upper molar teeth, particularly the first (*Fig.* 9.8), but symptoms of pain and periapical abscessation are rare. The infective processes seldom advance to expose the pulp tissues because secondary dentine steadily fills the pulp throughout life.

Fractures

Dental fractures, mainly of the canine teeth, may arise as a result of trauma or weakening of the dental tissues by abrasive wear. Iatrogenic

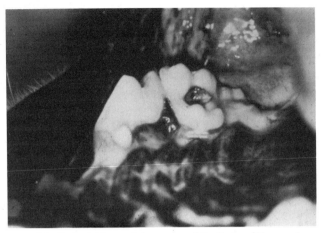

Fig. 9.8. Caries in the retaining centre of the first maxillary molar.

root fractures may arise during extraction and a dental sequestrum will result unless the fragment is removed. Whenever the pulp cavity is exposed (*Fig.* 9.9*a*) it is vulnerable to infection, necrosis and extension of suppuration to the soft tissues around the root (*Fig.* 9.9*b*). This process is not rapid in the dog and the application of a simple calcium hydroxide seal to the crown defect is an adequate first aid procedure prior to restoration.

If the tooth is to be preserved, radiographs should be taken to check for the presence of rarefaction around the root which would be an indication for apicectomy and root canal filling (*Fig.* 9.9*c*). The choice of conservation technique from the many available should take into account the occupation of the patient, the cosmetic consequences of the end result, the strength and retentive properties of the restorative materials and finally cost. Simple nickel-chrome caps (*Fig.* 9.9*d*) have proved very durable in spite of arduous work and they are well retained. Whenever retention on the residual tooth is likely to be poor a post and crown device is preferred.

Dental abscessation

Maxillary dental (malar) abscessation is a specific condition of dogs which present with a discharging sinus below the eye (*Fig.* 9.10). The focus of suppuration is usually, but not always, in the periapical tissues of the upper carnassial tooth. Periapical suppuration may arise elsewhere and the site of discharge will depend upon which tooth is involved, and in rare cases the pus may be voided at the nostril (*see Fig.* 3.5). Dental sequestra may have similar consequences. The aetiology of

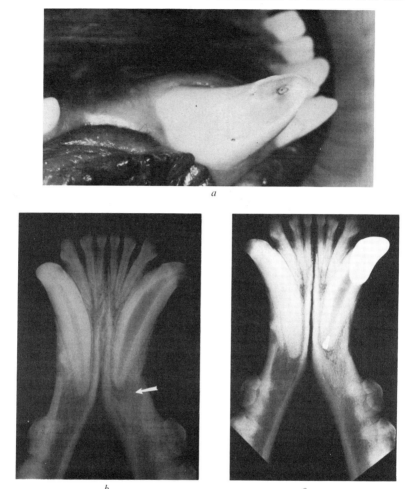

Fig. 9.9. Fractured canine. (*a*) Traumatic exposure of the pulp which is now dead.
(*b*) Radiograph of a longstanding fractured canine: note the wide pulp cavity and
the periapical rarefaction (arrowed). (*c*) Radiograph of a similar fractured canine
after apicectomy, root canal filling and capping.

maxillary dental abscessation is not known. One view is that it is a
sequel of pulp infection following flake fractures of the clinical crown.
Nevertheless, flake fractures may be present on the carnassial and other
teeth without producing periapical reactions and, furthermore, dental
abscesses arise around apparently normal teeth. Radiographic evidence
of periapical halo formation is not uncommonly seen around the roots

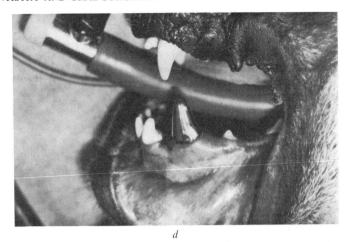

d

Fig. 9.9. Fractured canine. (*d*) Application of a nickel-chrome cap.

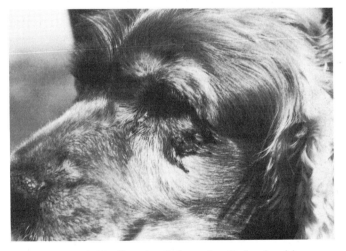

Fig. 9.10. Maxillary dental abscess in a Cocker Spaniel.

of the lower carnassial, and isolated cases of sinus formation are encountered. It is suggested that maxillary dental abscessation is the result of pressure necrosis around the roots of teeth that are subjected to considerable mechanical forces. Diagnosis of the disease is usually based upon the typical appearance and treatment is by extraction of the offending tooth. In those patients where there is doubt concerning the diagnosis or when extraction has not been succesful, radiographs

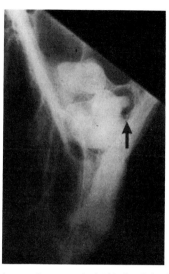

Fig. 9.11. Intra-oral view to show a periapical halo of the first maxillary molar.

should be taken to confirm which tooth is involved (*Fig.* 9.11) or whether a root remnant is present.

Ultrasonic dental therapy

Ultrasonic instruments have gained acceptance in veterinary dentistry during recent years because they offer distinct advantages over the conventional hand-held picks and scalers. Ultrasonic dental instruments offer an efficient means to scale teeth, clean periodontal pockets, plane roots and curette the supporting tissues, and although the thorough application of this technique may not be faster than with hand-held instruments, there is a lesser tendency to damage the tissues at the gingival margin. The final result should also be superior.

The primary function of ultrasonic instruments is to convert electrical energy into physical vibrations (*Fig.* 9.12a) that can be applied to the surfaces of teeth to remove calculus and plaque, to loosen carious dentine and necrotic cement and to curette and debride periodontal pockets. Instruments invariably incorporate a water spray which not only cools the ferromagnetic core but also provides a lavage medium to flush away debris. When ultrasonic energy is applied to a fluid medium tiny vapour bubbles are continuously formed in the fluid and these burst with great force. This 'cold boiling' effect enhances the overall mechanical action of ultrasonic therapy. Whenever a pressurized tank is used as the water source there is the added advantage that medication

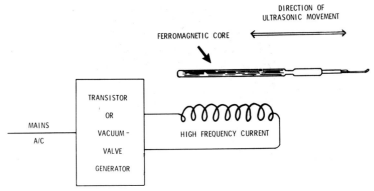

Fig. 9.12. Ultrasonic dentistry. Mechanism of an ultrasonic scaler.

such as antiseptic agents can be diluted in the flushing medium e.g. 1 : 5000 chlorhexidine, 1 : 350 sodium hypochlorite or thymol.

The high frequency ultrasonic movements occur along the long axis of the instrument so that the tip could be considered to be a miniaturized road drill and is thus well suited to break up hard supragingival calculus. None of the tips is intended to be pressed on to the treated dental tissues, nor should these instruments be used as dental picks. It can be appreciated that careless use will make for gross scratches on the surfaces of the enamel and cement which will provide a foundation for the recurrence of calculus.

Some instruments are promoted to veterinarians in advertising material on the basis of the 'power' delivered. The power output of the apparatus governs the amplitude of the vibrations but the ideal lies in a compromise between that which is necessary to disrupt thick calculus and that which will not provoke untoward damage to the dental of soft tissues.

Preparation of the patient (*Fig.* 9.13)

Dental procedures lead to the presence of loosened calculus and dental fragments in the mouth. There may also be haemorrhage from extraction sites and ultrasonic instruments spray water into the buccal cavity. Therefore, it is neglectful not to provide a cuffed endotracheal tube during anaesthesia for dentistry, as this prevents the possibility of inhalation of infected debris, blood and water. Once anaesthesia has been induced, the mouth is held open by a gag and the oropharynx is packed with a known number of swabs or a taped pharyngeal sponge. Dentistry should be performed on a tilted surface with the nose of the patient downwards and with the end of the table protuding over a suitable receptacle. The head of the patient should be supported on a

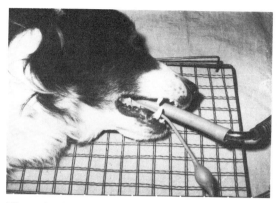

Fig. 9.13. Ultrasonic dentistry. Dog prepared for dentistry: note the cuffed endotracheal tube and the wire grid under the head.

wire grid, e.g. a baking grid, so that fluids can flow out of the patient's mouth, down the table and into the receptacle. This prevents the underside of the patient from becoming soaked in blood and water. After a thorough assessment of the state of the teeth and gingivae, a disclosure solution may be applied to demonstrate the distribution of calculus and plaque so that the full extent of the required treatment can be appreciated.

Preparation of personnel

When in use, ultrasonic instruments create a cloud of droplets containing particles of calculus and plaque and the operator and any assistants should wear face masks to prevent the excessive inhalation of microorganisms from this highly contaminated atmosphere. Spectacles are advisable to protect the eyes from flying fragments of dry tartar and tooth.

Technique

The instrument is prepared by adjustment of the water flow, tuning and selection of the appropriate tip configuration. In general, the tips of ultrasonic instruments are designed to be most effective when they are applied to the surfaces of the teeth at an angle of 15°.

Gross accumulations of supragingival calculus may be cracked away with forceps, provided that care is taken not to damage the soft tissues at the gum margins. However, when ultrasonic instruments are used for prophylaxis or for the removal of light calculus deposits, hand-held instruments should be avoided. The careless and inaccurate application of the sharper tips of ultrasonic scalers can themselves produce unnecessary trauma at the gingival sulcus and may lacerate the soft tissues of the mouth. The end piece is best gripped in a pen-holding fashion and it is important not to apply excessive pressure; this reduces the efficiency of the instrument and provokes undesirable abrasions on the surfaces of the tooth. Freehand movements of the end piece within the oral cavity should be avoided and the instrument should be supported at all times over the fingers of the opposite hand. Supragingival plaque and calculus are removed by vertical movements starting at the gingival margins and working towards the free border of the crown (*Fig.* 9.14). The tip of the end piece should be moved lightly over the surface of the enamel or calculus in a series of short, overlapping strokes, and continued until all the plaque and calculus,

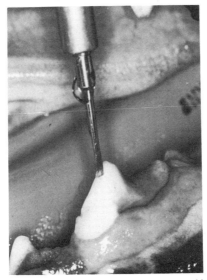

Fig. 9.14. Ultrasonic dentistry. Supragingival calculus removed by vertical strokes of the tip.

previously marked by the disclosure solution, has been removed. A finer tip is required for the cleansing of the inter-proximal spaces, and in this area a cross-hatching pattern of diagonal strokes should be applied. Subgingival calculus is removed with a fine attachment, using short horizontal strokes. The cavitation effect of the water flow over the ultrasonic tip assists in cleansing the pockets of debris and pus. Apart from the removal of the disclosure solution, smoothness of the crown and root surfaces and the absence of visible debris are signs of a successful treatment.

Root planing is an extension of ultrasonic scaling which aims to produce a smooth polished finish to exposed root surfaces. The objective is to encourage restoration of the supporting tissues and thus preserve the teeth. The reverse surface of the instrument is applied to the exposed root to produce an elongated contact area (*Fig.* 9.15). The power setting should be turned down and the operator should follow the contour of the root surfaces with a series of slow horizontal sweeping movements. This procedure is continued until a smooth surface has been produced. There is a tendency in ultrasonic dentistry

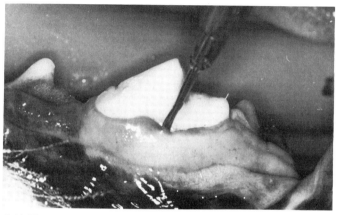

Fig. 9.15. Ultrasonic dentistry. Root planing using horizontal sweeps by the reverse surface of the tip.

to direct attention to the tooth surfaces only and neglect the supporting soft tissues. Curettage of the periodontal clefts is an important stage of the treatment and it is performed with a fine tip and at a high power setting. The tip of the instrument is placed between the gingiva and the tooth and withdrawn slightly from the base of the periodontal pocket and tilted against the gingiva. Gentle pressure is applied with the index finger to the outer surface of the gum over the position of the tip. Once the instrument is activated, the tip and finger are moved together in a series of horizontal sweeping movements.

At the end of the treatment session the disclosure solution should be reapplied to check for residual plaque and calculus.

Even when ultrasonic instruments are correctly used micro-abrasions are inevitable and the use of dental polishing pastes at the conclusion of the therapy is advocated. Although a coarse paste may be necessary initially, a fine paste is employed for the final polish; this is performed either with a rotating brush or rubber applicator, or with a soft tufted toothbrush.

Extraction techniques

Dental extraction may become necessary in established cases of periodontitis and, with the exception of some neoplastic lesions, this differs from other indications for extraction in that the attachments of the teeth are weakened already. Caries, dental fractures, periapical abscessation, dental malalignment and neoplasia are the other important reasons for removing teeth.

Extraction procedures aim to separate the offending tooth from the patient with the minimum damage to surrounding tissues. The procedure depends upon the disruption of the periodontal ligament which secures the tooth to the patient. Failure to break down the periodontal attachment adequately will result in fracture of the tooth, retention of roots and, possibly, suppuration.

The structure of the periodontal ligament of carnivores has been mentioned above. Its strength is such that the dentist's 'flick of the wrist' extraction technique is not successful for small animals and usually leads to root fracture. The principal instruments used to extract teeth are forceps and elevators. Unfortunately, veterinarians have been obliged to make do with equipment designed for human teeth. Elevators are curved chisels which are intended to cut through the periodontal ligament and to displace the tooth from its socket in a lemon-pip fashion. The human Coupland elevator is the most suitable instrument available at present but it is wide in cross-section and cannot be driven into the periodontal space without some disruption of the surrounding alveolar bone. Forceps are hinged elevators, and the technique of extraction is not to avulse the tooth by traction but rather to displace it from its socket by forcing the jaws into the periodontal space before employing a rotating, pushing and squeezing action. Only when the tooth has become thoroughly loosened should traction forces be applied.

In the selection of forceps and elevators attention should be directed towards the shape of the points. These should be sufficiently narrow in cross-section to be introduced into the periodontium and the curvature should match the tooth to be extracted. Forceps that meet the requirements of small animal extractions are not available and therefore their use should be limited to the removal of teeth that are already loose.

Specific extraction techniques

Upper carnassial

Although it is possible to remove this tooth intact by the thorough use of elevators to each root, extraction is greatly facilitated by division of

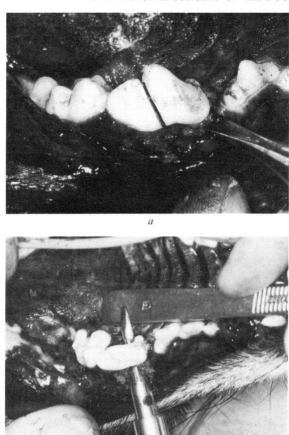

a

b

Fig. 9.16. Extraction of the upper carnassial. (*a*) Division of the tooth precedes the use of an elevator. (*b*) When the lever technique is used, the palate is protected.

the tooth with a saw (*Fig.* 9.16). In this way the two smaller anterior roots are separated from the large posterior radicle and the two small sections can be extracted individually.

Molars and premolars

There is no simple knack to the extraction of bicuspid and tricuspid teeth, particularly when the root attachments are healthy. The periodontal ligament around each root must be divided with the sharp point of the elevator which is chosen so that the concave surface fits the convexity of the tooth. This process can be laborious but impatience is likely to be rewarded with a root fracture.

a

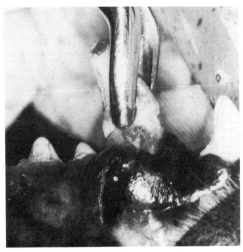

b

Fig. 9.17. Extraction of a canine. (*a*) A periosteal flap improves access to the root which is loosened with a curved chisel. (*b*) The loosened tooth is withdrawn along its line of curvature and the defect is closed with silk sutures.

Canines (*Fig.* 9.17)

Canine teeth are extremely deeply rooted, with approximately 65 per cent lying subgingivally. In order to expose sufficient root for a successful extraction a periosteal flap is made over the lateral aspect of the root. The tooth is thoroughly loosened by separation of the periodontium with a curved chisel and removed by forceps withdrawal along its line of curvature.

Feline teeth

These are notoriously brittle and difficult to extract intact. A satisfactory technique is to use a pointed scalpel blade as an elevator. The periodontal ligament of each root is incised carefully before using a conventional elevator.

Complications of dental extraction

Haemorrhage

Serious haemorrhage is unlikely to arise from the tooth sockets except in patients afflicted by dyscrasias. However, significant loss of blood may result from inadvertent injury to the soft tissues of the mouth inflicted by sharp instruments. The tongue is a highly vascular structure but the sublingual veins are additionally vulnerable to injury of this nature. Ligation of specific vessels and closure of lacerations with sutures may be required.

The palatine arteries are at risk when the lever technique is used to lift away the upper carnassial. This is a valid technique but protection of the palate should be provided otherwise the palatine artery, which lies immediately beneath the mucosa, is liable to be disrupted (*Fig. 9.16*).

Bacteraemia and septicaemia

Whenever the periodontal or periapical tissues are infected, extraction provokes a transient bacteraemia which may in turn produce more serious sequelae such as septicaemia or endocarditis. Prophylactic broad spectrum antibiotic therapy is indicated as an adjunct to all extraction procedures.

Root fractures

However careful they may be, all veterinary dentists encounter tooth root remnants from time to time. These may act as dental sequestra if left and it is neglectful not to remove them. The roots of extracted teeth should always be examined to be sure that they are complete. Whenever there is uncertainty, radiographs provide definitive information and the fractured remnants can be squeezed out of the alveolar sockets by the use of a fine elevator.

Mandibular fractures

Extraction of mandibular teeth, particularly the canines and carnassials, is never to be taken lightly in cats and small dogs. Painstaking

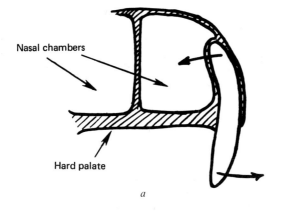

a

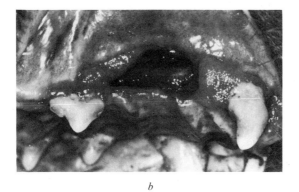

b

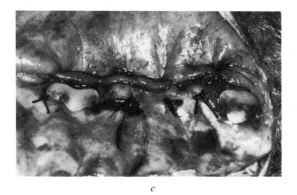

c

Fig. 9.18. Oronasal fistula. (*a*) Cause. (*b*) Result. (*c*) Correction with a gingival flap.

separation of the tooth is essential if fracture is to be avoided. Rough-and-ready forceps extractions are certainly contraindicated.

Oronasal fistula (Fig. 9.18)

This is almost invariably a sequel to extraction of an upper canine tooth. The technique described above emphasized that the loosened tooth should be withdrawn along its line of curvature. The clinical crown must never be levered laterally otherwise the root will be forced medially into the nasal cavity. Once a fistula is established it may be difficult to close. The edges of the defect should be freshened and an elongated strip of gingival mucous membrane is released laterally to the dental arcade. This is lowered to close the defect with interrupted sutures of 3/0 silk.

SUPPLEMENTARY READING

Bedford P. G. C. and Heaton M. G. (1977) A repair technique for dental abrasion in the dog. *Vet. Rec.* **101**, 327.

Ewen S. J. and Glickstein C. (1968) *Ultrasonic Therapy in Periodontics.* Springfield, Ill., Thomas.

Gibbs C. (1978) Radiological refresher. The head—Part IV: Dental disease. *J. Small Anim. Pract.* **19**, 701–7.

Lane J. G. (1977) Small animal dentistry and the role of ultrasonic instruments in dental care. *J. Small Anim. Pract.* **18**, 787–802.

Ross D. L. (1977) Infections of the oral cavity. In: Kirk R. W. (ed.) *Current Veterinary Therapy*, VI. Philadelphia, Saunders, pp. 918–26.

Shafer W. G., Hine M. K. and Levy B. M. (1974) *Textbook of Oral Pathology*, 3rd ed. Philadelphia, Saunders.

Chapter 10

Dentistry and Oral Surgery: II

STOMATITIS

Inflammation of the oral mucous membranes of dogs and cats often presents a major challenge to the small animal veterinarian, partly from an inability to make a specific diagnosis and partly from the lack of response to non-specific therapy. In many cases the intractable nature of the stomatitis stems from a poor understanding of the aetiological factors which precludes the implementation of rational treatment. The symptoms of stomatitis are obvious and include halitosis, pseudoptyalism, reluctance to eat, pawing at the mouth, bleeding at the commissures of the lips and constant rubbing of the jowls. Although an attempt is made here to classify the various recognized causes of stomatitis, in many instances such specificity cannot be achieved. At the initial examination it is helpful to make a written record of the distribution of lesions, first because this may suggest an aetiological factor and secondly so that the progress of the disease can be monitored accurately. An example of a record sheet for oral tumours is illustrated below (*Fig.* 10.9*a*) and this can just as well be used for evaluating the extent and progress of stomatitis.

Spread of local infections

Before enumerating the factors that predispose to stomatitis, two important local sources of infection must be mentioned. First, the most common cause of inflammation extending from the gum margins, but which may also involve the buccal and labial mucosae, is gingivitis and periodontitis. These have been discussed at length above and whenever generalized stomatitis is encountered routine ultrasonic dentistry is indicated to improve local hygiene. Secondly, stomatitis may be secondary to cheilitis and the labial fold conformation which predisposes to this disorder has been mentioned in Chapter 2. Cheiloplasty (*Fig.* 2.3) is an underpractised surgical technique but it can be commended in all cases of unresponsive stomatitis where an acute inflammatory process is present in the labial folds. In addition to these two local sources of infection, many clinicians believe that recurrent anal sacculitis and impaction play an important role in the infection and re-infection of the oral cavity and tonsils.

Viral stomatitis

Feline calicivirus (FCD) (*Fig.* 10.1) and to a lesser extent feline viral rhinotracheitis (FVR) infections may produce an acute stomatitis which usually resolves within 2–3 weeks, but the role of these agents in carrier cats with chronic gingivitis and stomatitis is not clear.

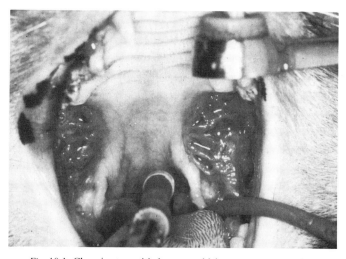

Fig. 10.1. Chronic stomatitis in a cat which was an FCD carrier.

Apart from viral papillomatosis, no specific viral causes of stomatitis have been recognized in dogs. Wart-like growths may be seen in the mouth in considerable numbers, not only in young dogs, but also in mature animals whose resistance may have been lowered by systemic disease. Oral papillomatosis is a self-limiting disorder and it is open to conjecture whether surgery or cryosurgery stimulate the immune mechanisms which cause the lesions to regress.

Bacterial stomatitis

Infections by fusiform and spirochaete bacteria can cause an acute necrotizing stomatitis in dogs. The condition responds well to potentiated sulphonamide or ampicillin therapy combined with supportive care, including frequent attention to local hygiene with dilute chlorhexidine mouthwashes, which are introduced into the cheek pouches and sloshed from side to side.

Mycotic stomatitis

Candida albicans may be recovered from the mouths of dogs with oral ulceration but it may not always be clear whether the organism is a primary cause of stomatitis or whether it is an opportunist invader. The practicalities of the administration of topical antifungal agents are not straightforward. The oral administration of thiabendazole ($20 \, mg \, kg^{-1} \, d^{-1}$) may be helpful but, as with other oral infections, there is no substitute for improving local hygiene.

Physical and chemical injuries to the mouth

Dogs and cats, especially when young, may chew live electric wires. Apart from the physical injuries to the contact sites where the circuit shorts, i.e. the hard palate, gingivae, tongue and commissures of the lips, acute pulmonary oedema may ensue. This complication is the cause of the high fatality rate in dogs but cats rarely succumb. The oral lesions are discrete and show a characteristic grey surface.

Fortunately, caustic chemicals are rarely imbibed by small animals. Nevertheless, owners may ring their veterinarian for first aid advice because they suspect that their pet has had access to household chemicals such as caustic soda or battery acid. Vigorous oral lavage with tap water to dilute the caustic solution is the most simple and effective advice. It is unlikely that neutralizing agents such as vinegar for alkaline or sodium bicarbonate for acidic products could be given in time to be beneficial.

In the face of physical or chemical injury to the oral mucosa the now familiar advice to maintain local hygiene pertains, although the careful débridement of necrotic surface tissues is more likely to be necessary here.

Systemic causes of stomatitis

The outstanding example of a systemic disease that predisposes to oral ulceration is uraemia. The possibility of an underlying nephritis should be considered in all cases of non-specific stomatitis. The halitosis of the stomatitis is exacerbated by the characteristic odour of urea but the diagnosis is confirmed by routine blood and urine biochemical assays.

Autoimmune (pemphigoid) stomatitis

The conclusion to be drawn from an increasing number of recent reports is that autoimmune-mediated disorders are responsible for many cases of intractable stomatitis. The clinical features of the external forms of pemphigus have been mentioned in Chapter 2 but it is unusual for the oral mucosae not to be involved in the various pemphigoid diseases. The lesions are by no means confined to the mucocutaneous junctions of the lips but may afflict the palate, gingivae and tongue. The changes range from patches of erythema, to localized desquamation of the surface epithelium, to discrete bleeding ulcers. The characteristic histological features of the lesions offer a simpler method of diagnosis than the demonstration of autoantibodies. Treatment depends upon immunosuppression, usually with oral prednisolone, but protracted therapy is frequently necessary.

Eosinophilic granuloma complex of cats

Although the most frequent expression of this idiopathic entity occurs on the upper lips (*see Fig.* 2.6), discrete raised white granulomatous lesions may be seen at the junction of the hard and soft palates and on the dorsal surface of the tongue. The first line of therapy consists of intra-lesional or oral corticosteroids. Although cryosurgery may be used speculatively for the palatine lesions, this technique should be avoided on the tongue unless a small site only is involved (*see below*).

MISCELLANEOUS LINGUAL LESIONS

The role of the tongue in deglutition is described in Chapter 7, and some of the disorders of this structure are mentioned there. Although the prehension of food and fluids and their propulsion from the oropharynx are the primary functions of the tongue in the dog, the feline tongue has an additional and essential role in the maintenance of bodily hygiene. Thus, a large portion of the tongue may be lost through infarction by a strangulating foreign body or by amputation for neoplasia or extensive laceration without insuperable ill-effects in the dog, but without the papillae which are generously distributed over the dorsal surface of the tongue a cat cannot groom itself and becomes unkempt in a short time (*Fig.* 10.2). An important component of the nursing of cats with FVR and FCD infections is regular grooming, but when the tongue deficiency is permanent, no amount of human care can substitute for the cat's own toilet activities. Thus, in this species

Fig. 10.2. The unkempt appearance of a cat with a major lingual deficiency due to excessive cryosurgery.

lingual surgery, including cryosurgery, must concentrate on preservation if serious long term complications are to be avoided.

Calcinosis circumscripta

The heterotopic deposition of calcium salts in the submucosa of the tongue and gingivae is most often seen in immature dogs of the larger breeds. The foci of calcinosis circumscripta have a characteristic gritty texture and their unsightly appearance is a source of anxiety to owners. The breed, age and appearance of the white grape-like lesions (*Fig.* 10.3) should be sufficient to suggest the correct diagnosis. Treatment depends upon local excision.

Cushingoid plaques

The plaques of calcinosis cutis are well-recognized features of Cushing's disease but similar plaques may be laid down in the lingual submucosa in the absence of cutaneous lesions. These flat, firm, white deposits are likely to be more extensive than those of calcinosis

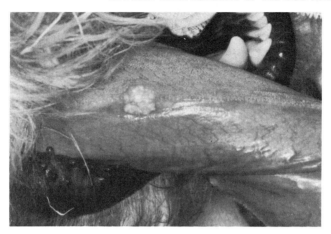

Fig. 10.3. Lingual calcinosis circumscripta in a 1-year-old Irish Wolfhound.

circumscripta, and the age of the patient also eliminates this alternative diagnosis.

Lingual haematomas in warfarin poisoning

The tongue is a highly vascular structure and its site renders it susceptible to minor contusions. The appearance of a haematoma beneath the lingual mucosa may be a feature of warfarin poisoning and is an indication to check the clotting time of the patient.

Actinobacillosis

Isolated cases of wooden tongue due to *Actinobacillus lignieresi* infection have been confirmed in dogs. Hard granulomatous swellings within the substance of the tongue can be palpated and a deeply sited foreign body is an alternative explanation. The afflicted dogs show considerable difficulty in swallowing and cannot lap. The discovery of club colonies on smears from biopsied material confirms the diagnosis. Prolonged treatment (4–6 weeks) with oral potentiated sulphonamides proved satisfactory in the single case presented to the author.

PALATINE SURGERY

Congenital palatine clefts

The aetiopathogenesis of clefts of the primary and secondary palates was discussed in Chapter 2. It is sufficient to repeat here that deficiencies of maxillofacial development may range from uni- and bilateral harelip, through variable degrees of cleft of the hard palate to small deficiencies of the soft palate. Animals with major congenital deformities are usually destroyed at birth by the breeders. However, some survive, often by dint of devoted nursing, and corrective surgery may be sought.

A diagnosis of a palatine cleft should be suspected if a puppy— kittens are rarely involved—is presented with a nasal return of ingesta, rhinitis, a rattling moist dyspnoea, inhalation pneumonia and unthriftiness. Confirmation of the diagnosis is usually straightforward but lesser palatine defects may escape attention until the patient is anaesthetized. Defects of the hard palate invariably consist of a midline cleft which may vary in width and length, and may arise with or without a cleft of the soft palate. Apart from simple midline clefts, the major deformities of the soft palate are aplasia, unilateral hypoplasia and pseudouvula formation (*Fig.* 10.4). Aplasia of the tonsil may accompany either of the latter anomalies.

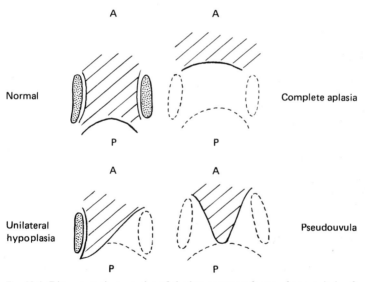

Fig. 10.4. Diagrammatic examples of the less common forms of congenital soft palate defects.

Corrective surgery should be deferred until the puppy is 12–14 weeks of age if possible, so that the patient will tolerate the general anaesthetic and so that the structures will have grown sufficiently to facilitate the operation. Once the patient has been anaesthetized the nasal chambers are flushed clear of food debris. A pharyngostomy tube is an invaluable

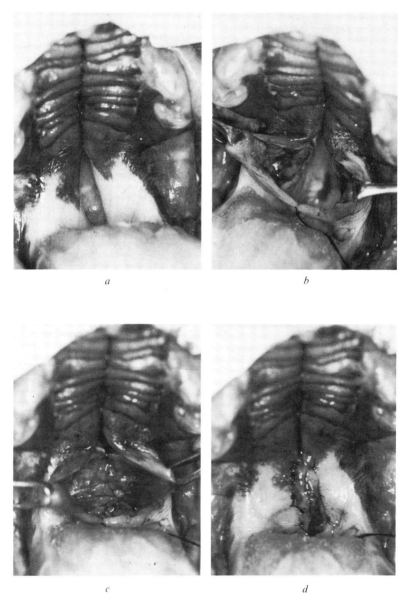

Fig. 10.5. Repair of soft palate cleft. (*a*) Preoperative appearance of midline cleft of soft palate which extends to involve the hard palate also. (*b*) A marker suture denotes the caudal limit of the repair. The soft palate is incised horizontally to create oro- and nasopharyngeal layers. Closure is in two stages, commencing with the nasal (*c*) and then the oral (*d*) layer.

aid in the aftercare of puppies that have been subjected to radical palatine surgery. The repair procedures are best performed with the patient in dorsal recumbency and the mouth gagged open. Gaseous maintenance of the anaesthetic via a bypass tracheotomy removes an additional encumbrance from the mouth.

Repair of soft palate clefts (Fig. 10.5)

Simple clefts of the soft palate are easily repaired. There is no tissue deficiency and therefore the laxity in the existing soft palate allows the edges to be drawn together without tension. The caudal limit of the tonsils provides a guide to the extent of the repair. A marker suture is placed before the repair commences (Fig. 10.5b). In many cases the distribution of the pigmentation of the mucosa is equally helpful. Linear incisions are made at the edges of the cleft so that the soft palate is divided into nasopharyngeal and oropharyngeal layers. The nasopharyngeal surfaces are closed with 3/0 Dexon (Fig. 10.5c) and the oropharyngeal mucosa with 3/0 silk (Fig. 10.5d).

Hard palate repair

Many veterinarians are familiar with the Langenbeck technique which comprises releasing the longitudinal strips of mucosa from the hard palate and sliding them together at the midline (Fig. 10.6a). The bone of the hard palate is exposed laterally but granulation and epithelization quickly follow. The viability of the strips depends upon the preservation of the vascular supply through the major palatine artery which emerges from the palatine foramen at the level of the upper carnassial tooth. The Langenbeck technique is usually effective to close the larger portion of clefts but there is a tendency for breakdown and persistence of a defect anteriorly.

In this respect the 'sandwich' method of repair is superior (Fig. 10.6b). On one side of the cleft a recipient bed is created by splitting the mucous membrane from the underlying bone at the edge of the defect (Fig. 10.6c). On the other, a strip of mucosa is released and rotated (Fig. 10.6d), using the edge of the cleft as a hinge, before it is sutured into the recipient site (Fig. 10.6e). On this occasion the vascular supply to the strip derives through the nasal mucosa at the margin of the cleft. Silk or Dexon 3/0 sutures are suitable for closure.

Unilateral hypoplasia of the soft palate (Fig. 10.7)

This congenital defect may be regarded as a lateral cleft because, again, there is usually sufficient laxity in the tissues to permit closure without

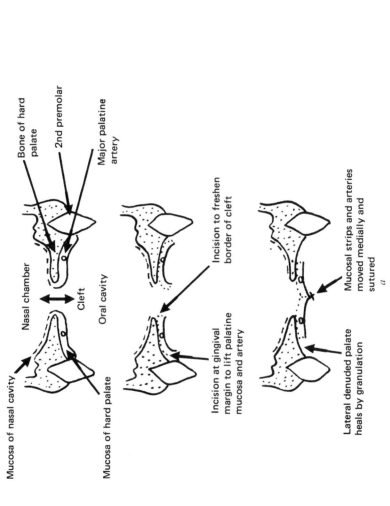

Fig. 10.6. Hard palate repair. (*a*) Principle of the Langenbeck technique. Diagram representing a transverse section of the palate in the premolar region.

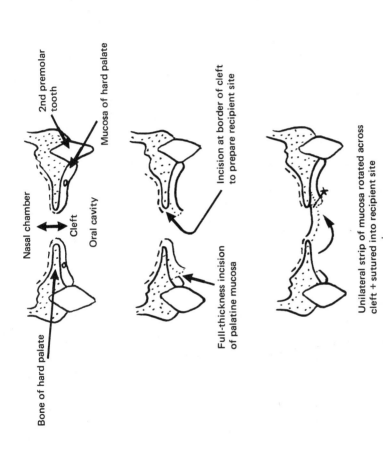

Fig. 10.6. Hard palate repair. (*b*) Principle of the 'sandwich' repair, again with a transverse section diagram.

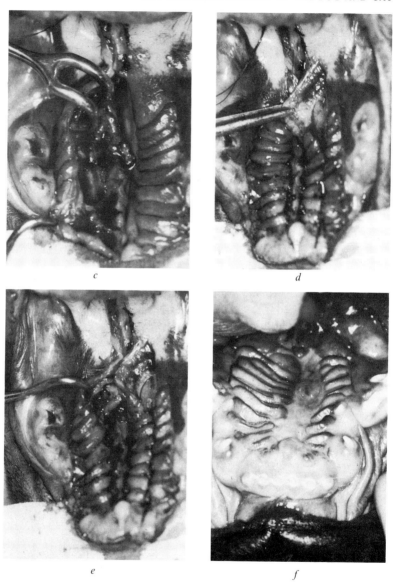

Fig. 10.6. Hard palate repair. (*c*) Sandwich repair: the recipient site is prepared by
a longitudinal incision at the edge of the cleft. The site has been opened with the
hooks. (*d*) The rotating strip has been formed after an incision of the hard palate
mucosa but the edge of the cleft remains intact to form a 'hinge'. (*e*) The rotated
mucosa strip is tucked into the recipient site and secured with Dexon sutures. (*f*)
Pug puppy 10 days after sandwich repair. Note that the entire length of the cleft is
successfully closed.

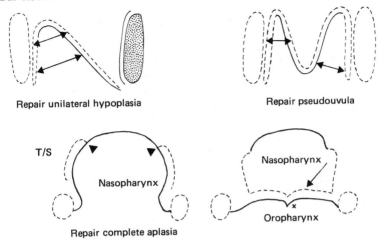

Repair unilateral hypoplasia

Repair pseudouvula

T/S

Nasopharynx

Repair complete aplasia

Nasopharynx

Oropharynx

Fig. 10.7. Diagram to show the concepts for closure of soft palate defects.

tension. The palatine tonsil may be absent on the affected side but the remnant of the tonsillar crypt can be identified. The repair technique is similar to that for a soft palate where an incision at the edge of the defect creates nasopharyngeal and oropharyngeal layers which are then brought together across the cleft.

Pseudouvula repair (*Fig.* 10.7)

The concepts of the repair technique are similar to those of the soft palate anomalies mentioned above. Pseudouvula may be considered as a bilateral hypoplasia but with a residual midline mass of soft palatine tissue. The repair utilizes the residual soft palate and the tissues at the tonsillar crypts, and the technique is, in essence, a bilateral version of a repair for unilateral hypoplasia.

Aplasia of the soft palate (*Fig.* 10.7)

In order to close a defect where there is an absence of soft palate a new palate is fashioned from strips of tissue separated from the lateral walls of the nasopharynx. The walls of the nasopharynx are left to heal by granulation and epithelization and the mucosal strips apposed with 4/0 silk.

Traumatic clefts of the hard palate (*Fig.* 10.8)

Cats frequently sustain direct compression injuries to the face which provoke a midline fracture and split of the hard palate as the maxilla is

Fig. 10.8. Traumatic palatine cleft in a cat.

spread by the force of the impact. A traumatic oronasal fistula is the result and this injury should not be taken lightly in the acute stage because these acquired clefts are difficult to treat if they are longstanding. The best opportunity for a successful repair is soon after the injury has occurred. The midline maxillary fracture should be reduced and wire fixation is applied across the dental arcades before the midline mucosal defect is closed. The usual explanation for the persistence of acquired clefts lies in the tension in the mucosal repair which is inevitable if no attempt is made to bring the maxillae together. Island grafts rotated on the major palatine arteries may be used for the repair of this injury.

Palatine foreign bodies

The predilection for foreign matter such as sticks and bones to become lodged across the hard palate has been referred to in Chapter 7 (*Fig.* 7.2). Rib bones are frequently involved and this disorder has increased in parallel with the popularity of Chinese take-away meals!

OROPHARYNGEAL NEOPLASIA

The general considerations pertinent to the diagnosis of visible neoplasia were discussed in Chapter 2.

CASE REFERENCE: BREED: AGE: SEX:

Duration of lesion:

Appearance: Ulcerated/Non-ulcerated   Texture: Firm/Friable
            Pigmented/Non-pigmented

Regional lymphadenopathy   Yes/No

Radiography: a) Local: Destruction: Minimal/Moderate/Severe
                          Proliferation: Minimal/Moderate/Severe

              b) Long fields: Metastasis: Yes/No/Maybe

Biopsy report:

Fig. 10.9. Record sheet suitable for oropharyngeal neoplasms. (*After* Todoroff
and Brodey.)

Oropharyngeal tumours constitute one of the major neoplastic
presentations encountered in small animal practice on the basis that
they frequently occur, they are often visible to the owner and many
carry a poor prognosis when they are not amenable to treatment.

Benign oral tumours

The most frequent soft tissue proliferation which occurs in the canine
mouth is the reactive fibrogranuloma or epulis. This lesion is not a true
neoplasm but consists of a firm chronic inflammatory swelling at the

gingival margin. An epulis rarely becomes ulcerated unless by traumatic contact with an opposing tooth. The cause of the inflammatory
proliferation is not known but dental malocclusion at the gingival
sulcus is often cited. However, a breed predisposition undoubtedly
exists in the Boxer, where it is exceptional to meet an elderly patient
which is free from some degree of epulis. The gross appearance of the
reactive fibrogranuloma varies from a linear gingival hyperplasia (*Fig.
10.10a*), usually on the lateral aspect of the maxillary or mandibular
dental arcades, to a gross localized mass which completely obscures the
adjacent tooth (*Fig. 10.10b*). The large focal lesions may be indistinguishable from malignancies, such as fibrosarcomas, on gross appearance and a biopsy examination may be necessary. A more friable

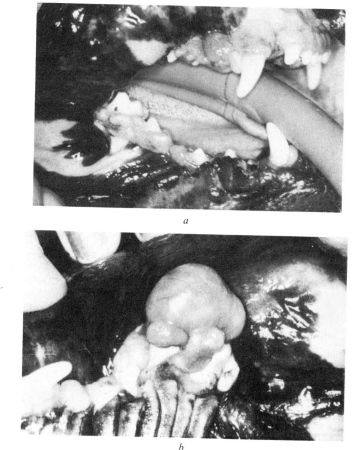

a

b

Fig. 10.10. (*a*) Generalized gingival hyperplasia. (*b*) Localized epulis in a Boxer.

variant of the fibrogranuloma, sometimes described as acanthomatous epulis, has been reported and the appearance is similar to the squamous cell carcinoma.

The treatment for both forms of epulis depends upon local destruction or extirpation, but recurrence is not uncommon. Scalpel resection to the level of the normal gum margin followed by diathermic cautery of the exposed surface is a satisfactory technique. When the site permits accurate cryosurgery this may be used in place of the cautery. Obvious dental disorders which may predispose to chronic inflammation should be corrected, if necessary by extraction.

Apart from the wart-like proliferations of oral papillomatosis, benign epithelial tumours are sometimes encountered, particularly on the tongue. A histological confirmation of a florid papilloma may follow the biopsy of a raised plaque with a spongy surface.

Oropharyngeal malignancies

Malignant oral tumours are not as frequent in cats as in dogs. Gingival, lingual and tonsillar squamous cell carcinomas occur occasionally, most often in the mouths of cats with predominantly white faces. Tonsillar lymphosarcoma may also be identified, but rarely as a solitary entity.

In order of frequency, the common malignant oral neoplasms of dogs are the squamous cell carcinoma (SCC), malignant melanoma (MM) and fibrosarcoma (FS). Lymphosarcoma of the tonsils (*see Fig.* 7.4) is likely to be an expression of a generalized lymphadenopathy where other superficial lymph nodes are palpably enlarged.

An extensive survey by Todoroff and Brodey (1979) confirmed earlier observations on the incidence and behaviour of oral tumours in dogs. Although older animals are usually involved, neoplasia does not respect the youth of its victims and dogs under 2 years old may be afflicted. Males are more susceptible than females, particularly to MM and to a lesser degree tonsillar SCC and FS. Smaller breeds tend to develop MM and tonsillar SCC whereas the larger breeds are more prone to FS and non-tonsillar SCC. The predilection site for MM and FS is at the gum margins but for SCC it is the palatine tonsil (*see Fig.* 7.4). Three-quarters of labial and buccal cleft tumours turn out to be MM. FS is more likely to be found on the maxillary (*Fig.* 10.11) than the mandibular gum margins. Todoroff and Brodey recorded the following frequencies of metastasis:

A. To the local lymph node or beyond:

MM	81%
Tonsillar SCC	77%
FS	35%
Non-tonsillar SCC	c. 5–10%

Fig. 10.11. Fibrosarcoma of the maxillary incisor region. Note that the teeth are spread and the nasal profile is deformed.

B. To the thorax, as demonstrated on radiographs:
$$\begin{array}{ll} \text{MM} & 14\% \\ \text{FS} & 10\% \\ \text{Tonsillar SCC} & 8\% \\ \text{Non-tonsillar SCC} & 3\% \end{array}$$

However, subsequent autopsy findings showed that thoracic radiographs provided false-negative results in 13 per cent of all cases.

The information presented above provides the bare bones on the incidence and behaviour of oropharyngeal malignancies and a knowledge of these data is invaluable for diagnosis and prognosis. Although there is no substitute for a histological examination of tumour material to confirm the tumour type, the gross appearance may provide a guide. By no means are all malignant melanomas melanotic (*Fig.* 10.12) and a diagnosis of MM cannot be eliminated simply on the grounds that the neoplasm is unpigmented. Fibrosarcomas tend to be firm, often with a pale non-ulcerated surface whereas gingival squamous cell carcinomas are often friable and ulcerated and are likely to arise anterior to the canine teeth (*Fig.* 10.13). Intra-oral radiographs show evidence of local bone destruction (*Fig.* 10.14)) in about half of malignant gingival tumours and this may be helpful to differentiate them from epuli. It is most unusual for oropharyngeal tumours to produce radiographic evidence of chest metastases in the absence of palpable enlargement of the local lymph nodes. Here is an opportunity to rationalize against the indiscriminate use of thoracic radiography to screen for secondary neoplasia.

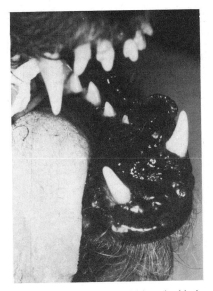

Fig. 10.12. Gingival malignant melanoma. Although this is melanotic, many melanomas are not pigmented.

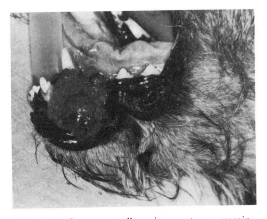

Fig. 10.13. Squamous cell carcinoma at gum margin.

The results of conventional local excision of oropharyngeal malignancies in dogs are very poor indeed, and for cryosurgery they are only a little better. The usual cause of failure of these treatments is local recurrence of the primary tumour. It remains to be seen whether

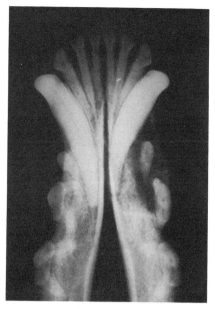

Fig. 10.14. Mandibular bony destruction by a malignant melanoma.

radiation therapy can offer a significant improvement on the very disappointing prognosis that must be offered with contemporary techniques.

SUPPLEMENTARY READING

Bennett D., Lauder I. M., Kirkham D. et al. (1980) Bullous autoimmune disease in the dog. *Vet. Rec.* **106**, 497–503.

Gaskell R. M. and Gruffydd-Jones T. J. (1977) Intractable feline stomatitis. In: Grunsell C. S. and Hill F. W. G. (ed.). *The Veterinary Annual*, 17th issue. Bristol, Wright–Scientechnica, pp. 195–9.

Howard D. R., Davis D. G., Merkley D. F. et al. (1974) Mucoperiosteal flap technique for cleft palate repair in dogs. *J. Am. Vet. Med. Assoc.* **165**, 352–4.

Kolata R. J. and Burrows C. F. (1981) The clinical features of injury by chewing electric cords in dogs and cats. *J. Am. Anim. Hosp. Assoc.* **17**, 219–22.

Ross D. L. (1977) Infections of the oral cavity. In: Kirk R. W. (ed.). *Current Veterinary Therapy*, VI. Philadelphia, Saunders.

Scott D. W. (1975) Observations on the eosinophilic granuloma complex of cats. *J. Am. Anim. Hosp. Assoc.* **11**, 261–70.

Todoroff R. J. and Brodey R. S. (1979) Oral and pharyngeal neoplasia in the dog: a retrospective survey of 361 cases. *J. Am. Vet. Med. Assoc.* **175**, 567–71.

Chapter 11

The Differential Diagnosis of Cervical Swellings

Whenever a patient is presented with a firm or fluctuating mass in the cervical region, it represents a test of differential diagnostic skill. Even if the diagnosis is straightforward, the subsequent surgical treatments, which are discussed in Chapter 12, may be challenging. In this section the net has been cast widely so that the term 'swelling' is used to include a range of conditions which extends beyond simple, discrete space-occupying lesions.

The loose skin which is a feature of the neck of dogs and cats and the long hair of some breeds of both species conspire to obscure lesions in this region. Thus, through no neglect on the part of the owners, progressive swellings may escape detection until they are sizeable. It is not uncommon for a clinician to be confronted with a patient with an extensive mass which has been discovered by chance and when there is no history to indicate the rate of onset.

Palpation plays an important part in the diagnostic protocol and yet this technique will be useless without a knowledge of the normal anatomy of the region and an appreciation of the range of normality which varies with the species, breed and bodily condition of the patient. Students, for example, are frequently confused between the normal submandibular salivary glands which lie at the junction of the internal and external maxillary veins and the local lymph nodes which are sited anteromedially.

Apart from the physical presence of the swelling, there may be other signs of disease. Any large mass, be it an abscess, haematoma or neoplasm, which arises adjacent to the pharynx, larynx or trachea, may distort or compress the airways and provoke respiratory distress. Furthermore, lesions which infiltrate or compress the recurrent laryngeal nerves may cause obstructive dyspnoea by secondary laryngeal paralysis; an altered voice may be an additional feature.

CONGENITAL ANOMALIES

Branchial cleft and thyroglossal duct cysts

Cystic remnants of the thyroglossal duct or branchial arches are frequently mentioned as the possible causes of fluid-filled lesions in the neck. In reality, each of these lesions is as rare as hens' teeth in canine and feline practice. Some authors believe that the formation of the embryonal thyroid gland is such that thyroglossal duct cysts are not possible in a dog; to date there have been no adequately documented reports of the condition in this species.

Cystic developments from the remnants of the branchial and pharyngeal clefts have been authenticated in dogs but they are very rare. It can be deduced that they would arise on the lateral aspect of the neck in the parotid region and that they are lined by an epithelium whose secretions contribute to the fluid within. Naturally, a successful surgical treatment necessitates total extirpation of the lining of the cyst.

In normal circumstances these rare congenital abnormalities would not warrant discussion in a book of this nature. However, an unfortunate confusion has arisen in the veterinary literature and amongst practising veterinarians between these anomalies and salivary cysts. Not only are the terms 'salivary mucocoele' and 'branchial cyst' used as if they were synonymous, perhaps because branchial cleft remnants are more common in people, but irrational treatment is frequently applied for the management of salivary duct leakages. The lining of a salivary cyst is non-secretory and does not contribute to the contents of the swelling; there can be no virtue in the painstaking dissection of such a sac.

DEVELOPMENTAL ANOMALY

Calcinosis circumscripta

Foci of metastatic calcification may develop in connective tissue to form firm, palpable and painless masses. Although the predilection sites for calcinosis circumscripta lie in the tarsal, carpal and elbow regions, as well as the oral submucosa (*see Fig.* 10.3), these discrete lesions may occur in the neck (*Fig.* 11.1). At this site calcinosis circumscripta may arise in the segmental muscles and it is usually firmly attached to the cervical spinal column. Irrespective of the site of origin, the concentrated calcium deposition renders the lesion radiodense. The aetiology of this developmental anomaly is not known, but dogs between 1 and 2 years of age and from the larger breeds, such as the German Shepherd and Irish Wolfhound, are usually involved.

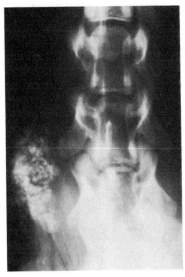

Fig. 11.1. Radiograph showing calcinosis circumscripta adherent to the cervical spine of a young German Shepherd.

ACQUIRED ANOMALIES

Haematoma

The loose skin of the neck is an ideal site for haematoma formation. The usual history consists of the sudden onset of a painless swelling, often after an episode of trauma. As the extravasated blood spreads between the fascial planes, the lesion becomes more pendulous. Nevertheless, the neck is not a common site for haematoma formation in dogs with deficiencies of the clotting mechanism, e.g. in warfarin poisoning. The possibility of a blood dyscrasia does not normally warrant consideration in a dog with a cervical haematoma unless the lesion is persistent or there is other evidence of prolonged bleeding or clotting times.

Abscess

Pyogenic foci may develop from contaminated puncture wounds following bites and scratches or around buried foreign bodies. The most likely route for foreign bodies to reach the neck is by way of oral or pharyngeal penetration; they may range from grass seeds to sizeable sticks. Those foreign bodies that penetrate the oral mucosa on either side of the lingual frenulum tend to migrate to the soft tissues of the intermandibular space; grass seeds are usually involved at this site and they account for abscesses in the anteroventral cervical region. Sharp metallic objects such as needles may be prehended by dogs or cats and some of those which are not ingested penetrate the lingual or oral tissues. These objects are not normally grossly contaminated and therefore the tissue response which follows is characterized by pain and low-grade swelling rather than acute suppuration. Dogs that chase sticks are vulnerable to oropharyngeal penetrations. A wooden fragment can pierce the oropharynx in one of three characteristic sites: (*a*) ventrally, between the tongue and the mandible; (*b*) dorsally, through the fauces towards the temporomandibular joint; and (*c*) caudally, lateral to the larynx into the para-oesophageal tissues. Although the stick may be removed by the owner or veterinary surgeon, splinters or larger fragments of wood may be left within the wound. A suppurative reaction will be provoked and the symptoms of the abscessation will depend upon the location of the foreign body. Sublingual penetrations will lead to an abscess in the intermandibular space which will point and discharge at that site. A retrobulbar abscess with proptosis may arise when the foreign body has entered through the fauces or tonsillar areas. Sinuses from foreign bodies in the paralaryngeal or para-oesophageal tissues tend to discharge at the ventral and lateral aspects of the neck (*Fig. 11.2*). Occasionally abscesses in this region discharge directly into the mouth or pharynx; halitosis may be observed by the owners. In the acute stages, following a retropharyngeal penetration, crepitation due to simple emphysema, as air is aspirated through the mucosal defect, or to gas gangrene due to clostridial infections may be detected in the soft tissues of the neck. Alternatively, a generalized inflammation of the connective tissue—cellulitis—may develop in the face of hyaluronidase-producing bacteria, most notably Streptococci spp. and *Staphylococcus aureus*.

Infected bites and scratches are common in cats and Pasteurella spp. are the usual contaminants recovered from feline abscesses. Painful fluctuating swellings develop rapidly and the parotid and sub-mandibular regions are frequently involved (*Fig. 11.3*).

Snake bites

The majority of snake bites are inflicted through the ventral aspects of the head and neck. The pathogenesis of bites by viperine snakes depends upon the action of enzymes which produce tissue necrosis. Hyaluronidase is a common ingredient and thus the typical appearance of a snake bite is consistent with cellulitis. There will be pain and oedematous swelling which extends quickly from the sites where the fangs have punctured. In untreated snake bites the necrotic tissue presents an ideal medium for the growth of secondary bacterial

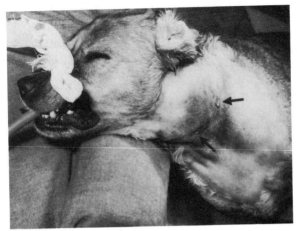

Fig. 11.2. Sinuses from a foreign body left after pharyngeal penetration by a stick.

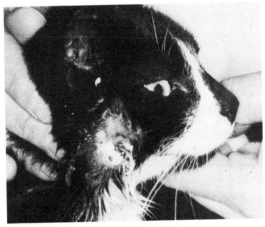

Fig. 11.3. Typical cat fight abscess. Note the site lies close to the parotid duct which could be damaged during surgical drainage.

infections which are invariably inoculated on the fangs. Clostridia are common inhabitants of the reptilian oral cavity and gas gangrene may develop.

Emphysema

Emphysema is the subcutaneous infiltration of air or gas. The circumstances under which the gaseous products of bacterial metabolism such as gas gangrene may accumulate in the tissues of the head and neck have already been described. Subcutaneous accumulations of air may arise following surgical or traumatic disruption of the conducting airways. Localized emphysema of the face is not uncommon following nasal surgery but it is more serious when leakage arises from the trachea. Most frequently, emphysema occurs as a soft, painless, crepitating but well-circumscribed swelling. However, when it extends to the region of the thoracic inlet, respiratory function may be embarrassed through pneumothorax. Once the site of leakage is closed off, either spontaneously or by surgery, air is rapidly resorbed.

OTHER ACQUIRED LESIONS

Lymphadenopathy

The submandibular and prescapular lymph glands cannot be palpated easily when they are normal. However, enlargement through inflammatory or neoplastic involvement may draw an owner's attention to these superficial nodes. Hyperplasia of the submandibular glands can be expected in the presence of many non-specific infections of the head. Diagnostic difficulties may arise when these local lymph glands are swollen in a patient with a known oropharyngeal neoplasm. Ulcerated tumours of the gingivae and tonsils are invariably infected and the lymph node enlargement may be a reflection of reactionary hyperplasia or tumour metastasis. Knowledge of the behaviour of neoplasms will help to determine the likelihood of metastasis, but in cases of doubt, a lymph node biopsy is required.

Iatrogenic lymphadenopathies may arise as a result of the use of intramammary antibiotic preparations in abscesses which have been lanced or in routine surgical wounds. It is the oil base of these products which can provoke a foreign body reaction at the site of application or a marked hyperplasia at the local lymph node. The prophylactic use of an intramammary preparation in any surgical wound is an unsound practice.

Staphylococcal lymphadenitis

This disease is sometimes known as 'puppy strangles' or 'big head' disease of puppies (*Fig.* 11.4) The disorder arises between 6 and 10 weeks of age and several members of a litter may be infected. The author has encountered this disorder in a variety of breeds, including the Labrador, Golden Retriever, Springer Spaniel, Basset Hound and Miniature Poodle. The mode of transmission of the infection is not understood but once staphylococcal lymphadenitis has occurred in a breeding premises, the frequency of outbreaks in subsequent litters may

Fig. 11.4. Staphylococcal lymphadenitis in a Retriever puppy.

reach ruinous proportions. One infected bitch puppy treated by the author was subsequently used for breeding purposes and every puppy in the two litters produced developed staphylococcal lymphadenitis. The implication is that either a carrier state of the condition exists or that there is an inherited predisposition.

The signs of staphylococcal lymphadenitis may be dramatic, with the sudden onset of gross enlargement of the submandibular lymph glands which eventually abscessate. At the same time, extensive facial pyoderma with multiple pustules, which tend to be concentrated around the orbit, and a purulent otorrhoea will be seen. Less frequent signs include a pustular dermatitis of the ventral abdomen and a purulent preputial or vaginal discharge. Apart from the obvious lymphadenopathy, a generalized oedema of the head may be evident, and hence the term 'big head' disease. Although the intensity of the condition might be attributed to a rampant *S. aureus* infection, some authors believe that a hypersensitivity reaction to Staphylococcal toxins may be involved. While intensive therapy may be successful in controlling the infection, affected puppies usually show extensive unsightly scars which render them unattractive for sale.

Oedema

Passive oedema of the head and neck due to compromise of the venous return is an uncommon finding in dogs and cats. Any cervical lesion which is large enough to cause venous obstruction will be obvious, but if none is to be found, the explanation for the oedema is likely to lie in the anterior mediastinum. Heart-based, aortic body, ectopic thyroid malignancies or thymomas may be implicated.

Goitre

Although 'goitre' should be used to denote all thyroid enlargements including neoplasia, it is used here to describe non-neoplastic swellings of one or both thyroid glands. A bilateral swelling of the thyroids, which are not normally palpable, can be expected in cases of iodine deficiency or where there is an innate dysfunction of thyroid hormone secretions. Modern trends in canine and feline nutrition render iodine deficiency an improbable cause of benign goitres today. Functional goitres are rare conditions which may be indistinguishable on palpation from bilateral neoplasia.

DISEASES OF THE SALIVARY GLANDS

Salivary cyst

Salivary cysts are a frequent cause of cervical swellings in dogs and occasional cases have also been encountered in cats. The condition develops when saliva leaks from a duct or gland and enters the surrounding soft tissues. Saliva contains digestive enzymes which are mildly irritant to connective tissues and thus accumulations of escaped saliva tend to be surrounded by a wall of inflammatory tissue which gives the lesion a cystic appearance. However, the lining of a salivary cyst is not composed of epithelium and it does not contribute to the secretions within the cyst. Excision of the cyst will not remedy the condition, but the solution to the disorder is either to repair the defect in the duct or to remove the glandular tissue which secretes the saliva. In practice, extirpation of the offending salivary gland offers a satisfactory treatment because it is not feasible to locate and to repair the site of leakage.

The aetiology of salivary cysts is not known. There is no confirmed breed or sex predisposition but dogs under 4 years of age are usually involved.

There are four pairs of major salivary glands in the dog (*Fig.* 11.5): the parotid, submandibular, sublingual and zygomatic (infraorbital) glands. Apart from these, salivary glandular tissue is generously distributed in the oral and pharyngeal mucosae. The surgical relationships of the major glands are discussed in Chapter 12, but for the purposes of some diagnostic procedures, such as contrast sialography, it is important to be aware of the location of the openings of the ducts leading from the glands. The parotid duct enters the mouth at right

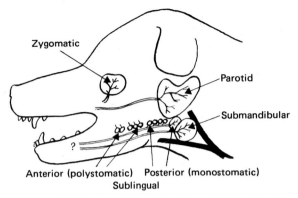

Zygomatic

Parotid

Submandibular

Anterior (polystomatic)   Posterior (monostomatic)
Sublingual

Fig. 11.5. Distribution of the major salivary glands of the dog.

angles to the labial mucosa, opposite the upper carnassial tooth. The duct turns through 90° immediately caudal to its opening before passing over the superficial face of the masseter muscle, where it is vulnerable to trauma. The submandibular duct opens immediately behind the tip of the sublingual caruncle and in those cases where there is a separate sublingual opening this lies a further 1–2 mm caudally. In some dogs the submandibular and sublingual ducts have a common orifice. Caudal to the parotid papilla and on a level with the last upper molar tooth is sited the zygomatic duct opening. Several small red dots lying on a ridge behind this major papilla mark openings of the lesser zygomatic ducts.

Although the cause of the salivary duct leakages is not known, sialographic studies have shown that cysts that occur in the cervical region (*Fig.* 11.6) and at the lateral aspect of the tongue (ranula or honey cyst) (*Fig.* 11.7) almost invariably arise from disruption of one of the small sublingual glands or ducts. In a significant proportion of cases, 20 per cent in one series, there may be bilateral involvement. Although a cervical salivary cyst may appear to be slightly lateral at first, as it increases in size it becomes more pendulous and comes to lie at the ventral midline. Unsightly pouches may develop with loss of hair and the overlying skin becomes thin. Nevertheless, spontaneous ulceration of the skin or perforation of the cyst wall is unlikely. The distension of a ranula may produce an obvious deviation of the tongue and the patient may find closure of the mouth difficult when the teeth tend to occlude on to the cyst. A small number of cysts which develop from the sublingual ducts arise at the level of the tonsillar crypts and at first glance may resemble carcinomas.

Salivary cysts rarely arise from the other major salivary glands or their ducts. Trauma to the parotid duct may cause stenosis, and initially there will be a palpable distension over the cheek region where

Fig. 11.6. Cervical salivary cyst in a Spaniel.

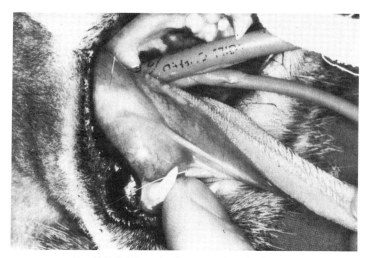

Fig. 11.7. Sublingual salivary cyst (ranula) in a cat.

the duct dilates. However, there will be a tendency for the glandular tissue to atrophy as pressure increases within the distension, except in the presence of low grade infection which stimulates the continued production of saliva. The parotid duct is more vulnerable to rupture by an incisive wound than the other major ducts, but under these conditions a fistula will develop with a discharge of saliva directly to the skin surface (*Fig.* 11.8). Rarely, a sialocele develops from the zygomatic gland to cause proptosis and this must be differentiated from a retrobulbar abscess or an orbital tumour. Obstructions in the small glandular aggregations in the mouth may give rise to blister-like cystic lesions, particularly around the palates.

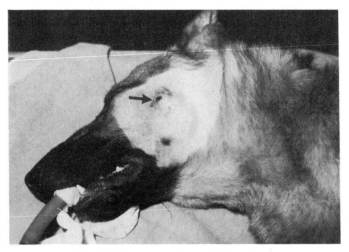

Fig. 11.8. Post-traumatic parotid duct fistula.

Saliva is saturated by calcium hydroxyapatite and this has several clinical consequences. First, saliva provides the matrix for the mineralization of dental plaque in its conversion to calculus. Secondly, calcium salts may precipitate within a salivary duct to form sialoliths which could occlude the channel. The obstructed duct will dilate to cause a swelling and may even rupture to present a typical salivary cyst. Nevertheless, this is an unusual occurrence and sialoliths are not implicated in the majority of sialoceles. Finally, the stagnant saliva which accumulates within a cyst often contains tapioca-like particles formed by calcium salts. The discovery of these particles at surgery confirms the diagnosis of salivary cyst.

Sialadenitis

Inflammatory lesions of the salivary glands are rare in dogs and cats and they are characterized by painful swelling of the affected gland. The parotid is usually involved and this may be explained by its position, which makes it vulnerable to penetration bite wounds. Other cases of sialadenitis are presumed to arise from the haematogenous spread of infection and there may also be a tendency to abscessation and discharge.

Salivary gland infarction

This is a specific variation of sialadenitis which consists of an inflammatory reaction with ischaemic necrosis of glandular and capsular tissues. All the cases reported to date have involved the submandibular glands and have presented as a painful swelling. Intercurrent systemic disease is usually present but the aetiology of the infarction is not known.

Ptyalism and hypersialosis

Hypersialosis is the excessive production of secretions by the salivary glands, whereas ptyalism is the symptom used to describe patients that appear to be producing excessive quantities of saliva, irrespective of the cause. For example, some patients which produce normal quantities of saliva show pain or difficulty in swallowing (e.g. rabies or megoesophagus); others are unable to close their jaws to swallow (e.g. mandibular neurapraxia or TMJ luxation) or are unable to contain saliva within the mouth (e.g. congenital lip deformities or cheilitis). Patients in each of these categories may be said to be afflicted by ptyalism. Hypersialosis may be stimulated by local inflammation (e.g. oral ulceration or neoplasia) or impending emesis, particularly in the presence of an oesophageal disorder (e.g. reflux oesophagitis or oesophageal diverticulum). Rarely is hypersialosis attributable to a specific anomaly of one or more of the major salivary glands. Isolated reports have implicated a congenital uni- or bilateral parotid gland enlargement as a rare cause of ptyalism in dogs. The diagnosis is confirmed by sialography and by the elimination of ptyalism after ligation of the duct of the offending gland.

NEOPLASIA

Surprisingly, the range of primary and secondary tumours that give rise to cervical swellings in dogs and cats is limited.

Lipoma

Lipomas may arise within the fascial planes of the neck of elderly dogs and on palpation they tend to be discrete and have a characteristic doughy texture. Similar lesions may be detected on other parts of the body, particularly in obese patients.

Thyroid neoplasia

In the dog thyroid tissue is usually found in a pair of fusiform glands which lie adjacent to the carotid sheath at the level of the cricoid cartilage. Parathyroid tissue is closely associated with these glands, from which it may be indistinguishable. The embryological development of the thyroid gland is such that ectopic foci of functional tissue may arise at any point on either side of the larynx and trachea between the level of the basihyoid bone and the anterior mediastinum. Therefore, it follows that thyroid tumours may arise from a wide range of sites.

Although there is no sex predisposition to thyroid neoplasia, the Boxer is significantly over-represented. Adenomas and carcinomas occur with approximately equal frequency, and in one extensive series thyroid tumours accounted for 1·6 per cent of all canine neoplasms. Although thyroid tumours usually present with a firm uni- or bilateral swelling in the paralaryngeal or paratracheal region, an occasional cystic tumour explains the soft consistency which is encountered occasionally. Adenomas are more likely to be unilateral but carcinomas show equal uni- and bilateral involvement. Tumours of either type are rare in dogs under 5 years of age. A palpable swelling is invariably detectable by the time an owner presents a patient for examination, but other signs, such as local pain or respiratory distress, may be evident. Thyroid carcinomas tend to infiltrate the thyroidal veins to produce intraluminal cords and it is through the venous system that metastasis to the lung fields occurs. At exploratory surgery the typical cording of neoplastic tissue within distended veins around the mass is pathognomonic. Approximately 20 per cent of thyroid tumours produce excesses of circulating thyroid hormones with signs of hyperthyroidism.

Recently benign, but functional, thyroid tumours have been identified as a cause of unthriftiness in elderly cats. The lesions may be palpable in clinical cases, which respond to removal of the neoplasm.

Salivary gland tumours

Primary tumours of the major salivary glands are rare in dogs and cats. However, this possibility should be considered when discrete swellings of the parotid or submandibular glands are encountered. The small number of recorded cases of neoplasia of salivary tissue limits the usefulness of any predictions regarding metastasis. Each tumour should be examined on its merits with particular attention to the local lymph nodes and to the possibility of secondary foci in the lung fields.

Lymphosarcoma

Neoplastic involvement of the mandibular and prescapular lymph nodes is not uncommon in dogs afflicted by multicentric lymphosarcoma. However, it is most uncommon to encounter single node involvement in the cervical region. Although lymphosarcoma is the most frequent tumour of cats, primary involvement of the superficial nodes of the neck is unusual.

SECONDARY NEOPLASIA

Oropharyngeal melanomas and tonsillar carcinomas show a tendency to metastasize via the local lymph nodes. A palpable lymphadenopathy of the mandibular nodes is an indication for a detailed oral inspection in the pursuit of a primary tumour. On occasions the local lymph node swelling may be disproportionately large when compared with the primary tumour, especially in the case of tonsillar carcinomas. The tonsils may also be affected by multicentric lymphosarcoma and this possibility should be taken into account when other superficial lymph nodes are enlarged.

DIAGNOSTIC PROCEDURE

Many of the presenting features mentioned in the preceding descriptions are sufficient to suggest a tentative diagnosis of the cause of a cervical swelling.

History

Known trauma or stick penetration of the oropharynx in the face of a painful cervical swelling suggest an abscess; crepitation with such a history may indicate emphysema from a pharyngeal or tracheal tear, or gas gangrene. A reluctance to eat with pain and lethargy are consistent with an infected site and with maturation of an abscess. A painless fluctuating lesion which fills rapidly is more likely to be a haematoma than a salivary cyst. Sialoceles develop slowly, either lateral to the tongue or, more frequently, laterally at the submandibular region. As the lesion increases in size, gravity tends to draw it towards the ventral midline. It is important to obtain the owner's impression of the earliest site of the lesion before surgery so that the glandular tissue on the correct side is extirpated. Inquiries about difficulty when eating and drinking are relevant if oropharyngeal neoplasia is suspected. Information should be sought concerning dyspnoea or alterations of the bark when an invasive space-occupying mass seems to be present in the cervical region. When cellulitis has developed rapidly around the head or neck and the cause of trauma remains obscure, the possibility of access to areas where snakes are endemic should be considered.

External examination

A detailed inspection of the integument should be made to seek evidence of external trauma, discharging sinuses, loss of hair, ulceration or softening of the surface tissues where an abscess may be pointing. Palpation readily differentiates between solid and fluid-filled lesions, although abscesses with a thick pyogenic membrane and surrounding zone of reaction may form an intermediate group. The surface tissues are palpated to test for the characteristic pitting on pressure of oedema and the crepitation of emphysema. The exact location of discrete lesions is determined so that they may be correlated with the position of normal structures. Lymphadenopathies correspond to the sites of the superfical lymph nodes and when there is neoplastic involvement they are not particularly mobile. The most common site for thyroid neoplasia is lateral to the larynx and these tumours may be quite mobile. Large thyroid tumours may distort the trachea and the position of this latter structure relative to the midline should be determined. Lesions of calcinosis circumscripta are very firm on palpation and may be fixed to the cervical spinal column. Suspected and pendulous salivary cysts should be elevated to identify any tendency to one side or the other; this may be facilitated by placing the patient in dorsal recumbency. Abnormal prominence of the submandibular and parotid salivary glands may be misleading. This need not necessarily be evidence of swelling of the glands but may result from displacement by a deeper mass. The oropharynx should be inspected for primary neoplasia, ranuli or other salivary cysts in the region of the tonsillar crypt. A general anaesthetic may be necessary for a detailed examination. Anaesthesia will also facilitate deep palpation of the structures of the neck; the introduction of an oesophageal sound may be helpful for orientation.

Aspiration

Lesions that appear to be fluid-filled should be prepared for aseptic needle puncture and aspiration of the contents. The choice of local or general anaesthetic for this procedure must depend upon the circumstances of each case. Saliva is very tenacious and difficulty will be experienced in its withdrawal through an 18 SWG needle; on the basis of viscosity it should be easily differentiated from pus or blood.

Clinicians should note that saliva from a sialocele may be bloodstained and the contents of the cyst will become thin if previous drainage has been performed; the reformed cyst then contains a mixture of serum and saliva. The pus collected from a canine foreign body reaction may be both watery and bloody; it is easily confused with whole blood. Nevertheless, abscesses are usually accompanied by a considerable soft tissue reaction and they are painful, unlike thin-walled haematomas.

Radiography

The contrast provided by air in the upper respiratory tract and the bone of the skull and cervical spine contributes to the value of radiographs of the throat region. Radio-opaque foreign bodies will be obvious but both lateral and ventro-dorsal projections are essential for precise location. Soft tissue lesions will also be identifiable and note should be taken of any distortion of the airway as this may be helpful for safe anaesthesia and surgery. In cases of primary and secondary neoplasia, chest radiographs provide information regarding metastases to the lung fields, but again, projections in two planes are required and the exposures should be taken with the lungs inflated to provide maximum contrast. Particular attention should be paid to the anterior mediastinum when a primary chest tumour could be the cause of passive congestion and oedema of the head and neck. The lesions of calcinosis circumscripta are radiodense and the diagnosis by radiography is straightforward.

In selected cases, there may be an indication for special radiographic techniques using contrast media, particularly in the diagnosis of some salivary gland disorders. Apart from these, the introduction of metallic probes into discharging sinuses may provide helpful clues to the location of a foreign body before embarkation into exploratory surgery. Liquid contrast media have no place in the delineation of sinus tracts; under these conditions the material inevitably leaks from the site of introduction and the result is more confusing than helpful.

Both water-soluble and iodine/oil positive contrast media are suitable for sialography (*Fig.* 11.9). The contrast medium is introduced through a blunted 25 or 26 SWG needle at the duct opening of the gland under investigation. It is helpful if the patient has not been premedicated with atropine but even this handicap can be overcome by placing a spot of lemon juice or ascorbic acid on the tongue. The indications for sialography are as follows:

1. To differentiate sialoceles from the rare congenital anomaly of branchial cleft cyst. In the case of salivary cysts, the contrast medium will be seen to leak from the sublingual duct into the cyst. (In practice, biopsy of the cyst wall is more accurate and more simple to perform.)

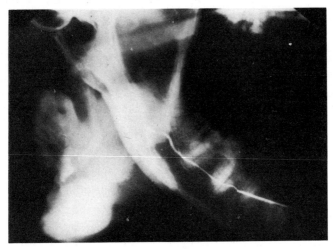

Fig. 11.9. Sialogram: in this case of sialocele, contrast material has been introduced into the sublingual duct but has leaked out into the cyst in the upper cervical region.

2. To demonstrate cases of dilatation and damage, particularly of the parotid duct. This technique is indicated in patients with a recurrent swelling or fistula.

3. To investigate the possibility of glandular enlargement in cases where hypersialosis cannot be accounted for otherwise.

4. To outline the glandular tissue in cases of neoplasia prior to surgery.

Sialography can be extremely tedious, particularly the cannulation of the sublingual and submandibular ducts. The most frustrating aspect of this technique is that it is usually not difficult to introduce the cannula into one duct but the identification of the second, usually the sublingual opening, requires great patience. There is little alternative when passing the blunt needle into the ducts at the sublingual caruncle to the use of fine thumb forceps, and yet the longer the procedure, the more this instrument distorts the mucosa to a point where identification of the ducts becomes impossible. There is a knack to the cannulation of the parotid papilla and this depends upon straightening the angle of the duct by tension to the mucous membrane immediately anterior to the papilla.

In the assessment of suspected cases of salivary cyst, the most common difficulty encountered is to confirm which side is involved, particularly when a cervical cyst is pendulous. In theory, sialography of each of the sublingual systems should present a satisfactory diagnostic solution, but in practice, this is difficult to perform and is time-consuming. In those cases where doubt continues to exist concerning the side of origin, it is unlikely to be detrimental to the patient and far more expeditious to the surgeon to perform a bilateral extirpation of the submandibular and sublingual glandular systems.

Exploratory surgery and biopsy

Surgical exploration may be necessary to differentiate inflammatory and neoplastic lesions. Tumours must be treated on their merits but the distinctive features of thyroid carcinomas are worthy of mention. These tumours are highly vascular, even the vessels encountered during the approach to the lesion will appear to be distended. Veins in the tumour capsule tend to be grossly engorged and palpation will reveal the characteristic cording within the vessels which has been mentioned above.

SUPPLEMENTARY READING

Brodey R. S. and Kelly D. F. (1968) Thyroid neoplasms in the dog. *Cancer* **22**, 406–15.
Glen J. B. (1972) Canine salivary mucocoeles: results of sialographic examination and surgical treatment of 50 cases. *J. Small Anim. Pract.* **13**, 515–26.
Harvey C. E. (1977) Parotid salivary duct rupture and fistula in the dog and cat. *J. Small Anim. Pract.* **18**, 163–8.
Harvey C. E. (1981) Parotid gland enlargement and hypersialosis in a dog. *J. Small Anim. Pract.* **22**, 19–25.
Karbe E. and Nielsen S. W. (1965) Branchial cyst in a dog. *J. Am. Vet. Med. Assoc.* **147**, 637–46.

Chapter 12

The Management of Cervical Swellings

This section concentrates upon the treatment of the more important disorders whose diagnosis was discussed in Chapter 11 but with particular emphasis on the surgery of the salivary and thyroid glands.

The prospects of a patient's survival of throat surgery are obviously improved if, first, the integrity of the airway, oesophagus, major blood vessels and nerves is maintained. By the same token, it is an elementary observation that these structures pass through the throat in a longitudinal direction and therefore surgical incisions which run parallel to these vital tissues are generally safe. Secondly, the use of sharp dissection techniques with scalpels and scissors in this area should be avoided unless the surgeon is absolutely confident of the anatomical relationships within the field and is sure that there have been no distortions by disease processes. Blunt dissection, possibly with fingers, to divide the loose facial connections is far safer. It is also helpful if patients are positioned so that the tissues of the surgical field are under slight tension (*see* Fig. 2.3). In order to avoid slackness of the tissues, for ventral midline incisions, the patients are positioned in dorsal recumbency with a sandbag behind the poll and the forelimbs extended caudally; for paramedian, ventrolateral and lateral incisions the neck is again extended over a sandbag but the underside shoulder is raised by a secondary bolster and the forelimbs are again drawn caudally. Adhesive tape passed across the operating table at the level of the patient's nose assists to retain the neck in an extended position. Although it is unlikely that special anaesthetic techniques will be necessary for the surgery described below, attention should be directed to the postoperative period. Surgery to extirpate a cervical mass is likely to leave dead space; tissue exudation, haemorrhage and possibly infection precipitate a distension of this space which could embarrass

221

respiration. The surgeon can prevent the prospect of asphyxiation in the postoperative period by paying particular attention to accurate haemostasis during the procedure and by the tactical use of implanted tissue (Penrose) drains. Whenever there is a likelihood that a wound will be left open to drain or that a Penrose tube will be used, it is helpful in the aftercare of the patient for the area which is clipped for surgery to be extended towards the manubrium of the sternum, particularly in long-haired breeds.

DEVELOPMENTAL ANOMALIES

Cervical calcinosis circumscripta

Although this lesion provokes a palpable firm swelling, usually closely related to the cervical spinal column, many are asymptomatic. Provided that the patient is showing no discomfort and that the forward movement of the scapula and shoulder joint is not restricted by the presence of the mass, calcinosis circumscripta at this site is best left untreated. Whenever a surgical excision is attempted care must be taken that the entire lesion is identified and removed. The procedure will necessitate extensive disruption of the segmental muscles of the neck before detachment of the mass from the periosteum of the cervical vertebrae.

ACQUIRED ANOMALIES

Haematoma

Most haematomas are best managed by conservative measures and these may extend to instructions to the owners to cage-rest the patient to prevent further trauma. Persistent haematomas may be treated by drainage at the most dependent point which may be maintained by the use of a seton.

Abscess

It is a fundamental principle of surgery that abscesses should be drained and that foreign material and necrotic foci should be eliminated. Antibiotics are contraindicated in acute abscesses prior to drainage and in the management of chronic discharging sinuses. As far as adjacent vital structures will permit, a wide incision is made into the most dependent point of an abscess so that gravity will assist drainage postoperatively. Apart from major blood vessels and nerves, the superficial salivary glands and their ducts are vulnerable to disruption when abscesses of the head and neck are lanced. The parotid duct in particular may lie adjacent to the acute lesions which are so common in the jowl region of cats (*see Fig.* 11.3). Whenever an abscess is drained, the initial incision is best extended bluntly by forcing scissors open within the site. The abscess cavity and the purulent material which is released are inspected for the presence of a foreign body. Fortunately, most foreign bodies will have been sequestrated by the suppurative response and therefore lie free within the abscess. Nevertheless, the pyogenic membrane should be searched for adherent foreign matter and secondary sinus channels. The site should be flushed with saline solution to improve visibility, and at the same time this provides a flotation medium for vegetable matter. In most cases an abscess incision should be left open to drain and to heal by granulation. Periodic irrigation by dilute hydrogen peroxide or povidone–iodine solutions prevents opportunist infections and assists in the maintenance of drainage. The implantation of a seton may also be considered at those sites where adequate drainage is not established easily. A simple loop of bandage is suitable for this purpose: a fresh bandage should be introduced daily by untying the old dressing and using it to pull through the new. The loop of the seton should not be tied too loosely because the patient's forefeet may become entangled.

Chronic sinus tracts almost invariably emanate from a deep foreign body. Considerable patience may be required to follow these sinuses using a surgical seeker as a guide. The surgeon should not be too enthusiastic to wipe or flush away pus as this is also a reliable marker leading to the foreign body. The earlier advice concerning the use of longitudinal incisions is especially pertinent in the dissection through fibrous tissue in the pursuit of foreign bodies in the neck. Again, the placement of an oesophageal sound will provide a useful landmark when the chronic inflammatory tissue extends deeply.

Snake bites

In these circumstances, apart from the administration of first aid attention, the intravenous or intramuscular injection of polyvalent antiserum would be ideal, but this is rarely on hand at veterinary hospitals. During the first aid attendance cold compresses reduce pain and swelling and at the same time limit the spread of venom through the lymphatics to adjacent tissues. Corticosteroids assist to reduce the inflammatory reaction but a broad spectrum bactericidal antibiotic is essential because all snake bites are infected, usually by gram-positive bacteria. Both antihistamines and analgesics are indicated during the first 12 hours after envenomation. Surgery to excise tissue from the bitten site is rarely needed.

Emphysema

Surgical interference to identify and close a focus of leakage of air from the upper respiratory tract is rarely indicated. On isolated occasions the area of crepitation may advance towards the thoracic inlet and the danger of pneumothorax arises. Fine sutures with 3/0 or 4/0 silk are suitable for the repair of tracheal wounds. A ventral midline incision offers the best line of approach (*see* Chapter 6).

MANAGEMENT OF OTHER ACQUIRED LESIONS

Lymph node biopsy

Enlarged submandibular lymph nodes may be biopsied to differentiate between inflammatory and neoplastic involvement. These may be excised entire through a simple longitudinal incision made through the skin and panniculus muscle which are tensed over the node in question. There should be no confusion between the appearance of an enlarged lymph node and a salivary gland: lymph nodes are more deeply coloured maroon, whilst salivary tissue resembles putty. The submandibular lymph nodes lie ventral to the external maxillary vein but the salivary gland lies dorsally in the fork formed between the external and internal maxillary vessels. The prescapular node is reached through an incision which runs parallel to the anterior border of the scapula but the overlying muscle layers must be divided to gain access to this node.

Staphylococcal lymphadenitis

The objectives of the therapy for 'puppy strangles' are to encourage abscessating lymph nodes to discharge and drain, to control the staphylococcal infection and to suppress the inflammatory reaction. The abscessating lymph nodes will usually point and discharge spontaneously but this process can be assisted by warm fomentations. An antibiotic effective against penicillinase-producing staphylococci should be administered for at least 2 weeks. Potentiated sulphonamides, lincomycin and cloxacillin are suitable. Corticosteroids assist to suppress the overall inflammatory reaction and it is a matter of opinion whether antihistamines are indicated. Although the regimen of polypharmacy suggested here may be effective to resolve the infection, many puppies are left with unsightly scars and breeders may find them difficult to sell.

SALIVARY GLAND SURGERY

Salivary cyst (*Fig.* 12.1)

The objective of the surgical treatment of cervical salivary cysts and ranuli is to remove the sublingual glandular system on the affected side and to drain the cyst itself. In practice the close relationship between

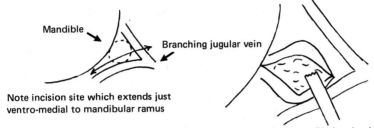

Mandible

Branching jugular vein

Note incision site which extends just
ventro-medial to mandibular ramus

Dissect on to capsule of submandibular gland.
Separate gland from capsule. Identify and
ligate blood supply

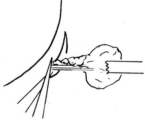

Dissect chain of sublingual glands
between digastricus and pterygoid
muscles. Drain cyst during this stage

Section sublingual chain as far
forward as possible. Avoid lingual
artery and hypoglossal nerve

Fig. 12.1. Correction of salivary cyst.

the submandibular and sublingual glands necessitates that both are
extirpated. During the excision of the salivary glands, communication
with the cyst is almost invariably established so that in most cases
drainage by suction can be performed without resort to a separate
incision. There are exceptional cases where the cyst is very pendulous
and the overlying skin has been stretched to a point where a cosmetic
procedure is necessary to excise the redundant tissue.

The submandibular salivary gland forms a palpable, spherical mass
which lies between the external and internal maxillary veins (*see Fig.*
11.5). It lies within a tough fibrous capsule which extends forwards to
envelope the sublingual gland also. The submandibular salivary gland
receives its blood supply through the capsule at the anteromedial
aspect. The duct leaves the gland from the anterior border and in its
course it is closely associated with the lobules of the sublingual gland. It
passes forwards between the pterygoid and digastricus muscles before it
comes to lie beneath the oral mucosa at the ventrolateral aspect of the

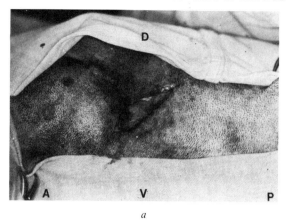

a

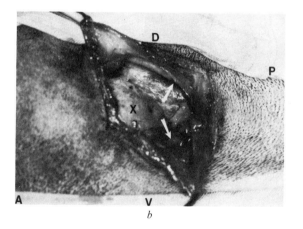

b

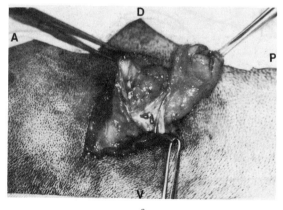

c

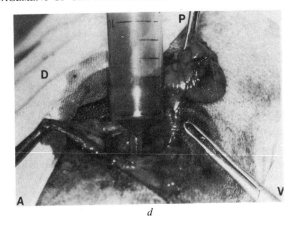

d

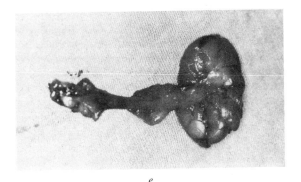

e

Fig. 12.2. Correction of salivary cyst. (*a*) The incision extends caudally and obliquely from just medial to the angular process of the mandible. (*b*) Submandibular salivary gland (**X**) lies within a capsule in the fork formed by the external and internal maxillary veins (white arrows.) (*c*) Capsule is detached and the submandibular gland is withdrawn by slight traction. (*d*) Submandibular gland and sublingual chain are freed. During the dissection, the cyst contents can usually be aspirated. (*e*) The excised material, consisting of the larger unilobular submandibular gland and multilobular chain of sublingual tissues.

tongue. The sublingual gland is composed of a series of lobules which form a chain as small ducts enter the larger sublingual duct. The most caudal lobule is quite large and is closely apposed to the submandibular gland. The chain of sublingual glandular tissue and both major salivary ducts follow the same course towards the oral submucosa. There is a separate series of sublingual glandular elements beneath the lingual mucosa and these have independent secretory ducts directly into the mouth. These latter glands are not involved in salivary cysts.

Surgical extirpation of the sublingual and submandibular salivary systems is performed with the patient placed in lateral recumbency and with the neck extended as described in Chapter 1. A 5–6 cm slightly curved skin incision is made which passes from the medial aspect of the mandible caudally over the submandibular gland to finish dorsal to the jugular vein (*Fig.* 12.2*a*). In obese patients it may be difficult to palpate the submandibular gland and it is helpful to raise the jugular vein so that its major division can be identified in the knowledge that the gland lies at the fork. The connective tissue is cleared and the panniculus muscle is split in the line of its fibres. The large veins lie in the loose connective tissue beneath this muscle and they may be identified (*Fig.* 12.2*b*). The submandibular gland has a putty-like colour and its capsule is identified, cleared and incised so that the glandular tissue within can be grasped with Allis forceps. Slight traction on the forceps is helpful while the capsule is pushed away by blunt dissection (*Fig.* 12.2*c*). Care should be taken to identify the arterial and venous supply on the medial aspect and these are ligated. Further traction applied to the gland tenses the submandibular duct to bring the sublingual tissue into view and the chain of glands is followed forwards towards the mouth. During this blunt dissection, saliva may well appear in the incision and it is usually possible to drain the cyst at this stage by a combination of external pressure and suction (*Fig.* 12.2*d*). Tapioca-like particles, typical of stagnant saliva, may be evident. The two major salivary ducts and the chain of sublingual glands are transected as close to the base of the tongue as possible and at this point good lighting is helpful to identify the lingual artery and the hypoglossal nerve which lie adjacent to the site of transection. The placement of a ligature around the salivary ducts is not necessary. Closure of the submandibular capsule, panniculus muscle, subcutis and skin is routine.

Only in exceptional cases is it necessary to excise the loose skin over a pouch-like cervical salivary cyst. Almost all sialoceles can be treated through a single surgical incision as described above. Owners should be advised that the dead space which exists where the cyst has been drained will inevitably fill with serum during the days following surgery. Without this briefing, an owner might suspect that the postoperative swelling indicates a surgical failure, but the distension can be expected to resolve within 2 weeks.

The prognosis for a successful surgical treatment of sublingual and cervical salivary cysts is excellent. Rarely, further salivary accumulations occur if inadequate sublingual tissue has been excised, if the incorrect side has been subjected to surgery or if the disease is bilateral. Confirmed or suspected cases of bilateral salivary cysts should be treated by bilateral extirpation of the submandibular and sublingual systems. The loss of glandular tissue bilaterally will not incapacitate the patient.

The treatment of parotid duct ruptures and fistulas

Harvey (1977) has rationalized the treatment of traumatic diseases of the parotid salivary duct and has suggested that there are four alternative approaches to surgery:

1. End-to-end anastomosis to repair the ruptured duct.
2. Implantation of the proximal segment of the duct by the creation of a new stoma in the oropharynx.
3. Ligation of the duct proximal to the site of injury and the induction of atrophy of the parotid tissue.
4. Extirpation of the entire parotid gland.

In practice, although it is technically feasible to anastomose the ruptured duct by the use of very fine suture materials the results of this surgery are disappointing, probably because strictures almost inevitably form at the site of repair. Re-implantation of the duct is rarely feasible unless the rupture is close to the natural papilla, leaving sufficient length of duct for placement into the buccal cleft without undue tension. In the hands of the present author this method has been disappointing because the new opening has no sphincter activity and ascending infections have provoked complications. Parotid gland extirpation is a difficult surgical procedure and provides the risk of damage to the facial nerve or great vessels. Thus, by a process of elimination, the most straightforward treatment for defects of the parotid duct is ligation: this technique is also suitable for the induction of atrophy of the salivary tissue in cases of glandular enlargement and hypersialosis. Prior to ligation, identification of the duct is facilitated by the introduction of monifilament nylon, either through the natural papilla when the duct is intact or through the fistula in cases of trauma. The duct is most accessible as it crosses the surface of the masseter muscle, but in other instances, it may be necessary to ligate the structure adjacent to the caudal border of the mandible, but before it divides to enter the gland itself. At least two ligatures of non-absorbable material such as 2/0 silk or linen should be used.

The parotid gland itself represents an inverted pyramid which is wrapped around the auricular cartilage dorsally and lies adjacent to the caudal border of the mandible anteriorly. Deep to the parotid gland lie the major divisions of the internal carotid artery and the internal maxillary vein. Branches of the trigeminal and facial nerves emerge between the mandible and the parotid gland. Fortunately the indications for excision of the parotid gland are rare and arise from inflammatory and neoplastic disorders of the gland itself. The procedure is performed through an oblique incision which runs from the caudal border of the auricular cartilage anteroventrally towards the angular process of the mandible. The overlying panniculus and auricular muscles are divided to expose the gland. Infusion of the glandular tissue with a dye such as Evans blue via the papilla can be helpful to determine the full extent of the tissues to be excised. Naturally every care is taken to avoid trauma to the vital structures which relate to the deep surfaces of the gland. Significant dead space is inevitably created when the glandular tissue has been removed and the implantation of a tissue drain is recommended.

Zygomatic gland excision

Removal of the zygomatic (orbital) gland is indicated for the treatment of the rare salivary cysts which arise in the orbital region. Although the zygomatic gland may be approached dorsally or laterally, the author's preferred technique is to make a single horizontal incision over the ventral border of the zygomatic arch. Once the subcutis has been cleared, the insertion of the masseter muscle on to the zygoma is identified. The insertion is sectioned prior to an osteotomy of the ventral half of the arch. This osteotomy can be performed with a handsaw or osteotome and should extend for no more than 2 cm from the anterior limit of the arch. It is important that a full-thickness osteotomy is avoided as this will disrupt the ventral border of the bony orbit. Once the bone window has been lifted away the zygomatic gland is identified deep to a layer of fascia. It is excised piece by piece, taking care to avoid trauma to the deep facial vein and maxillary artery. On completion of the excision, herniation of the orbital fat can be prevented by closing the periosteum of the zygomatic arch to the fascia of the masseter muscle.

SURGERY OF THE THYROID GLAND

The indications for surgery to the thyroid gland are biopsy for the confirmation of glandular inflammation and malfunction, and the removal of unilateral tumours. In cases of suspected thyroid adenocarcinoma chest radiographs should be made before surgery is contemplated so that unnecessary interference is avoided when metastases are already present. Even in those cases where the thyroid enlargement is represented by a palpable asymmetric swelling, a ventral midline incision offers the best line of approach. This should extend 6–8 cm caudally from the level of the hyoid bone but may need to be enlarged for the withdrawal of an encapsulated tumour. The sternohyoid muscles are divided at their midline raphe and there is inevitably a small vein to be ligated at this junction. The normal thyroid glands are located to the carotid sheath at the level of the cricoid cartilage. At first glance they may resemble a strip of muscle, but closer inspection will show that each flesh-coloured gland is 2–3 cm long and receives its vascular supply through the poles. The parathyroid tissue forms an

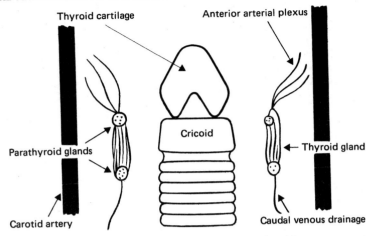

Fig. 12.3. Diagrammatic representation of canine thyroid anatomy.

integral part of the thyroid glands and usually cannot be distinguished (*Fig.* 12.3). For biopsy purposes the whole of the gland on one side is isolated and the arterial and venous tributaries are sectioned between carefully placed ligatures. The removal of thyroid tumours depends upon a fastidious process of dissection and ligation. These tumours are frequently highly vascular and the distended veins must be examined for the typical infiltrative cords of neoplastic tissue. The presence of such cords indicates a poor prognosis because there are likely to be metastases even in the absence of demonstrable densities on lung radiographs. Before a thyroid tumour is excised the contralateral glandular tissue should be inspected for lesser neoplastic involvement. Naturally, bilateral neoplasia carries a poor prognosis. It is not practicable to perform bilateral thyroidectomy in the dog without the simultaneous removal of the parathyroid tissue. Although the consequences of total thyroidectomy could be controlled by replacement hormone therapy, the metabolic derangement which follows parathyroidectomy is not so easily controlled.

The major indication for thyroid surgery in the cat is the removal of functional tumours.

SUPPLEMENTARY READING

Glen J. B. (1972) Canine salivary mucoceles: results of sialographic examination and surgical treatment of 50 cases. *J. Small Anim. Pract.* **13**, 515–26.

Harvey C. E. (1977) Parotid salivary duct rupture and fistula in the dog and cat. *J. Small Anim. Pract.* **18**, 163–8.

Harvey C. E. (1981) Parotid gland enlargement and hypersialosis in a dog. *J. Small Anim. Pract.* **22**, 19–25.

Chapter 13

Otitis Externa

It is convenient to divide the ear into three sections (*Fig.* 13.1).
1. The outer ear, comprising the external auditory meatus leading down to but not including the tympanic membrane. This is supported by the auricular and annular cartilages.
2. The middle ear, which is contained within a bony compartment of the petrous temporal bone but extends from the ear drum, via the auditory ossicles, to the oval foramen. The eustachian tube is included in discussions of the middle ear.
3. The inner ear or labyrinth, which consists of a system of membranous tubes—the cochlea, semi-circular canals, utricle and saccule—which are contained within the spaces within the deep portion of the petrous temporal bone.

Inflammatory diseases of the ear are described as otitis externa, media and interna respectively.

Surveys of small animal practice show that the treatment of otitis, particularly otitis externa, accounts for more than 10 per cent of veterinary professional time. Consequently, surgical procedures to the external ear are likely to be amongst the most frequent operations performed in general veterinary practice other than castration, ovariohysterectomy and treatments to traumatic wounds. In this chapter the aetiopathogenesis of otitis externa is described, together with a rational approach to treatment with particular emphasis on the role of surgery.

THE OTITIS CYCLE

Fig. 13.2 illustrates the 'merry-go-round' of events which occurs in the external ear canal once otitis has been initiated by one of the trigger

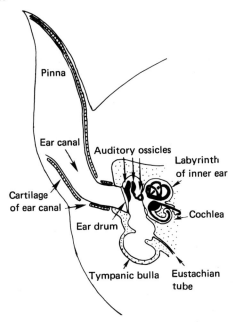

Fig. 13.1. Anatomy of the ear (diagrammatic and not to scale).

factors. The function of treatment, whether it be medical, surgical or a combination of both, should be, first, to identify and eliminate the trigger factors and, secondly to break the cycle of irritation, self-trauma and inflammation.

Trigger factors

Mites

Dogs do not tolerate the parasite *Otodectes cynotis* as well as cats. A small number of mites may excite a severe inflammatory reaction in the aural integument of a dog whereas a cat may carry a heavy burden of this parasite before symptoms develop. Cats have traditionally been labelled as the reservoirs of the infestation and, certainly, feline contacts of affected dogs should be treated whenever the condition is confirmed. The acute canine response to otodectic mange suggests a hypersensitivity reaction, possibly to mite saliva. Parasitism is a major cause of otitis in both dogs and cats—estimations range from 10 to 50 per cent of all cases—but a careful search is sometimes required before the diagnosis is confirmed.

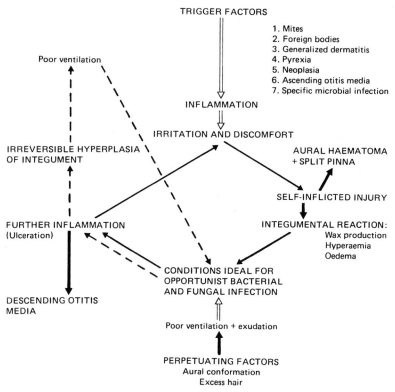

Fig. 13.2. Aetiopathogenesis of otitis externa.

Foreign bodies

Vegetable matter such as grass seeds and barley awns together with other dirt and debris are all familiar causes of otitis. Dogs with pendulous ears are more prone to trap particles in the ear canal, and a grass seed, for example, will tend to migrate towards the eardrum because its tail hairs prevent its being dislodged spontaneously. Foreign bodies cause great discomfort, especially when they come to lie in the pre-tympanic region, and the veterinarian's suspicions are aroused by the sudden onset of frenzied head-shaking. An aural foreign body should be regarded as an indication for urgent attention because the patient is often in considerable pain. The offending material should be removed without delay but this may require a general anaesthetic if a careful manoeuvre is to be performed on a distressed patient. Note that more than one grass seed may be present at any one time and the opposite ear should always be checked.

Generalized dermatitis

The epithelial lining of the ear is modified skin and this is just as susceptible to dermatitis as the skin of any other part of the body. Contact allergic dermatitis shows a distribution which corresponds to regions where there is a thin protective hair cover, namely the ventral abdomen, axilla and ear canal. Similarly, patients with parasitic dermatitis or generalized seborrhoea may be expected to show otitis externa and staphylococcal pustules may be present in the ear canal of dogs that are afflicted by more widespread impetigo. A general inspection of the skin is a necessary part of the examination of cases of otitis.

Pyrexia

Febrile diseases may initiate otitis in one of two ways, both of which permit opportunist infections to become established in the auditory canal. First, local immune defence mechanisms are likely to be depressed during systemic illness and, secondly, pyrexia provokes erythema, hyperaemia and swelling in the integument. In dogs with conformation defects, which prejudice good ventilation, any further change in the microclimate may favour bacterial or yeast infection.

Neoplasia

Neoplastic lesions in the ear canal cause narrowing and interfere with aeration of the microclimate. The surfaces of tumours may become ulcerated and this will contribute to conditions ideal for secondary infections. Otorrhoea and smell are often the first signs of aural neoplasia. Some will be obvious at the external orifice whilst other tumours are not identified until a deeper examination is performed. It should be noted that neoplasia may be a sequel to chronic otitis: glandular hyperplasia is a consequence of otitis and the hyperplasia may take the form of friable vascular polyps, particularly in the horizontal portion of the canal, and these lesions may progress to neoplasia. Most tumours of the outer ear of the dog are benign but occasionally carcinomas are encountered and the possibility of metastases should be investigated. Feline aural tumours range in gross appearance from small blue bubbles to ulcerated, fleshy protrusions and, again, most are benign. Occasionally tumours of the feline middle ear expand to occupy the horizontal portion of the external meatus.

Ascending otitis media

There is strong circumstantial evidence that a proportion of cases of canine otitis media arise following upper respiratory tract infections and the route of spread is via the eustachian tube. Otitis media may then break out through the eardrum so that an inflammatory reaction is initiated in the horizontal canal. It has not been possible to confirm the incidence of ascending otitis media in animals because they are not usually presented for diagnosis until the stage of otitis externa with otorrhoea has been reached. It should be appreciated that otorrhoea can arise in one of three ways: (*a*) primary otitis externa alone; (*b*) primary otitis externa plus secondary otitis media; (*c*) primary otitis media plus secondary otitis externa. Of these, the last two are likely to be clinically inseparable. Perhaps it is worth noting that in man the source of discharge from the external ear canal is almost invariably otitis media.

Specific microbial infections

It is the author's opinion that pathogens do not often become established in the ear canal as primary instigators of otitis and that they are more likely to be present as secondary opportunist invaders when conditions are made suitable by other trigger factors. The single exception to this view may be the infection typically seen in Labradors and Retrievers, which show an acute hyperaemic otitis with a thick yellow discharge. In this condition the aural integument becomes intensely inflamed within a few hours. No other primary factors can be identified on auriscopy and, thus, there is little chance for opportunism to have occurred. The acute onset of the condition together with the empirical response to topical antihistamine treatment suggests that a hypersensitivity reaction may be involved.

Many veterinary clinicians appear to be preoccupied by culture and sensitivity tests on swabs from cases of otitis externa. It is suggested that the more enlightened approach should be to investigate why microbes have become established in the ear canal as a prelude to therapy designed to change the conditions in the aural microclimate so that they no longer favour infection; this is in contrast to the more restricted pursuit of specific bacteria and yeasts prior to antimicrobial therapy based on sensitivity testing.

Factors that exacerbate otitis externa

Self-trauma

Scratching, rubbing and headshaking are all natural responses to aural irritation. These will not only intensify the inflammatory reaction within the ear canal but may injure the pinna to produce fissures of the tip of the flap or haematomas. Haematomas invariably arise between the integument of the ventral aspect of the pinna and the auricular

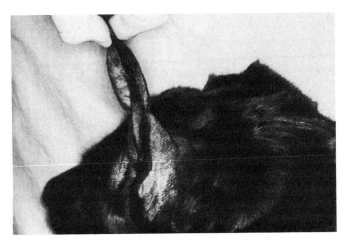

Fig. 13.3. Aural haematoma in a Labrador.

cartilage (*Fig.* 13.3). It should be obvious that there is little virtue in the treatment of these self-inflicted injuries in isolation, but that the first consideration must be to arrest the underlying otitis.

Natural tissue responses

The acute inflammatory response in the lining of the ear canal comprises hyperaemia, oedema and increased wax production. Thus, the canal becomes narrowed and ventilation is reduced. Contrary to popular belief, wax is not bactericidal but, rather, acts as a substrate for microbial growth. Inflammatory exudation into the canal leads to further constriction and again provides a suitable medium for the growth of pathogens. As the reaction intensifies ulceration of the epithelial surface may be seen.

In longer-standing cases of otitis the surface layers become grossly thickened and hyperplasia of the wax-producing glands is evident. These changes, which restrict the lumen of the meatus, are most obvious in the upper third of the canal. Irreversibly thickened folds may develop to give the lining a cauliflower appearance and this state is usually termed verrucose otitis (*Fig.* 13.4).

Aural conformation

The aural microclimate in dogs with pendulous ears or whose canals are excessively hairy does not ventilate satisfactorily so that in breeds such as Spaniels and Poodles local conditions favour opportunist

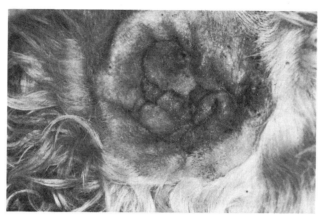

Fig. 13.4. Verrucose otitis: the vertical canal is obliterated by thickened folds of integument.

infections. Therefore it is not surprising that these breeds are over-represented in the incidence of clinical otitis externa. The erect carriage of the feline pinnae and the relative absence of hair within the ear canal may explain why the overall incidence of otitis externa is lower in cats than dogs.

Iatrogenic factors

Undoubtedly wax, dirt, foreign matter and exudates perpetuate and exacerbate otitis and it is reasonable, as a part of treatment, to attempt to cleanse the ear canal. However, the practice of screwing tissue paper, cotton buds or tufts of cotton wool wound on artery forceps into an inflamed channel is contraindicated. These materials are all, to some extent, abrasive and they will aggravate ulcers of the integument and this technique will distress the patient unnecessarily. The preferred method to cleanse ears is by gentle irrigation, either through a blunt-ended needle or with a water pick. The task can be facilitated by the preparatory use of a specific wax solvent or by loosening the wax-based debris with liquid paraffin or olive oil for a few days. The choice of irrigation fluid is important, as many antiseptic solutions are irritant or ototoxic. Cetrimide (0·5 per cent) is the author's agent of choice, but even at this concentration it is mildly irritant and must be flushed away with saline at the end of the procedure. A general anaesthetic may be required for all but the most cooperative patients.

Infections

Much has already been made of the role of bacteria and yeasts in otitis. Suffice it to say that a wide range of bacteria and yeasts may be recovered from healthy and diseased ears. Some organisms, such as staphylococci and pityrosporum, may be commensals which assume pathogenicity once the otitis is under way. Others, such as proteus and pseudomonas, are recovered from diseased ears only. When treatment is considered, the major aim of antibiotic therapy is to eliminate these secondary pathogens in order to break the otitis cycle. The notoriously limited sensitivity of pseudomonas renders it the most difficult infection to control.

THE DIAGNOSIS OF OTITIS EXTERNA

The signs of otitis externa are familiar to most pet owners and they include head-shaking, rubbing and scratching of the ear, excoriation of the skin at the base of the ear and between the ear and the eye, otorrhoea, smell, pain on contact with the ear, fissures of the ear flap and haematomas of the pinna. It will be seen in Chapter 14 that some of the signs of otitis externa are similar to those of otitis media.

The first objective of diagnosis is to identify the trigger factor so that specific treatments can be instituted to reverse these and, in early cases, resolution can be achieved quickly. It is important that the ear should not be examined in isolation but the general state of the skin of the patient should be taken into account. Apart from the identification of trigger factors, the purpose of diagnostic procedures is to establish the severity of the changes which have taken place in the aural integument.

Auriscopy

Effective auriscopy necessitates a cooperative patient, suitable instrumentation and a clear field of view. Inflamed ears are painful and, therefore, even placid animals may resent auriscopy when conscious. A thorough inspection of the ear canal will be necessary unless the cause of the otitis is obvious and can be rectified easily. It is better to resort to a general anaesthetic early in the course of the disease rather than late. The external meatus of a medium-sized dog such as a Labrador is approximately 10 cm long and therefore the human aural specula, which are still used in some veterinary practices, are entirely unsuitable for dogs—the longer veterinary specula are essential. All veterinarians are familiar with the frustrations of instruments with damaged bulbs and exhausted batteries. Auriscopes with mains supply or rechargeable batteries are widely available nowadays, and not only do these function more reliably, but they provide superior illumination to the conventional hand-held battery equipment.

The presence of a discharge in the canal may inhibit auriscopy. At the initial consultation it may be necessary to dispense treatment aimed simply at the dispersal of a wax-based discharge so that a thorough examination can be performed at a later date. Proprietary ceruminoly-tic agents have few advantages over olive oil, liquid paraffin and propylene glycol. There is a strong case for the revival of the art of materia medica as useful lotions can be made up in the practice pharmacy by the addition of agents such as sulphanilamide powder or iodoform to these oils. These lotions not only break up the wax aggregations but help to control the secondary infections.

The role of radiography in the investigation of otitis externa is limited but abnormalities in this region may come to light during the investigation of middle ear disease. Changes which may be seen in the external meatus on radiographs consist of narrowing of the canal and calcification of the annular and auricular cartilages (*Fig.* 13.5). To some extent it is normal for the cartilages of older dogs to show an organized pattern of calcification but in the face of longstanding suppuration metaplastic ossification of the cartilaginous elements may take place. This provides useful prognostic information because surgical inter-ferences to ossified canals are difficult and the prospects of success are reduced. The hyperplastic changes which occur in the lining of the ear canal in response to chronic inflammation cause narrowing of the meatus which is seen as a loss of air shadow on radiographs. Fortunately these hyperplastic changes are usually confined to the upper third of the ear canal and the horizontal portion remains patent. A small number of patients show strictures at the aperture of the horizontal canal after aural resections and radiographs can be used to establish the depth of the stenosis. The extent of soft tissue tumours may also be confirmed in this way.

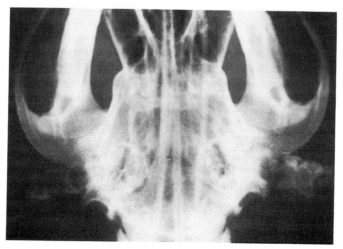

Fig. 13.5. Radiograph showing calcification of the aural cartilages. The dis-organized pattern of the change suggests that it is a response to chronic infection.

It is suggested that the value of culture and sensitivity tests on swabs taken from the ear canal has been overstated in the past. These tests add to the overall cost of treatment and yet it is only an exceptional case which is expedited by them. Microbiological tests are, however, indicated when otitis and otorrhoea persist in the face of rational medical or surgical treatment and when no trigger factors can be determined.

Biopsy sampling of soft tissue proliferations within the ear canals of dogs or cats is invaluable if a useful prognosis is to be given.

MEDICAL MANAGEMENT OF OTITIS EXTERNA

Fig. 13.6 illustrates a management protocol for otitis externa. Throughout this regime the aim is to identify and rectify specific causal factors if at all possible. By the time of presentation the trigger factors may long since have become masked or overrun by secondary changes. Polypharmacy should be avoided for as long as possible—proprietary drops containing several therapeutic agents prejudice the possibility of a successful diagnosis being reached. Some cases which could otherwise be treated medically will become surgical patients for the lack of specific therapy for a specific disease. Polypharmaceutical preparations almost always contain corticosteroids, which suppress the inflammatory response but also mask the underlying causes. A false impression of resolution may be achieved in the owner's eyes so that the patient is not presented for re-examination until a considerable time has elapsed and more serious changes have occurred within the ear canal. Calamine lotion or the astringent mixture of zinc oxide and surgical spirit are preferred for the suppression of the inflammatory response and self-inflicted injury.

SURGERY OF THE EXTERNAL EAR CANAL

Self-inflicted injuries

It has already been mentioned that attempts to treat self-inflicted injuries are likely to be unsuccessful if the underlying otitis is not resolved. In fact, splits of the pinna will usually heal without surgery if the predisposing headshaking is arrested. Drainage of aural haematoma is performed through a straight or sigmoid incision followed by compression sutures which are left in place for 14 days (*Fig.* 13.7). The compression may be achieved by discs of used X-ray film or narrow gauge polythene tubing; the traditional buttons are heavy and add to the general aural discomfort. Cruciform incisions are avoided because the subsequent scar tissue produces an unnecessary distortion of the pinna.

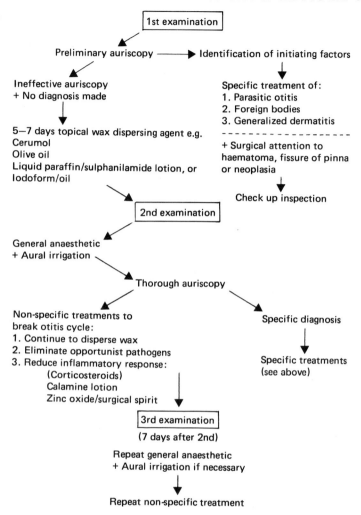

Fig. 13.6. Management of otitis.

Examinations should be repeated at weekly intervals until the discharge has been eliminated and the integument has returned to its normal appearance. Surgical treatment should be considered when the otitis externa persists.

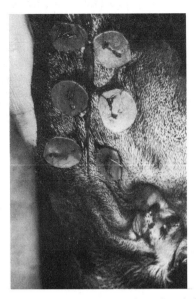

Fig. 13.7. 'Buttons' used to provide compression after drainage of an aural haematoma.

The objectives of aural resections

There are two quite different procedures collectively described as aural resections (*Fig.* 13.8) and their aims and indications are specific. First, the lateral wall resection (LWR) depends upon the removal of the lateral wall of the vertical canal. Its purpose is to improve the aeration of the aural microclimate and to facilitate drainage from the horizontal portion of the canal. In this way it is hoped that reversible inflammatory reactions in the lining of the meatus will subside. An LWR also serves to improve access to the horizontal canal for the treatment of otitis media, and tumours which are restricted to the lateral wall may be ablated by this technique.

The second procedure is the vertical canal ablation (VCA), which aims to do precisely that—to remove the upper portion of the external meatus while leaving a patent aperture directly into the horizontal canal. The tissues excised are likely to be most severely affected by the chronic changes of otitis, typically verrucose proliferations. There are techniques described in the literature which ablate the cartilaginous portion of the horizontal canal as well as the vertical segment but which leave no aural aperture. Such techniques are likely to enclose foci of infection and are contrary to the basic principles of surgery.

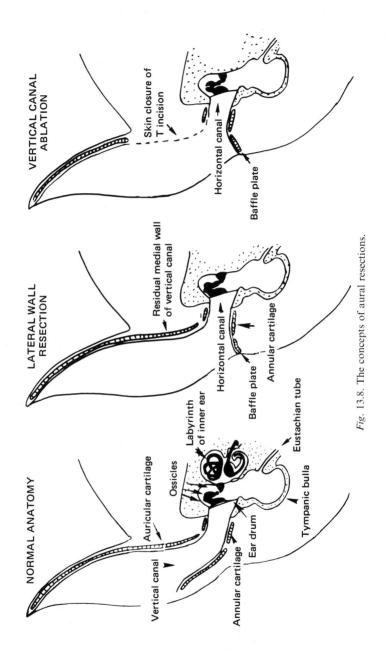

Fig. 13.8. The concepts of aural resections.

The indications for an LWR may be summarized as follows:

1. Persistent, non-responsive otitis externa where irreversible changes have not occurred. At this stage there is likely to be hyperaemia, oedema and ulceration of the integument.

2. Neoplasia of the lateral wall of the vertical canal.

3. Otitis media.

In contrast, the indications for a VCA include:

1. Irreversible, hyperplastic, otitis externa, e.g. verrucose otitis.

2. Neoplasia of the vertical canal.

Lateral wall resection (*modified Zepp technique*) (*Fig.* 13.9)

The skin around the ear is clipped and prepared for aseptic surgery in the normal manner. Contamination within the ear canal is reduced by preparatory irrigation with cetrimide solution as described above. For both LWR and VCA the patient is positioned in lateral recumbency with the head supported over a sandbag: this helps to draw the loose folds of skin away from the ear.

The level of the angle between the horizontal and vertical canals is located by the introduction of a pair of forceps into the meatus. A rounded skin incision is made 1 cm below this and approximately 1 cm wide (*Fig.* 13.9a). Parallel incisions are continued towards the notches on either side of the tragus at the natural opening of the ear. A finger-shaped skin flap is raised (*Fig.* 13.9b) and the soft tissues are cleared to expose the cartilage of the canal (*Fig.* 13.9c). Care is taken not to traumatize the parotid salivary gland at this stage. However, in spite of the large number of aural resections performed, parotid fistulas are very rare complications. The most crucial stage of the LWR is the incision of the cartilage. The spiral shape of the canal easily diverts the anterior cartilage incision from the lateral aspect of the tube towards its anteromedial surface. This will result in a restricted exposure of the horizontal canal and an inadequate baffle plate. This technical failure can be avoided if the cartilage incisions are made from the level of the ligamentous attachment between the auricular and annular cartilages (*Fig.* 13.9d). A scalpel is used to puncture the cartilage and integument at this point and the parallel incisions are continued dorsally aiming at the tragal notches mentioned above. The lateral wall of the ear canal can now be turned downwards (*Fig.* 13.9e) and a baffle plate is fashioned with rounded edges to fit the original skin incision. Provided that the incisions have been extended to the level of the ligament between the aural cartilages, the ligament will act as a hinge so that the baffle plate can be turned downwards to be sutured flush with the skin. The choice of suture material lies between 3/0 monofilament nylon and sheathed multifilament polyamide. Before the sutures are placed any gross cartilaginous projections should be filleted away, but when the sutures are placed between the skin surface and the integumental lining of the canal it may still be necessary to penetrate cartilage.

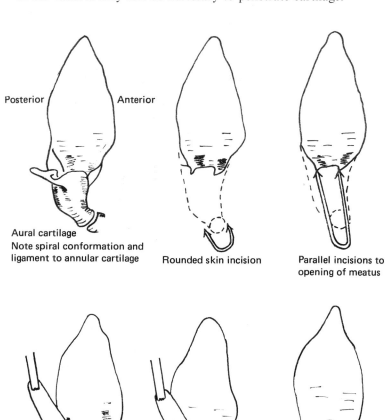

Posterior   Anterior

Aural cartilage
Note spiral conformation and
ligament to annular cartilage

Rounded skin incision

Parallel incisions to
opening of meatus

Lift skin flap, clear soft
tissue to expose cartilage
canal

Incise cartilage upwards from
level of junction ligament. Turn
down skin/cartilage strip

Resect cartilage to leav
rounded baffle plate.
Suture to skin

Fig. 13.9. Lateral wall resection.

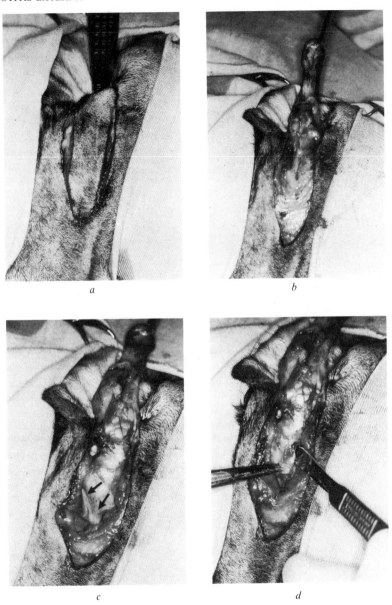

Fig. 13.9. Lateral wall resection. (*a*) Rounded skin incision extending 1 cm below level of horizontal canal. (*b*) Skin flap raised. (*c*) Cartilage canal exposed to show the ligament (arrowed) joining the annular and auricular cartilages. (*d*) The cartilage incision is made with a scalpel from the level of the junction ligament.

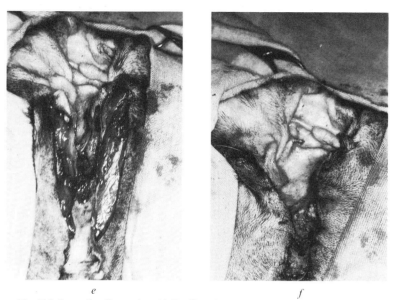

e   *f*

Fig. 13.9. Lateral wall resection. (*e*) Cartilage flap turned downwards. (*f*) The final
result: the horizontal canal is well exposed and the baffle plate lies flush with the
side of the head.

Aftercare consists of a 10-day course of broad spectrum antibiotics.
The patient is re-examined after 5 days so that the wounds can be
cleaned and checked. This may require a brief anaesthetic to replace
any sutures which are broken down. No attempt should be made to
dislodge healthy blood clots from the incisions. The sutures are
removed on the ninth day after surgery—the prolonged presence of
non-absorbable suture material at a site which is inevitably contaminated encourages the possibility of suture abscessation and wound
dehiscence. Sedatives and bandages are avoided during the time that
the sutures are in place but the patient's activities are restricted. Owners
should be advised that occasional headshaking is a normal reaction to
the presence of sutures. Head-shaking may also continue during the first
month after surgery whenever the patient is moved suddenly or taken
out into the fresh air.

Vertical canal ablation (*modified Tufvesson technique*) (*Fig.* 13.10)

Patient preparation is as for the LWR. In dogs with non-pricked ears a
T-shaped skin incision is made over the vertical canal (*Fig.* 13.10*a*).
However, in order to preserve the forward direction of the residual
pinna of prick-eared breeds, the skin incision should take the form of
an inverted L, where the angle lies at the caudal limit of the natural ear

opening. The base of the T or inverted L incision is marked with forceps introduced into the ear canal to the point where the vertical and horizontal sections meet. The skin flap or flaps are released and the underlying soft tissues are separated to expose the whole of the vertical

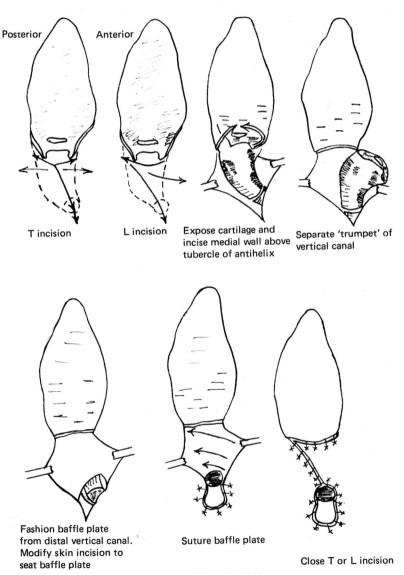

Posterior   Anterior

T incision   L incision   Expose cartilage and   Separate 'trumpet' of
                                        incise medial wall above   vertical canal
                                        tubercle of antihelix

Fashion baffle plate
from distal vertical canal.
Modify skin incision to   Suture baffle plate
seat baffle plate
                                                                      Close T or L incision

Fig. 13.10. Vertical canal ablation.

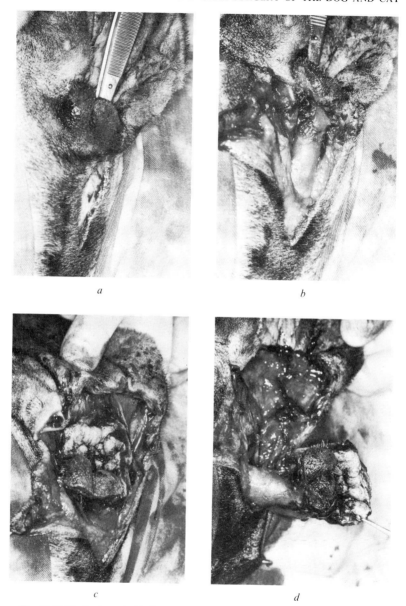

a

b

c

d

Fig. 13.10. Vertical canal ablation. (*a*) Vertical incision over canal: the forceps are used to locate the level of the junction between vertical and horizontal sections. (*b*) Inverted L skin flap drawn forwards: vertical canal exposed. (*c*) Incision through medial cartilage wall releases 'trumpet' of conchal cartilage. (*d*) 'Trumpet' freed from muscular attachments.

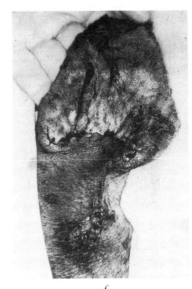

e   *f*

Fig. 13.10. Vertical canal ablation. (*e*) Creation of baffle plate before vertical canal
excised. (*f*) Closure of inverted L incision.

canal (*Fig.* 13.10*b*). The 'trumpet' of the conchal cartilage is separated
from the residue of the ear flap by an incision through the medial wall
of the vertical canal (*Fig.* 13.10*c*) at a level immediately dorsal to the
antihelicine tubercle. The muscular attachments are separated close to
the medial wall of the conchal cartilage so that the 'trumpet' is
mobilized (*Fig.* 13.10*d*). A baffle plate is fashioned from the lower
vertical canal (*Fig.* 13.10*e*) and lies in the same position as that
described for an LWR. Again, the ligament between the conchal and
annular cartilages acts as a hinge. The baffle plate is a valuable
innovation in this technique as it helps to maintain the long term
patency of the horizontal canal. The choice of suture materials is as for
an LWR but the soft tissues deep to the incised medial wall are included
in the sutures when the T or L incisions are closed so that dead space is
eliminated (*Fig.* 13.9*f*). Aftercare of the patient is similar to that for
LWR cases, although sutures are less inclined to dehisce after this
technique. Owners are advised that the ear carriage will be altered,
particularly in prick-eared dogs, because of the separation of the
muscular attachments from the medial surface of the vertical canal.
Nevertheless, some improvement in the appearance of the ear carriage
can be expected in the months following surgery. Long term aftercare
should include regular clipping of hair from the opening of the
horizontal canal.

When and why does an LWR fail to effect a cure?

Disappointing results may be obtained after an LWR through incorrect patient selection, technical failure and underlying untreated otitis media.

The temptation to defer surgical treatment and to continue with medical management of otitis, even when this is clearly ineffective, leads on to the pitfall of using an LWR when irreversible damage is already present. In this circumstance many of the signs of otitis will persist because of infection of the residual medial wall and exudation from it will continue (*Fig.* 13.11). It is possible to convert an LWR into a VCA by excision of the residual medial wall. Wound closure is achieved by a sliding flap which is obtained from the loose skin anterior to the ear.

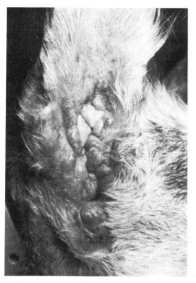

Fig. 13.11. An unsuccessful LWR: the operation has been delayed until irreversible changes had occurred in the medial wall.

Short term technical complications such as wound dehiscence are not uncommon with aural resections, and this is not surprising because the surgery is performed in a region where contamination is high and strict asepsis is not practicable. The most frequent long term technical error arises from a failure to establish satisfactory drainage from the horizontal canal. In the modified Zepp technique, this complication arises if a satisfactory baffle plate is not provided. In the absence of otitis media, the usual cause of persistent otorrhoea from the horizontal canal is a failure to extend the aural resection to the level of the ligament between the aural cartilages.

Whenever satisfactory exposure of the horizontal canal with a good baffle plate has been achieved and yet otorrhoea persists, a diagnosis of otitis media is likely. This is confirmed by palpation of the tympanic membrane and radiography (*see* Chapter 14).

When and why does a VCA fail?

The VCA technique gives rise to fewer complications and disappointments than the LWR. It is more difficult to select patients incorrectly for this procedure and the operation is so straightforward that technical failures are less likely to arise. Although cases of otitis may occur where a VCA is performed when an LWR would have sufficed, the patient will none the less be cured. Therefore, if there is doubt at auriscopy whether the changes in the ear canal will undergo remission through alterations in the microclimate, it is always correct to opt for the VCA procedure.

Postoperative stenosis of the horizontal canal can arise in the absence of a baffle plate and this latter modification is important because it helps to maintain the patency of the meatus. Preoperative stenosis due to inflammatory change in the integument of the horizontal canal is less easily resolved. Tight plugging with ribbon gauze impregnated with corticosteroid cream for 2- or 3-day periods can be helpful. In those cases where a stenosis takes the form of a narrow band, ablation of the stricture by cryosurgery may be considered.

Again, otitis media should be considered in those animals where otorrhoea persists but where the outer ear is healthy after a VCA.

OTHER CONDITIONS OF THE EXTERNAL EAR

Congenital anomalies

The attitude of the pinna is an important feature of the breed standard of dogs—German Shepherd, erect; Collie, semi-erect; Spaniel, pendulous—and shows a simple inherited distribution. The semi-erect is dominant over erect and pendulous factors and incorrect ear conformation is a serious fault in show specimens. Breeders may approach veterinarians with requests to change the aural conformation of their dogs. Such surgical corrections should be discouraged because they may promote defective stock and they are unethical. In the United Kingdom the cropping of ears is regarded as an unnecessary mutilation and it is not permitted.

Variations in the size of ears are encountered but most cases of macrotia and microtia do not cause concern unless they are very marked or involve show stock.

It is normal for the ear canal to be partly or completely closed by a membrane at birth but this recedes during the first 3 weeks of life. The membrane may lie at any level across the canal from the mid-horizontal segment to the natural orifice and, if it persists, it causes partial or total atresia. The consequences of an atretic canal range from nil to severe suppuration. Deafness may arise if the atresia is bilateral but this is very rare. Natural secretions accumulate in the blind canal and a typical suppurative process with sinus formation may follow. Some cases are asymptomatic and it is concluded that the drainage of the secretions occurs through the middle ear and eustachian tube. Others come to light when otitis media develops.

Canine aural dermatoses

The role of generalized dermatoses has already been stressed as a cause of otitis externa and the comments here merely highlight those skin disorders that show a predilection for the ear flap.

The rim of the pinna is a typical site for infestation by sarcoptes mites. Two features of this infection are constant—intense pruritus and recent direct or indirect contact with other dogs. Early skin scraping examinations are essential for confirmation of this diagnosis and effective treatment. The possibility of infection of human contacts should be considered.

Demodectic mange afflicts young dogs and the head as a whole is often covered with lesions of diffuse erythema and hair loss. Pruritus is not usually present but localized ear lesions may be seen. Again the diagnosis is established if adequate skin scrapings are taken for investigation.

Contact hypersensitivity reactions often involve the underside of the pinna where there is poor protective covering by hair. Other vulnerable sites such as the ventral abdomen and axillae will be involved.

Apart from papillomas, skin neoplasia involving the pinna is rare in dogs but mast cell tumours can occur at this site. Prompt diagnosis and amputation of the pinna may be necessary if metastasis is to be prevented.

Feline aural dermatoses

Poor circulation and a lack of hair insulation render the tips of the ears susceptible to frostbite injuries. Frostbite should be suspected if a cat, that has been outdoors in extreme climatic conditions is found to have cold, pale and painless ear flaps.

Notoedric mange tends to be most concentrated around the ear flaps but spreads to involve the dorsal surfaces of the head. The condition causes great irritation and self-mutilation and there is an over-representation in entire males. The diagnosis is confirmed by skin scrapings and treatment with non-toxic acaracides is rapidly effective.

Although lesions caused by fleas do occur on the earflaps of dogs, they are much more frequent at this site on cats.

Dermatophyte infection by *Microsporum canis* frequently occurs on the ears of cats and produces dry, scaly lesions with fragmented hair.

Cats with white hair are susceptible to solar dermatitis. In the absence of hair and skin pigment at sites such as the nares, eyelids and ear tips the ultraviolet component of sunlight produces areas of dermatitis, but in some cases this progresses to neoplasia. In the first instance, chronic inflammation of the ear tips is seen with ulceration and the presence of dried blood clots. The lesions may heal during the less sunny winter months but become progressively more severe with successive summers. The pinna may be deformed by scar tissue. The development of an ulcerated, bloody and friable surface denotes the onset of squamous cell carcinoma (*Fig.* 13.12). Although the progress of solar dermatitis may be retarded by the frequent application of sun creams, this is tedious and only temporarily effective. It is simpler to resect the vulnerable tip of the ear and, in cases of neoplasia, if this partial amputation is performed early, metastasis will be prevented.

Fig. 13.12. Squamous cell carcinoma on the tips of the ears of a white cat.

The cosmetic result of partial amputation can be improved if the skin of the dorsal surface of the pinna can be turned over the edge of the exposed cartilage. Linear carcinomas at the edge of the pinna are amenable to cryosurgery but this technique has little value for round or oval lesions because of the poor cosmetic results.

Amputation of the pinna

The indications for total amputation of the pinna include gross trauma, severe frostbite and extensive neoplasia. The surgical technique is similar to that described for vertical canal ablation, except that the medial incision is taken medial to the ear flap rather than across the wall of the vertical canal. After amputation the external meatus opens at the horizontal canal with a baffle plate. The cosmetic results achieved by this method are superior to those of a simple section of the pinna itself.

SUPPLEMENTARY READING

Coffey D. J. (1970) Observations on the surgical treatment of otitis externa in the dog. *J. Small Anim. Pract.* **11**, 265–70.

Fraser G., Gregor W. W., Mackenzie C. P. et al. (1970) Canine ear disease. *J. Small Anim. Pract.* **10**, 725–54.

Lane J. G. (1979) Canine aural surgery. *In Practice* **1**, 5–15.

Rose W. R. (1976) Otology: otoacariasis. *Vet. Med/Small Anim. Clin.* **71**, 1280–3.

Rose W. R. (1978) Otology: tumours. *Vet. Med/Small Anim. Clin.* **73**, 427–31.

Chapter 14

Otitis Media and Otitis Interna

Confusion has arisen in the veterinary literature owing to the terms 'otitis media' and 'otitis interna' being used as if they were synonymous. Whilst these conditions may coexist, a diagnosis of otitis interna should be reserved for those animals in which there is involvement of the organs of balance and hearing. These cases, which may also be described as 'labyrinthitis', show symptoms of ataxia, circling, loss of balance, nystagmus and deafness.

ANATOMICAL CONSIDERATIONS

The tympanic membrane or myringa forms the lateral limit of the middle ear and divides it from the horizontal canal of the external meatus. The middle ear cavity is air-filled and it is narrow dorsally where the epitympanic recess is traversed by the chain of auditory ossicles. Ventrally the space is bulbous and it occupies the thin-walled osseous bulla. The feline tympanic bulla shows an incomplete horizontal shelf so that on radiographs it appears to have a double-shelled structure (*Fig. 14.1*). The opening of the eustachian tube is sited on the anteromedial wall at a point level with the centre of the eardrum. Thus, the whole of the bulla lies ventral to this orifice and drainage from the middle ear will not be assisted by gravity.

The eardrum may be likened to a sandwich where the outer layers are formed by the continuation of the stratified squamous epithelium of the external auditory canal and the inner, the mucoperiosteal, lining of the tympanum. In the upper part of the drum, the pars flaccida, the filling of the sandwich consists simply of small blood vessels which gives this structure a pink appearance. The lower and larger portion, the pars tensa, is supported between the epithelial coats by collagenous con-

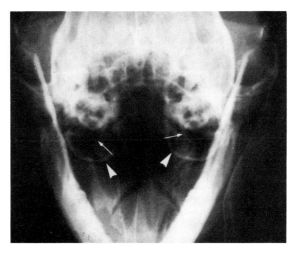

Fig. 14.1. Open-mouth projection of the tympanic bullae of a normal cat. Note the double-shelled configuration (arrowed).

nective tissue. The pars tensa is stretched between the manubrium of the malleus and the tympanic sulcus at the circumference. The fibrous tissue provides the pars tensa with an off-white appearance, much like rice paper. On examination with an auriscope the structures of the eardrum which are first seen are the larger posterior portion of the pars tensa, a small area of pars flaccida and the manubrium of the malleus curving forwards. In the region of the eustachian tube orifice the epithelium lining the tympanum is ciliated columna and it can be shown that movements by the cilia coordinate to move foreign material towards the eustachian tube.

The eustachian tubes themselves are divided into two parts, the upper of which passes through bone and is rigid. The lower, pharyngeal, section is weakly supported by cartilage and is usually flattened and closed. Cartilage flaps guard the pharyngeal openings and these open to permit air exchange within the middle ear during each deglutition sequence.

The middle ear serves two important functions. First, relatively compressible airborne sound waves are received at the tympanic membrane and are converted through the auditory ossicles into fluid vibrations of incompressible endolymph at the oval window. However, in the dog and cat, damage to the eardrum and ossicles leads to surprisingly little reduction of hearing. Therefore, it is likely that these species rely significantly on sound wave conduction through the bones of the skull (osseous conduction) and not only on ossicular conduction. The middle ear also has a protective role. The enclosed air space provides a cushion to loud sounds, especially those of low frequency which produce a wide amplitude of movement of the drum. The inco-malleolar joint yields elastically when sound waves become loud and at high amplitudes the stapes rocks laterally rather than moving through the plane of the footplate. The tiny stapedeus and tensor tympani muscles within the middle ear provide further protection by reflex tightening of the eardrum in response to loud sounds.

Provisions are made for the confined air space of the middle ear; small changes in pressure are catered for by the slack segment (pars flaccida) of the myringa. Major pressure adjustments, as well as long term air changes, are made through the eustachian tubes during swallowing.

The organs of hearing and balance are closely related anatomically and physiologically. The cochlea, saccule, utricle and semi-circular canals comprise a system of membranous tubes which are bathed in endolymph internally and cushioned from the bony labyrinth by perilymph. The vestibular apparatus and cochlea have a common embryological origin in the auditory sac. Therefore, it is not surprising that the cochlear and vestibular nerves should unite to form the auditory nerve. Both systems share a common fluid environment and this explains why the diseases which afflict one often afflict both, whether the causes be infectious, toxic, traumatic or more generalized degeneration.

ABNORMALITIES OF THE MIDDLE EAR

Spontaneous ruptures of the eardrum may occur in dogs that have no other evidence of ear disease. However, perforations are more likely to arise in patients with otitis externa where debris collects in the distal external meatus and comes to lie against the eardrum. In the presence of infection the eardrum appears to lose strength and ruptures more easily. Most simple ruptures occur in the central area between the tip of the malleus and the ventral tympanic sulcus; in longstanding cases of otitis small traces of degenerate membrane may remain. Spontaneous healing of simple ruptures of the eardrum readily occurs in the absence of infection.

The initial response of the middle ear to infection is one of thickening of the mucoperiosteal lining and hyperaemia. The middle ear may become filled by exudate; in those cases where the eardrum has ruptured, this usually consists of tenacious pus. In ascending otitis media it is often a viscous transparent secretion containing few leucocytes and bacteria. Occasionally, foreign material such as grass seeds migrates into the middle ear. Accumulations of granulation tissue may be encountered within the tympanic bulla but it is not always possible to associate this change with a protracted history of otitis. A more frequent long term sequel to otitis media is a diffuse thickening (sclerosis) of the bulla itself. In isolated cases a drastic osteomyelitic reaction ensues which extends to involve local structures such as the temporomandibular joint (*see Fig. 8.7*). Primary neoplasia of the canine middle ear is very rare but extensions of adnexal carcinomas of the external canal into the tympanum are encountered. In cats a pathological phenomenon has been recognized where inflammatory polyps arise within the middle ear and expand either by way of a stalk to the nasopharynx, or through the tympanic membrane into the external canal (*see* Chapter 5). The proliferative changes of craniomandibular osteopathy may be so localized around the tympanic bulla that they resemble neoplasia arising from that structure; the breed and age of the patient should, however, suggest the true diagnosis (*see Fig. 8.3*).

THE INCIDENCE OF OTITIS MEDIA

Otitis media occurs more commonly in dogs than may be realized. Most estimates suggest that the incidence of all ear diseases is about 10 per cent of the total canine cases presented at a first opinion centre. Further surveys indicate that, of these, 11–12 per cent will require specific investigations and treatment for otitis media. At second opinion centres it is unusual to find referred cases of otitis externa that have not advanced to involve the middle ear; this is undoubtedly related directly to the chronicity of the condition.

Although the association between otitis externa and otitis media is well established, it is surprising that the breed incidences of the two conditions are not compatible. That is to say that if a descending route of infection into the middle ear were the principal mode by which otitis media arises, this condition would occur most frequently in Poodles and Spaniels. This is not the case. It has been shown that the German Shepherd is significantly over-represented in the incidence of otitis media. On the other hand, this breed is under-represented in the incidence of otitis externa in general practice. Dogs are encountered in this and many other breeds where the eardrum is seen to be distended by exudate but remains intact without any sign of a healed perforation. Therefore it is concluded that ascending otitis media from the pharynx via the eustachian tube contributes significantly to the overall incidence of middle ear diseases.

Although otitis externa is a frequent occurrence in cats and otitis interna and the vestibular syndrome are well-recognized in this species, middle ear infections *per se* are seldom confirmed. No doubt they do exist and the middle ear acts as a stepping stone in the transition of infections from the external ear to the vestibular apparatus.

Veterinary interference in the treatment of otitis can have untoward consequences. Excessive force in the irrigation of the external canal can cause rupture of the eardrum. Provided that debris is not displaced into the middle ear and that infection is removed from the area of the drum, such an accidental myringotomy puncture will heal rapidly. Many antiseptic solutions are ototoxic and should not be introduced into the middle ear lest their absorption through the round foramen into the perilymph causes deafness or disturbances of balance. Cetrimide solution (0·5 per cent concentration) is one of the least toxic but even at this concentration it is mildly irritant and its use should be followed by irrigation with normal saline. Topical applications of chloramphenicol have been incriminated in the formation of granulations within the human middle ear; this may also occur in the dog. In those cases where a rupture of the tympanic membrane is suspected, the use in the external canal of solutions containing chloramphenicol should be avoided.

DIAGNOSIS OF OTITIS MEDIA

The presenting signs of otitis media are variable and depend upon the stage and route of development of the condition. Dogs with ascending otitis media still confined to the middle ear show lethargy, inappetence and sometimes fever; they tend to shake the head slowly and show a transient head tilt towards the affected side. When otitis media and otitis externa are present concurrently, the symptoms of the latter dominate—headshaking, scratching and pain on palpation of the external canal, as well as otorrhoea, may all be evident. A diagnosis of otitis media may be considered when one or more of the following features are shown:

1. Persistent otitis and otorrhoea, especially when appropriate corrective surgery on the external canal has failed to produce a cure.
2. Intermittent slow headshaking.
3. Characteristic head posture after headshaking—the affected ear tilted downwards transiently.
4. Concurrent labyrinthitis.
5. Susceptible breed, e.g. German Shepherd.

The specific techniques required to confirm the diagnosis of otitis media are best carried out on the anaesthetized patient.

Endoscopy

The diagnosis of otitis media usually hinges upon an evaluation of the tympanic membrane. Infection is likely to be present in the middle ear if the tympanic membrane is ruptured in an animal showing typical signs. However, dogs with healthy ears are occasionally found to have eardrum ruptures. A careful inspection of the eardrum through an auroscope is often unsatisfactory because discharges obscure the view and, even after cleansing, a fluid drop invariably seems to overlie the drum. Nevertheless, defects in the drum are occasionally seen and the majority occur in the area between the malleus and the ventral tympanic sulcus. It will be noticed that in the presence of longstanding infections in the outer ear, the drum shows grey discoloration prior to rupture.

Palpation of the tympanic membrane

Palpation of the eardrum using a blunt needle or probe is a reliable technique but it must be performed with care. The dog is placed in lateral recumbency and the probe is guided along the ventral wall of the horizontal canal to the pre-tympanic region. If the tympanic membrane is intact, the probe will balance softly on the drum. On the other hand, it will pass through a perforation before contacting the medial wall of the tympanum (*Fig.* 14.2). This produces a sharp bony tapping sensation unless granulation tissue is present, rendering it dull.

Eustachian tube patency assessment

This test should be performed only when a cuffed endotracheal tube is in place. Saline, possibly with fluorescein as a marker, is introduced into the middle ear. When the eustachian tube is patent, the fluid drains into the nasopharynx and appears at the nostril on the underside. The discrete use of an insufflator can achieve a similar result: air is puffed into the middle ear from the external canal and produces a character- istic whistle in the nasopharynx. However, this technique must not be attempted if there is any pressure resistance to the insufflation, otherwise an irreversible injury may be inflicted on the round foramen in the middle ear.

Radiography

Whole skull dorsoventral and the open-mouth projections are the most valuable in the assessment of chronic middle ear disease. The oblique lateral projection is less satisfactory because it is difficult to obtain consistent results. The normal tympanic bulla shows a thin snail-shell appearance (*Fig.* 14.3) but a diffuse thickening is a common finding after prolonged infection. Abnormalities that may be seen on radio- graphs include loss of the normal air shadow within the bulla (*Fig.* 14.4), sclerosis of the bulla wall (*Fig.* 14.5), bony destruction and gross proliferative changes with or without involvement of the adjacent temporomandibular joint. The normal air shadow within the middle ear may be replaced by empyema or by soft tissue proliferations of

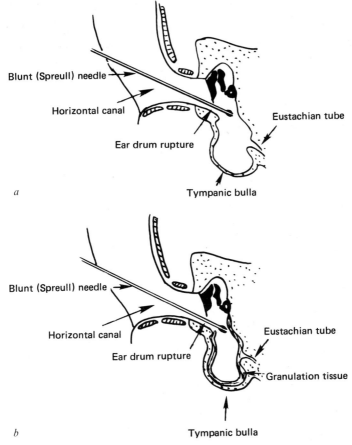

Fig. 14.2. Palpation of the eardrum for rupture. (*a*) Simple rupture providing bony tapping sensation. (*b*) Middle ear lined by granulation tissue rendering the sensation dull.

chronic inflammation or neoplasia. The expansion of an invasive adnexal carcinoma from the horizontal canal may lead to destruction of the bulla wall. The gross proliferative changes of osteomyelitis have been described above.

Surgical exploration

Exploratory surgery may become necessary in non-responsive cases when foreign material or neoplastic tissue may be identified and removed.

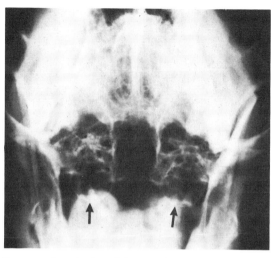

Fig. 14.3. Open-mouth projection of the normal tympanic bullae of a dog. Note the thin bony wall of the bullae which are air-filled. N.B., For this view the endotracheal tube is removed.

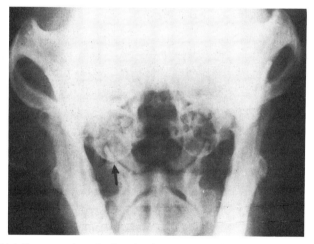

Fig. 14.4. Open-mouth projection showing empyema of the left bulla (arrowed). The bullae walls themselves are not sclerosed.

THE TREATMENT OF OTITIS MEDIA

Though much attention has been paid to the surgical management of otitis media, this condition usually responds to the relatively con-

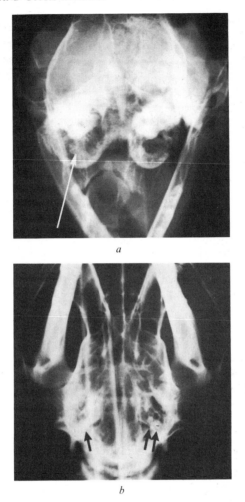

a

b

Fig. 14.5. (*a*) Open-mouth view of the bullae of a cat (compare with *Fig.* 14.1).
Both bullae are grossly sclerosed (arrowed). (*b*) Whole skull dorsoventral view
showing an increased density of the left petrous temporal bone due to sclerosis of
the bulla (arrowed). Compare with the normal side (double arrows) which
contains more air contrast.

servative regime of myringotomy and middle ear irrigation. In many
patients exposure of the horizontal canal will have been achieved
already by lateral wall resection or ablation of the vertical canal before
otitis media has been suspected or confirmed. In animals where this is
not so, a conventional LWR is indicated in order to expose the opening
of the horizontal canal. This will greatly improve access to the eardrum

and middle ear, and at the same time, allow ventilation and drainage to take place. Most middle ear irrigations are performed through a naturally occurring eardrum rupture but a myringotomy is indicated when acute otitis media is still confined to the middle ear and the eardrum remains intact. A blunt needle is used to puncture the drum in the central area between the malleus and the ventral tympanic sulcus. The technique to pass a blunted needle into the middle ear has been described above (*Fig.* 14.2) and mention has already been made to the selection of antiseptic solutions for lavage of the tympanum—0·5 per cent cetrimide in saline is suggested, provided that it is thoroughly flushed away by normal saline afterwards. This agent is chosen because of its detergent cleansing activity and its low ototoxicity but some clinicians prefer to use saline alone. The irrigations are performed until the excess washings overflowing from the horizontal canal are clear of debris. It is not unusual for this fluid to be bloodstained. At the conclusion of each stage of the irrigation the middle ear is drained by suction through the blunt needle. Finally, medication is infused into the tympanum and the passage of this solution into the eustachian tube may be assisted by the gentle use of an insufflator. The usual medication consists of a mixture of corticosteroid and appropriate antibiotic. The choice of antibiotic is determined by the results of culture and sensitivity testing of swabs taken before the onset of treatment. In the first instance, while awaiting the results of micro-biological investigations, a formulation containing polymyxin B is used because this is usually effective against *Pseudomonas aeruginosa*. The middle ear irrigations are repeated at 3–5 day intervals and resolution is usually obtained after two treatments, though on occasions up to five are required. Cases remaining refractory at this stage are exceptional and should be considered candidates for more radical surgery.

Middle ear irrigations may fail to effect a cure of otitis media under one or more of the following conditions:

Resistant infections within the middle ear.
Deficient function of the eustachian tube.
Granulation tissue within the bulla.
Disease of the bony wall of the bulla.
Foreign body in the middle ear.
Neoplasia.

The notorious antibiotic resistance of *Pseudomonas aeruginosa* tends to leave this organism in pure culture in the middle ear if non-specific broad spectrum antibiotics have been used. Medication containing neomycin and polymyxin B is more likely to be effective. Stagnation within the middle ear occurs when normal air exchange through the eustachian tube fails and evidence of obstruction of the tube should be taken as a poor prognosis for the immediate resolution of the infection. The detection of granulation tissue by palpation also suggests that conservative treatment may be unsuccessful but herein lies the rationale for topical corticosteroid therapy. Proliferative and lytic changes in the bone of the middle ear may be seen on radiographs and they are indications for bulla osteotomy. Foreign body debris may pass through an eardrum rupture into the middle ear, and grass seeds, for example, cannot be dislodged easily by simple irrigation.

The dangers of middle ear irrigation are underlined by reports of the sudden onset of deafness and vestibular signs after the technique. The potential hazards of subjection of the middle ear chamber to excessive pressure by overzealous irrigation or insufflation cannot be understated. The major barotrauma injury consists of a rupture of the round foramen with leakage of perilymph. This precipitates permanent damage to the cochlea and vestibular systems. The infusion of ototoxic drugs into the middle ear produces similar results. Strangely, although neomycin has been reported to produce deafness when administered systemically, there are no reports of adverse reactions after local administration in the middle ear.

Bulla osteotomy

The indications for bulla osteotomy are essentially those of failure of conservative treatments. Many veterinarians are deterred from this technique because they exaggerate the potential hazards. The surgical approach is straightforward and provided that the delicate structures of the middle and inner ears are respected, there should be no danger of provoking neurological deficiencies. The concept of gravity drainage of the bulla through a hole created in its ventral wall is sound but drainage is not easily maintained by the direct implantation of a tube. The depth of the tympanic bulla from the skin surface and the loose nature of the skin itself in the submandibular region make the prolonged retention of a simple tube unlikely. It is more satisfactory to pass a drainage tube from the horizontal canal, through the bulla and out via the osteotomy site (*Fig.* 14.6).

The patient is positioned in dorsal recumbency with the proximal neck extended over a sandbag. The surgical site is prepared in the normal way but the drapes should be applied to permit access to the horizontal canal of the affected ear. The site of incision lies anterior and lateral to the larynx and it is parallel with and medial to the mandible. Palpation will reveal a line of depression at this site (*Fig.* 14.7a).

The skin and a thin layer of muscle—the mylohyoid—are sectioned to reveal the belly of the digastricus muscle laterally and the muscles of the tongue-base medially. The large external maxillary and lingual veins are located at the caudal end of the incision but these are easily avoided. Simple blunt dissection between the muscle groups separates the loose connective tissue lateral to the pharynx. During this dissection

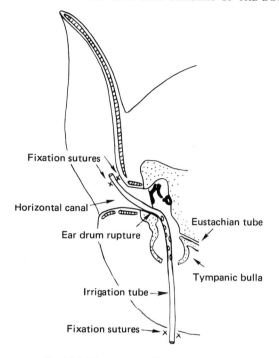

Fig. 14.6. The concept of bulla osteotomy.

the hypoglossal nerve and branching internal carotid artery are noted (*Fig.* 14.7*b*), but again, avoidance presents no difficulties. The bulla lies deep to the branches of the carotid artery and its smooth rounded outline is readily palpable (*Fig.* 14.7*c*). Should there be any difficulties of location of the bulla, the hyoid bones are useful landmarks—the bulla lies immediately anterior and medial to the site of articulation of the great cornu. The incision is held open with self-retaining retractors and the layer of soft tissue which overlies the bulla is cleared away. A square window is removed from its ventral aspect with an osteotome. The contents of the bulla are inspected, swabs are taken for culture and the cavity is flushed clear with saline. Care must be taken in curettage not to damage the ossicles or the medial wall which relates closely to the inner ear. A pair of curved forceps is passed into the middle ear from the horizontal canal (*Fig.* 14.7*d*) and these serve to retrieve the drainage tube (*Fig.* 14.7*e*), which has a series of holes in its wall to correspond with its intended position. Closure of the wound is routine. Sutures through zinc oxide plaster 'butterflies' secure the drainage tube at either end (*Fig.* 14.7*f*).

Postoperative care consists of twice-daily irrigation through the tube and instillation of an appropriate antibiotic solution for 10 days or until the washings are clear. Patients resent neither the presence of the tube nor the irrigation procedure and the tube is simply removed by release of the sutures. The long term presence of a tube may cause ulceration of the integument of the horizontal canal and, therefore, topical antibiotic drops are advisable for the first few days after removal.

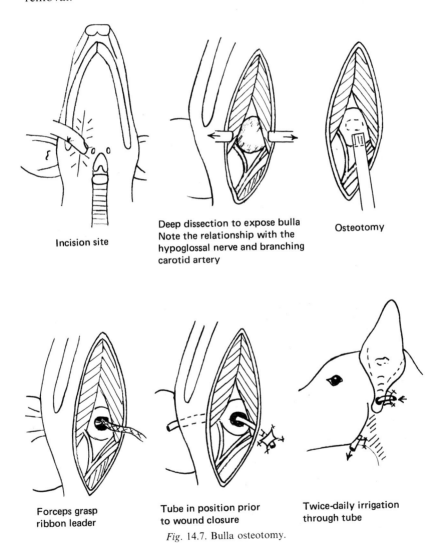

Incision site

Deep dissection to expose bulla
Note the relationship with the
hypoglossal nerve and branching
carotid artery

Osteotomy

Forceps grasp
ribbon leader

Tube in position prior
to wound closure

Twice-daily irrigation
through tube

Fig. 14.7. Bulla osteotomy.

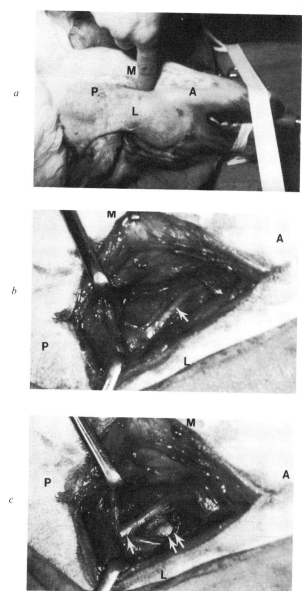

Fig. 14.7. Bulla osteotomy. (*a*) Site of incision. (*b*) Digastricus and tongue-base muscles separated to expose the hypoglossal nerve accompanied by the lingual branch of the internal carotid artery. (*c*) The hypoglossal nerve has been moved medially and the division of the internal carotid can be seen (single arrow). The bulla (double arrows) lies deep to the fork formed by the dividing arteries.

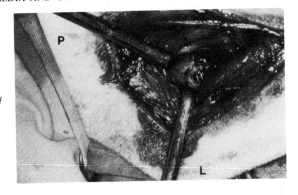

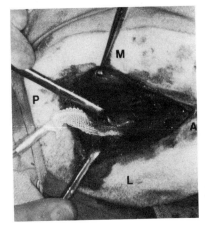

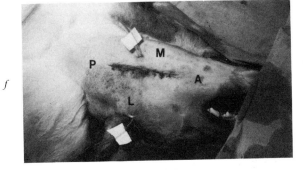

Fig. 14.7. Bulla osteotomy. (*d*) A window has been made in the bulla and the points of a haemostat passed from the external ear canal can be seen within. (*e*) A ribbon gauze 'leader' attached to the drainage tube is withdrawn by the haemostat through the bulla to the horizontal canal. (*f*) Drainage tube secured by adhesive plaster 'butterflies'.

OTITIS INTERNA (LABYRINTHITIS)

The inseparable relationship between the auditory labyrinth (cochlea) and the vestibular system (utricle, saccule and semi-circular canals) has already been emphasized, so that deafness and disturbances of balance usually occur concurrently in otitis interna. The diagnostic challenge, particularly where vestibular disturbances are apparent, is to differentiate between peripheral and central disorders and to identify the causal factors so that specific treatment can be implemented. In general, central vestibular disorders which afflict the vestibular nuclei, cerebellum and mid-brain are accompanied by additional CNS signs. Thus, in all cases of vestibular disturbance the diagnostic procedure should include appraisal of other cranial nerve responses including the distribution of sensation to the face (V), facial expression (VII), Horner's syndrome (sympathetic trunk), the gag response (IX), vocal capacity (X) and lingual function (XII). The ataxia of peripheral vestibular disease tends to be less severe than when central lesions are involved. Although righting reflexes are deficient with peripheral damage, deficiences of the hopping and placing responses are more likely to point to central vestibular disorders. Seizures of any kind provide obvious evidence of higher CNS abnormalities and, if recent in onset, they provide an indication for cerebral spinal fluid tapping to check for pressure, white cell count and protein concentration.

The signs of unilateral vestibular disturbances are dramatic, including head tilt with the affected side down, circling towards the affected side, rolling, falling towards the affected side and nystagmus in which the fast component is directed away from the affected side. In contrast, unilateral deafness may go undetected unless sophisticated audiological tests are employed.

Bilateral vestibular disturbances are most unusual and therefore whenever an animal is afflicted by unilateral labyrinthitis, the contralateral normal side provides a foundation for compensation. The value of therapy for otitis interna may be difficult to assess because during prolonged treatment simultaneous compensation through the normal labyrinth aided by visual orientation takes place.

Congenital cochlear deafness

A hereditary, partially sex-linked deafness of variable penetrance has been recognized for many years in several breeds of dog, including the Dalmatian, Old English Sheepdog, Blue Merle Sheepdog, English Setter and English Bull Terrier. Bitch puppies are slightly more at risk than males and the association between congenital deafness and coat colour is obvious; white-coated Boxers are frequently deaf. Similarly, white cats with blue eyes are often deaf. In recent years congenital deafness has been recognized in individuals where there is no obvious white or merle coloration, including English Cocker and Springer Spaniels as well as brindled Boxers. The cause of deafness is a degeneration within the organ of Corti which takes place between the fourth and tenth day after birth, but the deafness is not always complete and there may be residual hearing in the low tone range.

Although breeders try to identify and cull affected animals, deafness may not be suspected until they have been sold and their new owners find them difficult to train. An inspection of the external canals and eardrums shows no abnormality and radiographs of the middle ears are unremarkable. Under practice conditions deafness is assessed by challenge with a variety of natural sounds covering the normal hearing range. Tests for pure tone impairment with tuning forks or audiometry tend to be of academic merit only. The breeders of stock afflicted with congenital cochlear deafness should be informed and advised not to breed from known carriers. The owners of deaf dogs must be advised of the additional responsibilities which arise when their pet cannot respond to audible commands, particularly in those countries where owners may be held responsible at law for the damages precipitated by their animals.

Congenital vestibular disease

A congenital vestibular disorder has been recognized in the Dobermann, German Shepherd, English Cocker Spaniel and Burmese and Siamese cats. These animals show obvious signs of vestibular disturbance during the first weeks of life and they may be partly deaf. Some of the afflicted cases show a spontaneous improvement due to compensation. There is no effective treatment.

Labyrinthine infection

Infection may reach the membranous labyrinth by way of the middle ear or by haematogenous spread. In all cases where there are acquired vestibular signs or deafness the possibilities of otitis externa and otitis media should be thoroughly explored. Cats appear to be more prone to the spread of infection from the external meatus to the labryinth without obvious signs of intermediate otitis media. Information should be sought regarding recent trauma or veterinary attention to the ears. During the spread of infection from the middle ear the facial nerve and sympathetic trunk which lie adjacent may be infiltrated and the function of these two pathways should be evaluated. In all instances of combined otitis media and otitis interna systemic antibiotic therapy with chloramphenicol and corticosteroids should be supported by vigorous local therapy to the external ear canal and tympanic bulla. In fact, if there is radiographic or palpable evidence of established infection within the middle ear, a bulla osteotomy should be performed without recourse to conservative middle ear irrigation.

Ototoxicity

A number of drugs are known to produce irreparable damage to the sensitive structures of the membranous labyrinth and in this respect cats are particularly susceptible. The antibiotics streptomycin, dihydrostreptomycin and neomycin are the best known examples of ototoxic drugs, but other agents such as salicylates, mercurials and arsenicals can provoke a similar result.

Although quaternary ammonium and iodoform antiseptics are not ototoxic at weak concentrations, other antiseptics including chlorhexidine may provoke deafness or vestibular signs when used to irrigate the middle ear.

Trauma

The circumstances under which barotrauma with rupture of the round foramen can arise have already been described. When this lesion occurs in man, the round foramen is repaired by microsurgical techniques. At the time of writing, these techniques have not been described for animals for the correction of what is usually an iatrogenic disorder. Trauma to the head is occasionally the cause of peripheral vestibular disease and, provided there are no central deficiencies, there is a good prospect of resolution with supportive therapy alone.

Idiopathic feline vestibular syndrome (*Fig.* 14.8)

A unilateral vestibular disorder with an acute onset is common in mature cats of any age. The disease is typically seen during the summer months and, as the name implies, the cause is not known. Clinical examination merely reveals a patient with a severe tilt, incoordination and apparent discomfort. There is no evidence of external or middle ear infection and a complete spontaneous resolution can be expected within 10 days.

Idiopathic vestibular syndrome of senile dogs

This disorder is similar to that described above in cats but it is peculiar to geriatric dogs. Although the disorder has been termed 'stroke' in the past, there is no autopsy evidence to support such a suggestion. Most patients show a steady improvement and return to normal within 10 days.

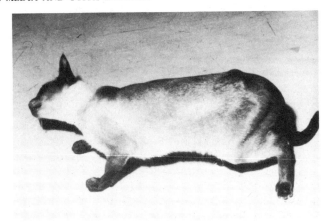

Fig. 14.8. Idiopathic feline vestibular syndrome.

Idiopathic senile deafness

Apart from the congenital cochlear deafness described above, acquired deafness of dogs, even in the face of severe otitis externa and media, is surprisingly uncommon. Nevertheless, one encounters dogs of all breeds from late middle-age onwards which show deafness apparently of sudden onset. The case history reveals no clues to toxic or traumatic causes and a detailed endoscopic and radiographic examination fails to reveal an explanation. Perhaps it should be noted that cholesteatoma and otosclerosis, which are common causes of deafness in adult humans, have not been authenticated in dogs.

Neoplasia

Neoplastic disorders within the petrous temporal bone are most unusual in dogs or cats. A diagnosis of neoplasia should be suspected in animals that show insidious and progressive signs of central vestibular disease. A detailed evaluation of cranial nerve function will usually show that the anomaly is not confined to the eighth nerve alone.

MISCELLANEOUS RELATED NEUROPATHIES

Facial paralysis (*Fig.* 14.9)

The signs of facial paralysis are essentially motor and consist of drooping of the upper lip and muzzle, drooping of the ear and a deficiency of the corneal protection reflex through paralysis of the eyelids. However, there may be an attempt to protect the cornea by the

Fig. 14.9. Cocker Spaniel with idiopathic facial paralysis. In the chronic state the paralysed muscles contract by fibrosis to raise the lip and the ear on the affected side. The upper eyelid remains partly closed.

nictitating membrane. In the acute stages of facial paralysis there will be an overflow of tears and drooling of saliva from the affected side. In the chronic state, the facial asymmetry persists but with contracture of the lip on the paralysed side due to atrophy and fibrosis of the facial muscles.

The close relationship between the facial nerve and the middle ear makes it vulnerable to damage in the presence of otitis media. However, the nerve is also vulnerable to injury after it emerges from the facial canal and continues its course over the ventrolateral aspect of the horizontal ear canal and the lateral border of the vertical ramus of the mandible. Veterinarians who perform surgery in this region should be wary of the facial nerve, for example during extirpation of the parotid salivary gland. Dogs that habitually push doors open with the side of the face may cause contusion to the facial nerve when it is pinched against the mandible. The subsequent paralysis may or may not be permanent.

Idiopathic facial paralysis—Bell's palsy—is a well-recognized entity in man but it has also been described in dogs. The mature Cocker Spaniel is most prone and the paralysis may be bilateral although not necessarily of simultaneous onset. In spite of the most extensive clinical and neurological tests, no explanation has been provided for the syndrome, which is also similar to Bell's palsy in that partial spontaneous amelioration can occur.

Horner's syndrome (*Fig.* 14.10)

Horner's syndrome is characterized by retraction of the eyeball (enophthalmos), drooping of the upper eyelid (ptosis) and constriction of the pupil (miosis). It arises through disruption of the sympathetic pathways by lesions in the cervical or anterior thoracic spinal cord, the anterior mediastinum, the carotid sheath, the petrous temporal bone, the floor of the cranium or in the retrobulbar structures. Whenever Horner's syndrome is recognized, the diagnostic procedure aims to identify the site of denervation so that appropriate treatment, if any, can be instituted. The close anatomical relationship between the postganglionic sympathetic fibres and the middle and inner ear explains why the syndrome often occurs concurrently with vestibular disturbances, facial paralysis or hemifacial spasms. In the diagnostic procedure it is important to eliminate the possibilities of traumatic injury at the cervico-thoracic junction or in the deep tissues of the neck and to check for the presence of neoplastic or inflammatory lesions in the anterior mediastinum and neck which could infiltrate the sympathetic trunk. An examination of the middle ear including radiography is also indicated.

As often as not, Horner's syndrome serves as a signpost to the location of another, more sinister condition and it is unlikely to be an isolated correctable entity.

Fig. 14.10. Horner's syndrome in a cat. Note the ptosis and pupillary constriction on the affected side.

Hemifacial spasm

Intra- and extracranial irritation of the facial nerve may produce facial asymmetry due to unilateral spasm of the facial muscles with a wrinkled expression. The diagnostic examination follows the course of the facial nerve to its emergence from the facial canal. Severe otitis media is the usual explanation, the treatment for which is discussed above. Hemifacial spasm may be accompanied by Horner's syndrome and by vestibular disturbances due to the close anatomical relationships described above. In the differential diagnosis of hemifacial spasm the possibility of contralateral facial paralysis should be considered. It should also be noted that the muscular atrophy which accompanies chronic paralysis also produces a wrinkled facial expression. Rare cases of idiopathic hemifacial spasm have been encountered and partial crushing of the facial nerve as it crosses the face of the masseter muscle is said to be an effective remedy.

SUPPLEMENTARY READING

Bedford P. G. C. (1979) Congenital vestibular disease in the English Cocker Spaniel. *Vet. Rec.* **105**, 530–1.

Blauch B. and Martin C. L. (1974) A vestibular syndrome of aged dogs. *J. Am. Anim. Hosp. Assoc.* **10**, 37–40.

Braund K. G., Luttgen P. J., Sorjonen D. C. et al. (1979) Idiopathic facial paralysis in dogs. *Vet. Rec.* **105**, 297–9.

Chrisman C. L. (1980) Vestibular diseases. *Vet. Clin. North Am.* **10**, 103–29.

Denny H. R. (1973) The results of surgical treatment of otitis media and interna in the dog. *J. Small Anim. Pract.* **14**, 585–600.

Hayes H. M., Wilson G. P., Fenner W. R. et al. (1981) Canine congenital deafness: epidemiologic study of 272 cases. *J. Am. Anim. Hosp. Assoc.* **17**, 473–6.

de Lahunta A. (1971) Feline vestibular disease. In: Kirk R. W. (ed.) *Current Veterinary Therapy*, IV. Philadelphia, Saunders, pp. 484–5.

Lane J. G. (1976) Canine middle ear disease. In: Grunsell C. S. and Hill F. W. G. (ed.) *The Veterinary Annual*, 16th issue. Bristol, Wright–Scientechnica, pp. 160–6.

Roberts S. R. and Vainsi S. J. (1967) Hemifacial spasm in dogs. *J. Am. Vet. Med. Assoc.* **150**, 381–5.

Rose W. R. (1976) Otitis interna—1: general considerations. *Vet. Med. Small Anim. Clin.* **71**, 1673–8.

INDEX

279

M.④y

Acute. Afebrile.

Mouthbreath.

Chest ◊◊ sounds (N).

White froth retched up.

Depressed. Dehydrated.

(Tapeworms, No flu.

the PDSA possible.